To Logan —

Bullish and Best Wishes

D. Craig [illegible]

9/21/88

How To Profit From The PSYCLE

by

D. CRAIG FECEL

How To Profit From The PSYCLE

by

D. CRAIG FECEL

Foreword and Market Theory Consultation by
Robert J. Farrell

Richardson & Snyder
25 Broad Street
New York

I.S.B.N.: 0–0943940–08–7
L.C.C: 83–062175

Library of Congress in-publication data:
1. Author: D. Craig Fecel
2. Investing in Stock Markets, U.S.
3. Psychology of Investors
4. Economics of Investment

Book Design and Typography by Stephen H. Severson

Dedication

This book is dedicated to

NORRIS W. BARRY

who graciously showed me the basics of
how to buy low and sell high.

My sincere thanks goes to
Bob Farrell
whose valuable contributions
helped make this book possible.

Contents

Foreward

Know thyself and knowledge of the stock market will soon follow. Ego and emotions determine far more of our stock market decisions than most of us would be willing to admit. For years, I have dealt with the leading professional money managers in the country and found they were as much subject to crowd following and other irrational emotional mistakes as any novice investor. They were for the most part better informed but facts alone are not enough to make profitable decisions. The human element encompassing a range of emotions from fear to greed plays a much bigger part in the decision-making process than most of us realize. The first accomplishment of this book is to take you through a market-related psychological and ego-state analysis that should help both the novice and professional investor better understand why wrong investment decisions are made. Moreover, there is a positive contribution in providing an understanding of the psychological motivation that can lead to more profitable decision making.

In a practical sense, most investors go exactly opposite to the instinctive wisdom of buy low, sell high just because of very predictable emotional responses to rising or falling prices. Falling prices that at first appear to be bargains give way to generating fear of loss at much lower prices when opportunities are greatest. Rising prices that at first appear to be good opportunities to sell ultimately become the trigger to greed-induced buying at much higher levels. Reason is replaced by rationalization and emotion with such cyclical regularity that those who recognize the symptoms can profit very well from this knowledge. Thus it has been over the entire history of markets and thus it ever will be. The following chapters will help you understand this psychological part of the investment process and then show you how to recognize the cyclical process in the market that takes stocks from overvaluation to undervaluation and back again.

There are some very basic principles that are discussed by the author that I have found to have stood the test of time. The most important of all is to have a discipline and the patience to stick to it. If you have not done well in the market over the years, it is very likely that you have not had a plan and have let emotions govern your investment decisions. If the average unsuccessful investor would take the time to examine the record of his past investment transactions, he would most likely find that his purchases increased in a rising market and decreased in a falling market. It would also be apparent that early in a bull market he tended to trade in and out for small profits and later, after prices had advanced substantially and risks were much higher, decided to become a buy and hold long-term investor. This pattern of behavior has always existed and is why the emotional majority does not do well in the stock market. The PSYCLE was written to help the average investor understand these universal errors and provide a discipline to accumulate wealth. It is not a "get rich quick" scheme nor an intellectual exercise beyond the average investor's understanding. It is plain common sense.

Some may wonder why someone who has spent his professional career practicing market timing would endorse a book that emphasizes selecting undervalued stocks with little regard for overall market timing. The primary reason is that I believe the average investor can follow an undervalued stock selection discipline more consistently than he can time the market. Moreover, the principles involved in undervalued stock selection are very similar to the basic premises of good market timing. In the last analysis concentration on the practical aspects of timing stock purchases is what the investment game is all about.

Bob Farrell

1
Accumulating Wealth

THE CROWD IS ALWAYS WRONG

Buy low and sell high. That's how you make money in the stock market. Everybody knows what you're supposed to do, but very few people do it consistently. What is the reason for this unhappy state of affairs? It's because of one unchanging rule of stock market dynamics: *The majority of investors will always be wrong at important turning points*. This is true of the stock market in general and of individual securities.

Of course, major turning points are only confirmed in retrospect. Yet, when the feelings of investors become emotionally one-sided, the price action of stocks often becomes volatile. Conversely, it is this sharp, and sometimes vertical price movement that is frequently the most visible reflection of extreme crowd psychology and may be the beginning of an important change of direction.

What is "crowd psychology"? The term is used to describe the conditions when investor sentiment forms a consensus and the majority begins to act in unison. Once the emotional extremes of optimism or pessimism have been reached by the majority of investors, most of the urgent buying or selling has been consummated. The price movement has usually discounted the perceived events of the future, and the stage is set for unforeseen surprises.

Fear and greed motivate most investment decisions because price movement is the major stimulus to investor sentiment. As prices move up, positive feelings are reinforced and greed motivates "buy" decisions. As prices move down, negative feelings are reinforced and fear motivates "sell" decisions. This phenomenon explains why the majority of investors is the most optimistic, and therefore fully invested at the top; and they are the most pessimistic and sold out at the bottom of any price cycle.

What makes investors produce the phenomenon of crowd psychology? These are some of the factors:

1. They don't have a consistent decision strategy of when to buy and when to sell.
2. They make investment decisions based on emotion. They buy motivated by greed and sell motivated by fear.
3. Their ego makes them believe that they can predict the events of the future and then interpret those events regarding stock price movements.
4. They do not understand risk and are unknowledgeable about the random price fluctuations that can influence their decisions.
5. They are extremely impatient and unwilling to give their investments the time needed to work out successfully.
6. They are unrealistic about the return they should receive on their capital.

Investors who desire capital appreciation generally seek out "growth stocks." This rationale is that increased earnings and dividends will produce appreciation in the price of the security. This is often true for a period of time. But inevitably, at some point, the price of the stock discounts all anticipated positive future events. Meteoric rises are often followed by frightening declines. Most investors don't think about selling a growth stock until it's too late.

Periodically the floor of the New York Stock Exchange is strewn with the corpses of former "high flying" growth stocks that have dropped precipitously from their peaks. To name just a few: Brunswick, from $77 to $8, Memorex, from $175 to $2, Xerox, from $171 to $41, Litton, from $80 to $3, and Gillette, from $66 to $21. The names of recent casualties may be more meaningful: Homestake Mining, from $88 to $17, Standard Oil of Indiana, from $99 to $34, and Halliburton, from $86 to $21. In some cases the earnings collapsed and in some cases they didn't. But almost by definition, at the apex of each price movement, the majority of investors were the most bullish.

Such price movements can only be explained by a dramatic shift in the psychology of the majority of investors toward a particular stock. Therefore, it must be concluded that the psychology of investors runs in cycles. Since price movement is the major stimulus to investor expectations, the Psychology of a Stock cYCLE or PSYCLE (pronounced Psyc'ill) will show definite characteristics. It is important to understand exactly how fear and greed interact with price movement to produce different attitudes among investors. Once it is understood that emotional extremes often preceed important price reversals, more profitable investment decisions can be made.

At the bottom of the price cycle of a stock, fear is the predominant emotion. Since the majority is much more worried about losing money than making it, the stock is viewed with *contempt*. The news about the company is very negative. The consensus reality is that the stock will go down further in price. As the stock eventually begins to move higher, *caution* is prevalent because investors are still motivated by fear. As the price of the stock continues to move upward, *confidence* in the continued uptrend becomes apparent. Little by little, fear begins to turn into greed. At the top of the price move, enthusiasm is at its peak. The *conviction* of the majority is that the price can only go higher. They will become intoxicated by the sharp, upside price volatility of this phase. Unfortunately, their pleasure may be short-lived.

Now, greed has become the overriding emotion among investors. They are no longer worried about losses, their focus is gains. As the price peak passes and movement begins to have a downward bias, investor *complacency* with regard to the stock is widespread. However, as the stock continues to react, greed melts into fear. The majority now feels *concern* about losing money. As prices accelerate to the down side, some of the staunchest holdouts are forced into *capitulation* and they join the panic selling. Now fear has returned as the predominant emotion and the PSYCLE can begin again.

To the rational investor, it may seem incredible that this phenomenon could repeat itself over and over again. But you must realize that it may take a period of several years completely to evolve. The PSYCLE is a model that could easily apply to the price movements in almost any financial market. It is not perfect, but it seems to be a fairly accurate analysis of the phases of crowd psychology.

There are many ways that you can profit from the PSYCLE. First of all, you will learn a consistent and conservative technique for investing your hard-earned money. This approach should produce very positive results over the long term. As a successful investor, you will be able to accumulate wealth with a minimum of aggravation or involvement on your part. Second, you should have a dramatic increase in your time and energy to pursue the other important aspects of living. This is because you will be able to turn your back easily on all other "investment opportunities" with a clear conscience. Once you embrace this approach as *your* reality of the stock market, the resulting peace of mind can be euphoric.

Before you rush out to order your new Rolls-Royce, you should be aware that there is a small "catch" involved. You will have to challenge and disregard many of your ill-conceived perceptions about stock market investing. You will have to master certain basic concepts of stock market dynamics. You will have to clearly understand what motivates people's behavior. Finally, you will have to learn to make investment decisions opposite to what your emotions tell you to do. This means you will have to buy when you are almost paralyzed with fear and sell when you are choked with greed. To make money consistently in the stock market, you will have to change your behavior. That will not be easy.

Successful experiences reinforce behavior. When we do something "right" we tend to repeat the behavior. An unsuccessful experience is the only thing that will stimulate us to change our behavior. This usually involves some kind of pain. Most people do not want to change their behavior. They will only do it when the *pain* of their actions becomes unbearable. The alcoholic won't quit drinking until his personal life is in shambles. The cigarette smoker won't quit smoking until the doctor tells him that there's a spot on his lung. The speculator won't quit trading until he's lost all his money. Rarely will behavior change without pain. Think about it.

So in order for you to become a successful investor, you'll have to go through some discomfort. Hopefully, most of it will be benign. Of course, many of you have already experienced the emotional and financial pain that can accompany unsuccessful investing. Believe it or not, it is necessary to learn a different perception of reality in the stock market.

There is no "quick" or easy way to do it. You can't get something for nothing. You must go through the entire process in order to change your thinking to become a successful investor. This means taking a step-by-step series of actions that will produce the desired end result. As you participate vicariously in the mistakes that I and other investors made, you will find yourself. Hopefully this will keep you from having to make costly mistakes. It may be the most exciting journey in self-awareness that you've ever experienced.

This has been written from a man's point of view, since that is the only way that I can perceive it. However, this strategy is very well suited for the woman investor. In fact, it's my feeling that they can probably accept and use it more readily than men. This is because they won't have some of the ego hang-ups of male investors. Regardless, the crowd has no gender. Anyone who wants to become a successful investor must avoid being caught in the vortex of crowd psychology.

The use of this investment approach has empowered me to accumulate wealth at a rate faster than I would have ever believed possible. In order to accomplish this, I have been forced to understand myself and the world around me. Also, a clearer perception of reality has helped me become a much happier person that I've ever been before in my life. It will do the same for you, if you take the process step by step. So let's start at the beginning.

THE THRILL OF RISK

Some five thousand million years ago, our planet was just beginning to become a solid mass. Four thousand million years ago, it was just cool enough for water to exist on its surface. Only then was it possible for the simplest forms of life to exist. Scientific data have proved that the human species called *Man* has evolved from the earliest forms of life. It doesn't build one's ego to confront the fact that we are all direct descendants of one-celled creatures that begin life in tidal pools. The ascendancy of Man from the lower forms of life over many millions of years was a dramatic and miraculous series of events. Yet, during that vast expanse of time, many forms of life came into being, lived and then perished. Why has Man evolved to be master of his world?

The answer to this question can be found in a process called Natural Selection or *Survival of the Fittest*. It applies to most species. It means that the stronger and more intelligent individuals will survive and reproduce themselves. They will be better able to hunt and to defeat their enemies. The weak perish. As cruel as it may seem, it is nature's way.

Each member of a species has an instinct to achieve in life. Through the millenia as Man rose to higher and higher levels of consciousness, he developed a creative success mechanism within himself. This power of analysis and determination enabled him to become the "king" of all other creatures on Earth. It is this driving force that has brought him out of the caves and into the skyscrapers.

Ever since Man began walking erect, he instinctively tried to better himself. Initially, he was concerned about survival in a hostile environment. He worried about food, shelter, and clothing. Later, he domesticated animals, farmed the land, lived in houses, and began to educate himself about the world around him. More recently, he flies in airplanes, harnesses the atom, and uses computers to help control his environment. In today's society his lower-level needs are virtually assured, yet his internal drive for success still pushes him forward.

Every human being is both "blessed" and "cursed" with this ambitious inner force that tries to propel him ahead to continuous achievement. Of course, it is much stronger in some individuals than in others. Nevertheless, it makes Man naturally restless, so he must continue to seek challenge and take risk; otherwise, he is bored and unfulfilled. Accomplished goals produce only temporary satisfaction. They eventually become only a frame of reference for further advancement. Throughout history, Man's willingness to "take a chance." has been the propellant of human progress.

Risk means *a chance of encountering harm or loss*. Usually, you cannot achieve gain without risk. They go hand in hand. This is especially true in financial markets. However, when an individual is trying to achieve some kind of gain, he isn't really thinking about losing. He thinks only of winning.

Of course, he is aware of the "risk" involved, but it is unlikely that he thinks the true "chance of loss" is applicable to him. This too is nature's way. Because if it were possible always fully to comprehend the magnitude of possible loss, the motivation for achievement would be substantially quieted.

In our cosmopolitan society, Man's life-force often can be directed toward acquiring wealth, power, and status. This is especially true of high achievers. These would be individuals who have the intellect, motivation, and persistence to seek accomplishments substantially beyond what is necessary for day-to-day existence. They are driven to be at the top of their profession, the most respected in their peer group, to have considerable influence over other people's lives, or to be rich. Of course, not all will be completely successful and, unfortunately, many will fail. But this is nature's way. As quoted in the Bible, "many are called, but few are chosen."

Another dimension of achievement is not so well understood. While the pure risk involved is exhilarating, the anticipation of rewards is usually more exciting than the end results. When one assumes risk he can often escape from reality. High risk requires high concentration. For the moment, you cannot think about business problems, family strife, or personal inadequacies. The intense excitement of risk can be its own reward.

Everyone craves the feeling of self-satisfaction that a "successful event" produces. Besides the stimulation of the risk involved and the possible tangible rewards, just being a "winner" at anything can be an instant affirmation of one's own self-worth. The dream of the reward usually overshadows the penalty of failure, no matter how severe it may be. You can expose yourself to risk in a variety of ways. It can be as harmless as an afternoon of bridge, or a "serious money" Friday night poker game. One of my clients likes to go on African safaris, even though some "Bwanas" have never returned. Paul Newman became a race-car driver in his mid-forties with the awareness that he could be killed, or seriously injured in a car crash. A friend of mine loves to "bomb" down ski slopes. He ignores the fact that a wrong move could paralyze him for life. Others will bet thousands of dollars on the roll of the dice or on a breathtaking plunge into a financial market, realizing the possibility that they could be wiped out. The thrill of risk sure keeps life interesting.

Let's look at the risks involved in the stock market. Because this is the arena in which the "instincts" of many individuals will compete. Remember, that in order for a few to be right, many must be wrong.

In today's stock market environment, there are essentially two types of investors. The most dominant is the Institutional Portfolio Manager (IPM). This is a group of individuals who invest large pools of money. They might manage a mutual fund or corporate retirement plans. Their full-time job is to try to outperform everyone else, given their risk parameters. There is also the Private, Part-Time Investor (PPTI), who makes his livelihood at some other job. Yet, he (or she) is very interested in making his investment capital increase in value. Our objective is to help the PPTI exploit the forces of the marketplace, instead of being victimized by them.

When someone is in the process of assuming financial risk he could be gambling, speculating, or investing. Although there are considerable differences in each category, few people really understand the distinctions between them. One of the most misused words in the financial world is "investor." Everyone is called an *investor* regardless of the magnitude of the risk he assumes.

Actually, the proper term is Risk-Taker (RT), so called because of the risk involved every time one puts money to work. It could be very high risk, or low risk, depending on the type of financial vehicle invested in, and the time frame involved. For instance, the IPM may consider that he is making an investment in a stock. However, in reality, it could be construed as rank speculation. The PPTI may feel that he has engaged in an exciting speculation, whereas it may be just a pure gamble. Often, it is not possible to make a clear distinction between the gambler, speculator, or true investor. Because the term *investor* is so widely accepted, we'll use it to mean a risk-taker of any type. (When we are using the term correctly, the word true will be placed before it.) Now, let's try to understand how random, raw chance can affect the outcome of each decision to assume risk.

THE RANDOM PROCESS

Pick up a quarter and flip it into the air. Watch it turn end-over-end as it travels higher and higher. As the upward momentum is overcome by the downward force of gravity, it will be momentarily suspended in space just spinning and spinning. Quickly, before it falls back to earth, try to describe what will happen when it does. Will you call heads? Perhaps you called tails. If you said either heads or tails, you may have been wrong.

Actually, at the apex of the toss, the outcome was uncertain because there are two possibilities. Mathematicians use the term *probability* to describe the outcome of events. The probability of this coin landing on heads would be expressed as one chance in two or 1/2. It is more commonly expressed as .5, in its decimal form. It would also be correct to state that the odds of the event (heads) in a coin flip would be one chance to two chances. More simply, it would be stated 1 to 2.

The flip of a coin is a simple example of a random process. Its outcome is determined by *pure chance*. Assuming it is well-balanced and symmetrical, the coin is equally likely to land either on heads or tails. However, there is no predictability other than in terms of mathematical probabilities. The probability of heads is 1/2 and the probability of tails is 1/2. The probability of tossing either heads or tails with one coin is

1/2, plus 1/2, which equals 1. This is an example of a certainty. Conversely, if it was impossible for an event to occur, its probability would be zero.

The most important thing to understand about the Random Process is that the events of the past have absolutely no influence on future events. This means that you could observe and analyze ten years (or ten minutes) of data of a random process and the value of your efforts would be worthless in predicting what would happen in the future. But, this is a concept that is very hard for many people to comprehend. They become conditioned by past events and believe they will continue in the future.

Let's go back to your quarter. Please pick it up and study it carefully. Does it have eyes so that it could see how it landed in the past? Of course, the answer is no. Does it have a mind so that it remembers the outcomes of its previous flips? Again the answer is no. Close observation would lead you to conclude that the quarter was an inanimate object that was devoid of sight, memory, or other senses. Therefore, it is impossible for the outcome of the events of the past to have any influence on the outcome of the events of the future.

Look at it another way. Suppose that you've been flipping your quarter for several hours to record and observe the outcome. All of a sudden the coin begins to land on heads and continues to do so nine straight times. Amazed, you pause to wonder what the probability of the coin landing on heads on the next flip would be. Could it be very low because there have been so many heads previously? That seems to make sense. On the other hand, perhaps the coin is on a "hot streak" and will continue to land on heads. Now, it's getting confusing.

Believe it or not, the lifeless chunk of metal you are holding in your hand has no idea that it landed on its side called "heads" the last nine times it was flung into the air. So, there is a 1/2 chance that the tenth flip will be heads. But, you're still bothered. Because it seems that the probability of throwing ten heads in a row, out of say 1,000 tosses, would be pretty low. That is correct. It is very low, but it is also a very different question.

The *theory of probability* is the mathematical science that deals with the random process. Through the use of formulas, it is possible to describe the expectation of events. If we flip ten different coins 100 times, we could determine that the probability of getting ten heads in a row was about .001. We could also expect that about 25% of the time we could get an equal number of heads and tails each time we flipped ten coins. The theory of probability provides the tools to predict mathematically what will happen in the future if you accurately know the probability of each event and are given a large number of chances. However, the actual results could deviate substantially over the short run.

Man lives in a world that is highly affected by chance. In an earlier time, superstitions explained accidents and coincidences that were out of the ordinary. However, the theory of probability helps one understand that certain phenomenon can be explained by the workings of natural law. The theory of chance affects all men with the power to make decisions concerning any type of resource. They could be a general of an army, a president of a corporation, a scientist working on an atomic bomb, or a private investor managing his stock portfolio. This is because these men of action must come to concrete conclusions based on factors that are uncertain or problematical. Man can live and thrive more effectively only if he can learn to take chances more intelligently.

Much of what we (superstitiously) call luck is simply the natural laws of the random process in action. We all know someone who seems to be lucky beyond all rational reason. The streaks of good luck and bad in every series of events can be explained in most cases by the laws of chance. For instance, more than one roulette wheel has produced a series of at least 25 red numbers in a row. That is explainable within a very large number (millions and millions) of chances. However, if you had been betting on red, you would have considered yourself very lucky; but, if you had been betting on black, you probably would have felt unlucky. Sometimes luck depends on your point of view.

One definition of luck is *preparation meeting opportunity*. So, there are many things an individual can do to increase the number of favorable events that he encounters. One of my friends is fond of quoting the old saying "the harder I work, the luckier I get." The more prepared you are for any endeavor that has an unknown element of chance, the higher the probability of a favorable outcome. However, people can occasionally have disastrous runs of luck in their professional, personal, or financial lives. When this happens, they may become more superstitious or religious, or search their past "wrongs" to try and understand why they are being "punished." Their predicament may be nothing more than an unfavorable swing in the natural laws of chance. Unquestionably, in financial markets, the less risk you assume, the less likely you are to be "unlucky" and be wiped out.

But, raw chance affects your life more than you realize. For instance, you probably met your wife by happenstance. Your sex was determined in a random manner at the moment of conception. It depended on whether the X-chromosome or Y-chromosome made contact first. Will you have a successful business career or be a welfare recipient? It would have a lot to do with the random determination of being born in a suburb or ghetto. How you depart from this life is subject to chance. Will you be killed in a freak accident in the prime of life or simply die of old age? No one really knows.

Each of us must expose ourselves to risk on a daily basis. The modern machines that provide comforts and conveniences can become vehicles of destruction. No matter how cautious an individual may be, he is still taking chances. In order to escape risk, he could avoid travel in airplanes, automobiles, boats, or even elevators, but that would mean he couldn't earn a living in modern society. But, whether we are crossing the street, rolling the dice, or buying and selling stocks, it is important to understand that pure chance does affect the outcome of our endeavors.

GAMBLING, SPECULATING, OR INVESTING

"They're coming out! Get your bets down!" the stickman cries, and the players nervously place their chips on the crap table. Las Vegas dice is a game of pure chance. Although many gamblers would disagree, there is no skill required other than a factual knowledge of the game. It is also man's oldest known gambling device. It is a game that big bettors can easily play. This author has personally watched a gambler walk up to a table, sign a marker for $5,000 worth of chips, and lose the total amount within sixty seconds. Whether he had any fun in doing so was not immediately apparent. This author has also been playing at a table where an individual won over $40,000 on a very long roll of the dice and hardly cracked a smile.

If you doubt that the thrill of risk is something inherent in the nature of Man, then go to Las Vegas sometime. There you will see blue-collar workers and successful businessmen pitting themselves against raw chance and random fluctuation with thousands and thousands of dollars. Why do they do it? For the pure excitement that is produced by the high tension of winning and losing, followed by the inevitable letdown? For an escape from reality that comes from putting money at risk? Just to prove to themselves they can win some easy money? Who knows for sure? Yet, there are more hotels built each year to accommodate the players.

The action in Las Vegas represents only a small fraction of the amount of money bet annually in the United States at various games of chance. The total amount is probably well over $1 trillion. That's a mind-boggling amount when you consider that probably most of it is gambled illegally. That number was extrapolated from the $500 billion figure that gambling expert John Scarne estimated in a careful survey he made in the late 1950s. Since many of the same dollars are bet over and over again, the figure only represents the "action" (amount bet) not how much was lost.

If the $1 trillion estimate is even close to being accurate, then gambling is by far the largest industry in America today. That seems impossible, doesn't it? But the total Gross National Product (GNP), which is the dollar value of all goods and services produced in this country, was $1.67 trillion in 1980. So, gambling was about 60% of our GNP. Let's look at it another way. In 1980 Exxon Corporation had sales of $108.5 billion. So gambling action was about nine times as large. Of course, comparing gambling action with the sale of goods and services is not totally accurate.

Gambling should be considered a huge, but highly fragmented financial market. In 1980, the total dollar volume of shares traded on the New York Stock Exchange (NYSE) was $3.75 billion. So there was almost 270 times as much money gambled. Of course, comparing the gambling industry to the NYSE would send some of its members into shock and outrage. Nevertheless, the distinction is clear. An individual exposes himself to risk only when he believes that he can gain. In other words, he takes a chance of losing part, or all, of what he already possesses to try to attain something of greater value. A market of any kind is simply a mechanism that facilitates the trading of particular goods or services. On the NYSE, it's the stock of a corporation. On the gambling tables of Las Vegas or on the streets of Harlem playing the "numbers," it's purc cash. All markets are the same. They are just people trading goods, services, or cash in hope of gain.

There are many kinds of gambling markets. The casino is the most formalized and the smallest. Perhaps less than 10%

of the action occurs there. Within its walls you will find many mechanical games of chance. That is, a game in which there is no element of skill involved other than a factual knowledge of the game. Included in this category would be roulette, craps, keno, wheel of fortune, slot machines, faro and Las Vegas baccarat. Other such games played outside the casino that represent a much larger piece of the action would include bingo, policy numbers, lotteries, and other raffles. No matter how experienced and talented the gambler may be, or regardless of his betting technique, there is nothing he can do to overcome the expectation of loss built into the game.

Most gamblers believe that their skill will help them win in sports betting. This occurs when an individual wagers on such athletic contests as football, baseball, basketball, prize fights, or horse racing. Most of this money is bet illegally and represents an enormous amount. However, sophisticated handicapping by bookies and other professionals reduces the game to random events. Therefore, that is the commonality that separates gambling from other forms of risk-taking.

Whether gamblers believe it or not, they are risking money based on purely random events. Since most games of chance are biased toward the "house" or gambling professional, most individuals will lose over the long run. But the expectation of loss does not account for the great losses (in percentages) of most gamblers. Their belief in systems of betting techniques usually accelerate their ruin. Rarely can they manage their bankroll in an objective manner. Even if they have a prudent approach, it usually breaks down in the heat of the game and, of course, at any time, random fluctuations could produce a disastrous run of luck. By the way, these ingredients are also the downfall of most speculators.

If you don't believe it, then call your faithful stockbroker (if you have one) and make the following statement: "I'd like to gamble on a stock. What do you have that looks good?" The sequence of events should follow something like this. First of all, he would sound shocked. He may indignantly reply that people don't gamble in the stock market. Of course, they may *speculate* on occasion. He may even lecture you on the immorality of gambling. What's the difference? Is there a difference? Well, in some ways yes and some ways no.

One definition of speculation is to buy or sell in expectation of profiting from market fluctuations. Fluctuations? That sounds familiar. Can it be the same kind of fluctuations that you can get by flipping a coin or rolling the dice? The word speculation sounds like a high-minded adventure whereas gambling brings to mind something sinister and immoral. Another element of speculation is that the individual usually believes he possesses some element of knowledge associated with the venture that differentiates the risk from a pure random fluctuation, such as in gambling.

After your stockbroker has informed you as to the difference between the two, the conversation may go like this: "Mr. Speculator, I'm glad you called because I'm looking at a situation right now that seems very interesting. Hotshot Electronics may be bought out by the Rock of Gibralter Company. The stock has been moving up a little bit (40%) in anticipation, but I think we could buy it here and perhaps catch a 3 or 4 point move. Why don't we go ahead and get a thousand shares? I think something's going to happen this week in the stock." Does that sound like an intelligent speculation? Or, do you think that your chance might be just as good at the tables in Las Vegas?

Why do people speculate? Well, you don't have to be a psychologist to know that everyone is looking for easy money. The lure of instantaneous riches is a strong primary motivation. Most people secretly have a desire to "make a killing" without much work or effort. Their Child Ego State can dream of the opulence and prestige of being a big-time gambler or a successful stock market speculator. To experience the thrill of making thousands of dollars just by the roll of the dice, or the sale of a stock, is a familiar dream for almost everyone. *Wealth without toil* is the illusion that drives people to gamble and to speculate in financial markets.

Will they all be successful? Think about it this way. How many tennis players achieve the status of a Rod Laver? How many West Point graduates become a General Patton? How many heart surgeons attain the fame of Dr. DeBakey? The point is that every occupation has only a few outstanding achievers from among many other talented and dedicated professionals. But, all have achieved their status through hard work, seasoning, and sacrifice.

You will agree that it would be unrealistic for a top tennis player to simply read a book on medicine and then be competent to perform open heart surgery on a dying patient. It is almost equally presumptuous for a doctor or a lawyer to believe he can make money speculating in the stock market. The same superb performance realized in one's own professional endeavors will not necessarily be reflected in success in financial markets.

There are a few very talented and very knowledgeable individuals in the stock market who can speculate and make money at it. But they have a game plan, they do their homework, they know when to take losses, and they can handle their decisions in an objective manner. Yet, speculation is far from being easy money. It's a gut-grinding, tough occupation. The people who do well at it are highly seasoned, experienced, and have "paid the price" in many failures to achieve their expertise. Most speculators are novices and do not possess the same kind of credentials. They are usually undercapitalized and make highly emotional decisions. They are "looking for something for nothing." That's why the majority of them nearly always lose over the long run.

There is a tremendous difference between the abilities of people to make money. The *informed speculator* takes a risk with his capital only if it appears justified after a thorough analysis of the pros and cons of the venture. The *uninformed speculator* makes almost a casual decision without an adequate evaluation of the reality of the risk. Therefore, the latter is much more likely to be wrenched about by the random price movements of the marketplace.

"Don't fight the tape!" "Let your profits run and cut your losses short!" "Keep your winners and sell your losers!" These old Wall Street adages advise the speculator to respect the trend of stock prices. The business section of every library is full of books on how to make money speculating in the stock market. If you don't have time to read them, then there are a number of investment advisory services that you can purchase for a reasonable fee. Reasonable, that is, compared to how much money you *should* make. They all will gladly expose their excellent trading record. All you have to do is carefully follow the strategy in the book or the advice of these sages, and you will profit handsomely. How can you lose?

Unfortunately, the uninformed speculator will find many different ways to lose his money. Almost all decision techniques are based on the ability to identify the trend in prices or anticipate the change of a trend in prices. In effect, everyone claims, in one way or another, to be in "harmony" with the stock market momentum. Of course, this defies common sense. They lead you to believe that everything will be great most of the time. But, they somehow forget to tell you about the disastrous effects of getting "whipsawed."

In timber country, before the advent of power tools, trees had to be cut down by the use of a two-man crosscut saw with jagged teeth. In the process of being felled, the tree could often bind the saw and suddenly stop its motion. When that happened, the lumberjacks's forward momentum would coil the blade like a spring. It would then lash backward violently as if it were a whip with the person on its end. Hence, the name whipsaw. They have been known to break bones and throw 200-pound men over 10 feet. In timber country, getting whipsawed could be physically painful.

In the stock market, getting "whipsawed" can be financially painful. This occurs when you buy a stock after a sharp rise and it then drops almost equally as sharply. The whipsaw movements of stock prices on a near-term basis could be construed as being absolutely random.

No gambler or speculator consciously puts his money at risk in a haphazard manner. He believes that he possesses a unique skill (or has access to some special information) that will enable him to profit from his venture. Although he doesn't expect to win every time, he certainly would not believe that the outcome of his decision was heavily influenced by pure chance. Substantial evidence, provided by an examination of the results of these risk-takers, would suggest that they may have a distorted perception of reality.

There was a study done at one time that estimated that only 5% of all private, part-time investors made and kept any money over a full market cycle. It also concluded that another 15% only managed to break even. The remaining 80% actually lost money. Whether it was totally accurate can never be proven. However, it's probably a lot more right than wrong. Certainly, the biggest problem for most investors is losing money, not relative performance.

In speculating, the future value versus the market price is of primary consideration. Buying stocks with "good long-term growth prospects" usually means the speculator is anticipating a rise in the price of the security. The evaluation may focus on the potential for the company's products and the strength of management. These factors, along with others, may be used to predict increasing earnings over a number of years in the future. If the analysis is thorough and the time frame long-term, wouldn't the decision be considered investing? The answer is NO. It is merely informed speculation.

One dimension of investing requires that the so-called "intrinsic value" of the company be less than the market price. Determining the intrinsic value of a company is an inexact science that requires an analysis of such factors as assets, earnings, dividends, capital structure, and others. The end result will enable you to buy "value" at a distressed price. Herein lies the fundamental difference between speculating and investing. The speculator focuses on what he will have in the future, whereas the true investor is concerned with the value he gets now.

One traditional way of identifying an investment is to say that its current income is important. For instance, perhaps the safest long-term investment would be a United States Government Bond. Unless something like a nuclear holocaust happens, the investor would be guaranteed his interest and principal. This is because the government could print money, if necessary, to pay him off. A U.S. Government Bond could be considered the "safest" type of an investment in the truest sense of the word. But, this is a fixed income investment with no opportunity for growth of principal.

An equity investment can produce a "reasonable return" through price appreciation, income, or a combination of both. However, for it to truly be categorized as an investment, there should be a safety factor of the purchase price over intrinsic value. Because future earning power is a function of the quality of the assets of the corporation, stockholder equity per share is a benchmark of this investment strategy. (This will be thoroughly explained in the next chapter.) So, if the true investor can buy the assets of a viable company at a substantial discount to stockholder equity, then by one measure, he has a safety factor.

Another important aspect of investing is to have broad diversification of your capital. No matter how thorough the analysis, no equity can be considered absolutely safe. Every stock is subject to a sharp price drop. Of course, in rare circumstances, the company may simply go out of business. We will explore these types of risk very shortly. But, for the time being, let's just underscore the fact that the speculator tends to concentrate his capital to achieve high returns; whereas, the true investor diversifies his capital to spead his risk of loss.

In the final analysis, the *attitude* of the decision-maker may determine the amount of his risk exposure. The speculator is attempting to maximize gain while the true investor is concerned with minimizing risk. The focus of the speculator is on making profits. The focus of the true investor is on avoiding losses. With all the pitfalls in the stock market, does the private, part-time investor even stand a chance? The answer is yes, if he can keep himself from being caught up in the vortex of crowd psychology. However, to do so, he must become disciplined and conservative in his approach. Rather than trying to predict future stock prices, perhaps he should accumulate quality companies when they are out of favor with the majority of investors.

WHY BUY STOCKS

Equity ownership of the shares of a publicly traded corporation offers a number of important advantages over other investment vehicles. First of all, you are, in fact, a partial owner of the company as represented by the number of shares that you possess. You may have a call upon a portion of the assets of the corporation and you may vote on important proposals that may affect your company. Your representation is in direct proportion to the number of shares that you own as a percent of the total number outstanding.

A corporation is an entity unto itself. As a common stock owner, you have no personal liablility for any of its actions. Also, you can never lose more than your original investment. A new company that needs capital to develop its products or a seasoned company that needs capital for expansion, may sell shares to the public to raise the money. After the offering, the shares begin freely trading in the open market. The buyers hope to participate in the profits generated by the corporation.

The profits of a corporation can benefit the investor in two ways. First of all, they can be reinvested back into the further expansion of the company. This should increase its earning power and therefore, the value to the investor. As the company earns more money, other investors will want to participate and their buying should increase the share price. Second, part of the profits can be paid to the investor in cash dividends. This money can be used for living expenses or reinvested in other opportunities. As the company grows, the earnings should increase. As the earnings increase, so should the dividends. Increased earnings and dividends should provide an appreciation in the value of the shares of the company. This is the economic rationale behind common stock ownership.

Stocks ultimately give more protection against inflation than fixed-income investments. Although earnings and dividend growth may be eroded temporarily during high inflationary periods, stockholder's equity can continue to increase. This is because the replacement value of the assets of the corporation becomes more expensive. For instance, during the late 1970s, a number of takeovers ensued. This was because it was much cheaper to buy whole companies than to start them from scratch.

In the inflationary environment of the 1970s, collectibles such as art, antiques, stamps, coins, old cars, and even bubble gum cards seemed to appreciate in price much more than many stocks. They have certain attractions that would include their aesthetic value for the enthusiast. For most people, they cannot be a real alternative to the stock market because they are too risky. They are highly illiquid and the difference between the "bid" and the "offer" price makes their real worth highly questionable. They are a game only for an individual that is very knowledgeable about the values in the respective markets.

Hard assets are no "investment panacea" either. Silver

hit a high of over $40 an ounce in early 1980. It then dropped to $10 an ounce several months later. In 1980, the price of gold dropped about 50% from its highs. These markets can be treacherous for all but the most seasoned speculator.

Neither hard assets nor collectibles can generate profits. Therefore, they cannot produce any income. They can only provide a return if the asset appreciates in price and is sold. Since worth in the future assumes an increase in price because of scarcity, they must be categorized as speculations.

Tax advantaged investments, usually in the form of limited partnerships, is the last investment alternative for most private, part-time investors. Real estate sydications, oil drilling programs, and equipment leasing would be included. Because these ventures are usually highly leveraged and often depend on the general partners' ability to perform, they must also be considered speculative. The transaction costs are often very high (usually over 10%). Also, you might ask yourself this question: If its's such a good deal, why are the general partners trying so hard to raise money?

There is a fallacy in so-called tax shelters that most investors don't seem to understand. First of all, Congress has closed most loop-holes in the tax laws. Now, there is no way to write off more money than you have "at risk." The leveraged deals in which you could get your cash out through tax savings are gone. You must write a check to somebody. If it's to put into the tax shelter, you still have aftertax dollars invested. If it's to the IRS, you have aftertax dollars available for investment. The real question is what will your return on your aftertax dollars be, given the risk exposure.

Let's assume that you have $10,000 of incremental income and you are considering putting that money into an oil drilling program in order to "save taxes." If you write a check for $10,000, they will "drill up" the money and you have a $10,000 write-off against ordinary income. This will save you from paying $5,000 in taxes, but you still have $5,000 of after-

Exhibit 1.1 ***Tax Advantaged Investments (50% Tax Bracket)***

Sheltered		
Incremental Ordinary Income		$10,000
Oil Drilling Program		($10,000)
	Tax Savings	$ 5,000
Invested Aftertax Capital		$ 5,000
Unsheltered		
Incremental Ordinary Income		$10,000
	Tax Liability	($ 5,000)
Aftertax Capital Available for Investment		$ 5,000
Opportunity Cost		
Assume an Aftertax Compound of 12.25% for six years		$ 5,000
	Opportunity Cost	$10,000

tax dollars invested. Exhibit 1.1 "Tax Advantaged Investments" shows the alternatives.

Of course, you could pay Uncle Sam his $5,000. As painful as that might be, you would still have $5,000 left to invest or spend. Assume you could make a aftertax return of 12.25% compounded every year for six years; you would then have $10,000 after taxes. That may not seem spectacular, but that's your opportunity cost. If your drilling program hit all dry holes, you will lose all of your cash. There has probably been more money lost trying to save taxes than for any other reason.

Liquidity is an important consideration in any investment. Although you may not get your original purchase price, just being able to "get out" could be important at a future date. This is extremely difficult, if not a virtual impossibility, in most real estate sydications, oil drilling programs, or other types of limited partnerships. On the other hand, common stocks usually provide a high degree of liquidity. The prices are quoted every day and they can be bought and sold freely.

Stocks can accommodate both small and large investors. This is especially important to the individual who is just beginning to accumulate equities. He can buy as little as one share and also diversify his capital easily over a number of companies.

There is no direct involvement by the investor. That is, common stocks are a passive investment. Once they are acquired, nothing has to be done until the appropriate time to sell them. At that point, the transaction costs are usually very little compared to other forms of equity investments. The investor has full control of his assets. He can decide when to buy or sell without the interference of other people such as in a partnership. Common stock ownership gives the investor ultimate flexibility with a minimum of bother.

The tax rates heavily favor the equity investor. The government takes only a small amount of the profits of a long-term capital gain. This would apply to someone who held his position more than one year. The maximum amount the government can claim is 20% of the profits for even the highest income investor.

There is another very important tax benefit for the equity investor, which is that he does not pay taxes until the asset is sold. So, there is an additional compounding effect of the unrealized profits. The reason for this is because the final outcome of a profit or loss will not be known until a sale is consummated.

Examine Exhibit 1.2, "Inflation Risk." It assumes a constant 8% interest payment on a fixed-income investment. Exhibit 1.3, "Equity Investment" assumes the same 8% return in the form of price appreciation. By comparing the results, you can see the positive effects that the tax laws can have on a real rate of return. When you own stock, there is no dampening effect of taxes on the appreciation every year. Therefore, the profits are compounded at a higher level. When taxes are the finally paid, they are only 20% versus 50%. So, the equity investor keeps much more of his profits.

Of course, an 8% increase every year cannot be guaranteed for an equity investment. But, neither can fixed-income rates. But for comparison purposes, you can see that the tax effects dramatically change the results for the equity investor. After adjusting for inflation, the fixed income investor had a negative rate of return of 20%. The equity investor has a real rate of return of 11%. Although that doesn't sound very exciting, there is a substantial difference in performance. The tax advantages are heavily weighted toward the equity investor and against the fixed-income investor.

Now, think about the word *wealth* for a moment. What images appear in your mind? Do you think about piles of money, a big mansion with servants, or a chauffeur-driven limousine? Most people think about vast riches, but this is not completely correct because almost everyone has some wealth.

Exhibit 1.2 ***Inflation Risk***
12-Year Example

In 1967 the Consumer Price Index was adjusted to 100. The government does this every 10 or 12 years so the public doesn't know how bad inflation really has been over the long term. Assume that you had $10,000 in 1967 and that you could invest this money in a fixed-income investment that would earn 8%. But, assume you are in the 50% tax bracket so you only keep 4% after taxes. The 8% rate was high for the late 1960s and early 1970s. It would be too low for the mid- to late 1970s. The average overall rate is approximately correct.

Exhibit 1.2 ***Inflation Risk***
12-Year Example (Continued)

Year	Principal	Aftertax Earnings
1967	$10,000	$400
1968	10,400	416
1969	10,816	433
1970	11,249	450
1971	11,699	468
1972	12,167	487
1973	12,654	506
1974	13,160	526
1975	13,686	547
1976	14,223	569
1977	14,792	592
1978	15,384	616
1979	16,000	

At the beginning of 1979 you had accumulated $16,000, or 160%, of you 1967 $10,000. Unfortunately, the Consumer Price Index had gone up over 100% so it took $20,000 to buy what you could have bought in 1967 for $10,000 aftertax.

$$\begin{array}{r} (\$20{,}000) \\ 16{,}000 \\ \hline (\$\ \ 4{,}000) \end{array}$$

$$\frac{(\$\ \ 4{,}000)}{\$20{,}000} = (20\%)$$

Over 12 years you not only didn't make any real return, you lost 20% of your wealth. Fixed-income securities often produced a guaranteed aftertax loss in buying power. You have more money, but it won't buy as much.

Exhibit 1.3 ***Equity Investment (8% Return Per Year for 12 Years)***

Year	Beginning Principal	Plus 8% Appreciation
1967	$10,000	$10,800
1968	10,800	11,664
1969	11,664	12,597
1970	12,597	13,604
1971	13,604	14,693
1972	14,693	15,863
1973	15,863	17,138
1974	17,138	18,509
1975	18,509	19,990
1976	19,990	21,589
1977	21,589	23,316
1978	23,316	25,181
1979	25,181	

Sale Price January 2, 1979	$25,181
Original Principal	($10,000)
Profit	$15,181
Capital Gains Taxes at 20% of Profit	($ 3,036)
Aftertax Profit	$12,145
Original Capital	$10,000
Total Aftertax Capital	$22,145
Inflation Rate 100%	($20,000)
Real Increase in Capital	$ 2,245

Real Rate of Return:

$$\frac{\$\ 2{,}245}{\$20{,}000} = 11\%$$

The economic definition of wealth is all *property possessing monetary value*. Wealth could take many different forms such as your home, personal property, stocks, certificates of deposits (CD), or other investments. The important point to realize is that wealth must be able to be converted into monetary value. Money is the medium that nations use to exchange for goods and services. In the case of the United States, it is dollars. As you know, in an inflationary period, the same dollars buy a little less every year. Unless your assets can be converted into monetary value with greater purchasing power, then you are not accumulating wealth.

Let's go back to our two previous examples. With the CD, about 20% of the purchasing power was lost. With the equity investment, about 11% of purchasing power was gained. In the first example, wealth was decreased and in the second example, wealth was increased. Now, let's reword the definition: *Accumulating wealth occurs when the aftertax monetary value of assets increase greater than the inflation rate.*

For the vast majority, gambling and speculating are not realistic avenues for accumulating wealth. The randomness of raw chance, the expectation of loss, the unpredictability of the future and, as we shall examine later, the emotions of fear and greed all make it nearly impossible for the gambler or speculator to achieve consistent capital growth. Therefore, any vehicle or approach that, by its very nature, would be considered a pure gamble or speculation must be eliminated as a viable alternative for the accumulation of wealth.

Have you ever read the first few pages of a prospectus on a limited partnership? These words usually appear somewhere: *there is a high degree of risk...* Remember that the true investor is concerned with minimizing risk. If there is a reasonable possibility that you can lose part, or all, of your money, the vehicle must be considered a speculation. This means that you should avoid oil and gas programs, raw land syndications, highly leveraged income real estate, and most equipment leasing partnerships.

There are other kinds of speculation. This includes anything that requires an accurate prediction and interpretation of the future. So, you shouldn't put money into precious metals, collectibles, and small growth companies. Since staying power is important, any approach that does not have a long-term time frame must be disregarded. This would include options, short-term trading, and highly leveraged stock positions.

Because a vehicle is considered low risk, it doesn't mean that it can be used to accumulate wealth. Investing in short-term financial instruments and long-term bonds are excellent ways to preserve capital and generate income. However, by their very nature, they cannot ever produce growth of capital. For this reason, and because taxes virtually assure negative real rates of return for high income individuals, these alternatives must also be deleted. If it seems that the above rationale has elimінted all but one way to increase monetary value, you're exactly right.

Common stock is the only realistic vehicle that most private, part-time investors can use to accumulate wealth. It is possible to make decisions based on intrinsic value with a margin of safety. Diversification is easy to accomplish. A long-term time frame can be considered with a minimum of involvement. Can all these criteria really be met? The answer is yes. All you have to do is learn how to profit from the PSYCLE.

2

Investment Techniques

FINANCIAL TOOLS

In order to invest intelligently in common stocks, it is necessary to understand basic measures of value. This does not mean one has to become a Certified Financial Analyst. It means that you should have a working knowledge of the terminology. To appreciate the strengths and weaknesses of fundamental security analysis, it is important to comprehend the financial tools that are used to reach conclusions.

The analysis of the balance sheet of a corporation is one of the most important tools used to determine the financial health of a corporation at any given time. All publicly traded corporations publish an in-depth balance sheet at the end of each fiscal year. This is done by the annual report. Although there are many intricacies in balance sheet analysis, we will consider only the basic structure.

If an individual takes the cost of all the assets he owns and then subtracts all the money he owes to other people, the resulting figure would be his net worth. This is exactly what is done for a corporation to generate a balance sheet. Notice that the value of the assets used is the cost basis, not the market value. In a corporation, the assets (except land) are *depreciated*, or reduced in value, every year. This is an accounting technique to allow for wear and tear. Because of inflation, it is possible that the market value is greater than the depreciated cost basis (called book value).

Look at Exhibit 2.1, "Balance Sheet." It explains the structure in a simplified format. Don't be confused by the dollar signs with a subnumeral like this ($\$_1$). They just represent a variable in a dollar amount. The key point to remember is that assets equals liabilities plus stockholders equity.

One important ingredient in determining the viability of a corporation is the amount of money it owes. The capital

Exhibit 2.1 ***Balance Sheet***

Equation:

$$\text{Assets } (\$_1) - \text{Liabilities } (\$_2) = \text{Stockholder's Equity } (\$_3)$$

From algebra, add Liabilities ($\$_2$) to both sides of the equation:

$$\begin{aligned} \text{Assets } (\$_1) - \text{Liabilities } (\$_2) &= \text{Stockholder's Equity } (\$_3) \\ \text{Liabilities } (\$_2) &= \text{Liabilities } (\$_2) \end{aligned}$$

Now the original equation is adjusted to read:

$$\text{Assets } (\$_1) = \text{Liabilities } (\$_2) + \text{Stockholder's Equity } (\$_3)$$

But accountants like to read vertically so:

$$\begin{aligned} \text{Assets } (\$_1) &= \text{Liabilities } (\$_2) + \\ &\quad \text{Stockholder's Equity } (\$_3) \\ \hline (\$_1) &= (\$_2) + (\$_3) \end{aligned}$$

Assume the Assets ($\$_1$) of XYZ Corporation were \$10,000,000. Let's also assume that the Liabilties ($\$_2$) of the company were \$3,000,000 and the Stockholder's equity ($\$_3$) was \$7,000,000, then:

Balance Sheet
(000)

Assets		Liabilities	
Assets $10,000		Liabilities $	3,000
		Stockholder's Equity $	7,000
$10,000 =			$10,000

Putting a few items in each category, a very simplified balance sheet might look like this:

Balance Sheet XYZ Corp
December 31, 1980
(000)

Assets		*Liabilities*	
Cash	$ 1,000	Bank Loans	$ 1,000
Inventories	2,000	Bonds	2,000
Equipment	2,000	*Stockholder's Equity*	
Factories	4,000	Original Capital	1,000
Land	1,000	Retained Earnings	6,000
	$10,000		$10,000

structure of most corporations is made up of both debt and equity. A big debt as a percentage of total assets indicates high leverage and reduced staying power in the event of hard times. In the case of XYZ Corporation, the debt is 30% of total capital. The maturity of this debt is also important because banks and bondholders become impatient for their money when it is due. These are items the investor should be aware of when making his decisions. However, an in-depth balance sheet analysis is both complex and subjective. It is also beyond the scope and requirements of this strategy.

Stockholders equity can be determined from the balance sheet. It represents how much money would be left if the assets of the corporation could be sold for their depreciated financial cost and all of the debtholders paid in full. This figure would then be distributed to the shareholders according to how many shares they owned.

For a viable corporation, shareholders equity may be worth much more than its stated value. The replacement cost of these working assets may be much greater in an inflationary environment. Shareholders equity does not account for an organizational value, that is, the people operating the assets. It also cannot take into account the acceptance of the company's products that have accumulated over the years. Whereas these last two factors are subjective, shareholders equity is clearly an objective and calculable number.

Stockholders equity is one of the most important factors in determining intrinsic value. A fundamental security analyst would argue that intrinsic value would be determined by the future earning power of the assets. However, determining the future earning power of a corporation requires many subjective conclusions. Investors are interested in what they get for their money now, as well as in the future.

In the final analysis, there are only two ingredients necessary for a corporation to make money. The most important one is assets. The company must have the plant and equipment to produce products for sale. It is true that the assets must be managed properly in order to make a profit. If you have good assets that are being managed poorly, the shareholders can replace the management. However, the best managers in the world cannot produce salable products without good assets. Management is a subjective evaluation whereas stockholders equity is an objective evaluation. So, if you can buy the assets of a corporation at a substantial discount, then you have acquired intrinsic value.

You also have established a margin of safety in case of insolvency. Although it would be extremely rare for a seasoned manufacturing company to go out of business, it could happen. In a liquidation or a distressed takeover, the assets may be worth less than the stockholders equity. By acquiring the assets at a discount, you have given yourself some protec-

Exhibit 2.2 ***Stockholder's Equity***

Equation:

Assets ($\$_1$) − Liabilities ($\$_2$) = Stockholder's Equity ($\$_3$)

Now divide Stockholder's Equity by total shares outstanding:

$$\frac{\text{Stockholder's Equity } (\$_3)}{\text{Total Shares Outstanding } (SHS_1)} = \frac{\$}{\text{Share}}$$

Now, let's determine the stockholder's equity for XYZ Corporation:

$10,000,000 − $3,000,000 = $7,000,000

Let's assume that there are 350,000 shares outstanding.
Divide this figure by the total number of shares outstanding:

$$\frac{\$7{,}000{,}000}{350{,}000 \text{ shares}} = \$20/\text{share}$$

tion of your capital.

Look at Exhibit 2.2, "Stockholders Equity." It is the amount of money that could be distributed to the owners on a per-share basis. This assumes the assets could be sold for their exact depreciated cost basis and all of the debts of the corporation paid from the proceeds. The stockholders equity for XYZ Corporation is $20 a share. So if the investor could buy the stock for $12, then he would have bought assets at a discount with a safety factor of almost 1.66 times. But assets are only valuable if they can produce profits. Let's see how this happens in a corporation.

A corporation produces goods or services for sale. These sales revenues generate income. All expenses required to produce these goods or services are then subtracted. What is left is called profits. In the United States, the government is a silent partner in every corporation; Uncle Sam takes his share of the profits and calls it taxes.

What remains is called profit after taxes. (The two words profit and earnings have the same meaning.) These profits are for the owners (stockholders). This money can be reinvested into the company or paid out in the form of cash dividends. Total aftertax profits are divided by the total number of shares so that it can be expressed in a dollar per share figure. This is the common denominator of all publicly traded corporate earnings.

Exhibit 2.3, "Income Statement" shows a very simplified format. For XYZ Corporation, the earnings for 1980 are $2,100,000. They paid $700,000 in dividends to stockholders and there was $1,400,000 available for reinvestment into the company. But, to be meaningful, these figures must be expressed on a per share basis. Exhibits 2.4 and 2.5 show that the earnings per share for XYZ Corporation were $6 per share and the dividends per share were $2 per share.

These figures must be compared to the market price to have additional meaning. The price to earnings ratio confuses many people. It is simply a pure number that is determined by dividing the market price per share by earnings per share. In the case of XYZ Corporation, the market price is 8 times earnings. The dividends per share is the amount of cash distributed to the investor. To calculate the current yield, the dividends per share are divided by the market price. These financial tools, along with many others, are used to evaluate the fundamental worth of the corporation.

FUNDAMENTAL SECURITY ANALYSIS

What is the price of stock really worth today? What will it be worth in the future? How does that compare with its present market price? Fundamental security analysis is a process that attempts to evaluate the future profitability of a company as an ongoing business. Unfortunately, it is not an exact science.

The fundamental security analyst uses many financial tools, as well as a number of assumptions about the future in order to predict the price movement of a stock. One of his tasks is to try to anticipate changes in the economic environment in which the company is operating and then to deter-

Exhibit 2.3 *Income Statement*

Equation:

Sales Revenues ($\$_4$) − Expenses ($\$_5$) = Profits ($\$_6$)

But accountants like to read vertically, so:

Sales Revenues	($\$_4$)
Expenses	−($\$_5$)
Profit Before Taxes	($\$_6$)
Taxes	−($\$_7$)
Profit After Taxes	($\$_8$)
Dividends Paid	−($\$_9$)
Retained Earnings	($\$_{10}$)

Let's assume XYZ Corporation had sales of $20,000,000, expenses of $17,000,000, profits of $3,000,000, taxes of $900,000, and paid dividends of $700,000 to shareholders. Now, a simplified income statement would look like this:

Income Statement XYZ Corp.
January 1, 1980 to December 31, 1980
(000)

Sales Revenues	$20,000
Expenses	−$17,000
Profits Before Taxes	$ 3,000
Taxes	−$ 900
Profits After Taxes	$ 2,100
Dividends Paid	−$ 700
Retained Earnings	$ 1,400

Exhibit 2.4

Earnings Per Share

Equation:

$$\frac{\text{Earnings After Taxes } (\$_8)}{\text{Total Shares Outstanding } (SHS_1)} = \frac{\$}{\text{Share}}$$

For XYZ Corp:

$$\frac{\$2{,}100{,}000}{350{,}000 \text{ Shares}} = \frac{\$6}{\text{Share}}$$

Price to Earnings Ratio

Equation:

$$\frac{\text{Market Price of Stock } (\$/\text{Share})}{\text{Earnings per Share } \quad (\$/\text{Share})} = \text{Ratio}$$

For XYZ Corp., assume a market price of $48 Share

$$\frac{\$48/\text{Share}}{\$\ \ 6/\text{Share}} = 8$$

or expressed another way:

Market Price = P/E Ratio × Earnings per Share

For XYZ Corp. you could say the stock was selling at 8 times earnings per share:

$48/Share = 8 × $6/Share

---

mine the effects on profitability. He then must decide if the company is overvalued, fairly valued, or undervalued in relation to its market price. In order to arrive at these conclusions,

Exhibit 2.5

Dividends Per Share

Equation:

$$\frac{\text{Dividends Paid } (\$_9)}{\text{Total Shares Outstanding } (SHS_1)} = \frac{\$}{\text{Share}}$$

For XYZ Corp.:

$$\frac{\$700{,}000}{350{,}000 \text{ Shares}} = \frac{\$2}{\text{Share}}$$

Current Yield

Equation:

$$\frac{\text{Dividends per Share } (\$/\text{Share})}{\text{Market Price per Share } (\$/\text{Share})} = \%$$

For XYZ Corp.:

$$\frac{\$\ 2/\text{Share}}{\$48/\text{Share}} = 4.2\%$$

---

he must carefully examine a large number of factors based on established principles and sound logic. This in fact, is the meaning of the word *analysis*.

But no matter how thorough the analysis, it can never be precise. The skill of the individual analyst and raw chance are important elements in determining the ultimate success or failure of the decision. Of course, the same would be true in other professions such as medicine or law. Unfortunately, the fundamental security analyst must consider a relatively large number of complex, interrelated variables in order to arrive at his conclusions.

Here are some of the questions that must be answered:

- What will be the overall economic environment in the United States for the next several years?
- Will it be expansionary or recessionary?
- Is there any impending legislation that could affect the company?
- How will the industry of the company be affected?
- Will there be an overall increase or decrease in the demand for its products?
- How strong is the company relative to its competition?
- Is there any technological development that could change its competitive position, either positively or negatively?
- What is the depth and quality of management?
- Have they had a good track record and are they flexible enough to adapt to changing environments and circumstances for the company?
- What are the financial strengths and weaknesses of the company?
- Do they have too much debt?
- Are they well capitalized to take advantage of future growth opportunities?
- Can they survive an unforeseen downturn in the economy?
- What has been their past earnings record?
- Has it shown steady growth or has it been erratic?
- Can the earnings be predicted with regularity?
- How influenced are they by the cyclicals of the economy?

- What has been the return on invested equity?
- Are there reasons to believe that it will increase or decrease over the next several years?
- How secure is the dividend?
- What can it be increased?

Once these questions have been answered, the analyst must decide if his conclusions have already been "discounted" in the price of the stock.

Where does the analyst get the information on which he bases his decisions? First of all, he would examine closely all the financial reports of the company and other companies in the industry. This would include the annual report and quarterly reports. Since a security analyst must know so much about the overall industry in order to make an informed decision on a particular company, it only seems natural that he should "follow" or evaluate all the important companies in that industry.

Where else does he obtain data? He will usually go to visit the company personally at least once a year. There he will have in-depth discussions with senior management. He will also explore pending problems or opportunities or the profitability of the company. Many times, companies will have meetings especially for security analysts in order to more efficiently disseminate their information. Of course, he will also carefully study certain economic reports, government reports, and trade publications. From this extensive reading, he must decide what is and what is not important to his final conclusions.

He must now compare the current market price of the stock against three different measures of value. *Future value* is his projected price assuming the outcome of his assumptions is correct. *Intrinsic value* is the price-based worth of the assets of the corporation and their ability to earn money under ordinary circumstances. *Relative value* shows how this stock is priced compared to other stocks in the marketplace. Of course, an individual analyst may attach different levels of importance to each measure of value.

The analyst must now make a recommendation regarding the future price movement of the stock. He has processed a large amount of data. He now draws upon his expertise and past experience to come to a conclusion. He will recommend a buy on the stock if he thinks it could appreciate significantly. He will recommend a hold on the stock if he thinks it will move with the overall stock market. A sell recommendation will be placed on the stock if he believes it has significant downside risk. Of course, as new data becomes available, he reserves the right to change his mind, and his recommendation.

Evaluating the fundamental value of a stock based on its business prospects is one basis for an investment decision. But, high asset evaluations, low P/E ratios, or increasing earnings and dividends cannot directly make stocks go up and down in price. People do. It is investor perception regarding the outlook for the stock that stimulates buying and selling.

PRICE MOVEMENT

As elementary as it may seem, it is important for the investor to understand that security prices reflect the basic laws of supply and demand. Simply stated, it means that if a company has a fixed number of shares outstanding, then the price will rise as the demand increases and that the price will fall as the demand decreases. When demand absorbs all the supply at a certain price, the price will go up in order to bring out sellers at a higher level. Conversely, when supply is absorbed by buyers at a certain price, the price will go down in order to attract buyers at a lower level. On any given day, this battle between supply and demand is reflected by the volume of the stock traded. It is very important to keep in mind that *for every buyer there is a seller*. When you buy a stock, you buy it from somebody. When you sell it, you sell it to somebody else. It means that whoever is on the other side of your trade is thinking exactly opposite to you. One of you is right and one of you is wrong.

The most important tool used by the market analyst in plying his trade is the price chart. This gives him a picture of how the forces of supply and demand are affecting the price movement of a security or the market averages. Although there are several different types of charts, we will focus on the bar chart, which is the most common.

The bar chart has two dimensions. Price is the vertical axis and time is the horizontal axis. In its simplest form, it is made by drawing a vertical line between the high–low price range for the period of time chosen. It can be kept on a daily, weekly, or monthly basis or, in some cases, a yearly basis.

The type of chart used would depend on the focus of the risk-taker. The short-term trader would be interested in the daily price action. The intermediate-term trader would be more likely to use the weekly price chart. The long-term investor would be more concerned about monthly price movements, if not longer term moves.

Because this investment strategy has a long-term time frame, the only type of price charts needed are the monthly bar charts. These charts generally show about 15 or 20 years of past price movement adjusted for splits and stock dividends. Exhibit 2.6, "Monthly Bar Chart," shows a partial enlargement of a hypothetical stock. The price action for the last three months of 1980 and the first three months of 1981 is revealed. In reality, the chart would be much smaller and the lines closer together.

Exhibit 2.6 ***Monthly Bar Chart***

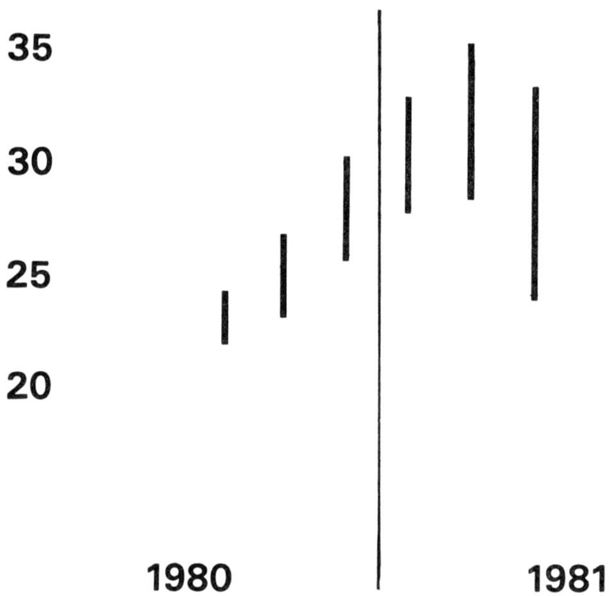

	high	low
1980		
Oct.	24	21½
Nov.	26¼	23
Dec.	30	25¼
1981		
Jan.	31½	28
Feb.	34	29
Mar.	32	24⅜

The basic use of the monthly bar chart is to determine long-term support and resistance levels. A support level is where demand can absorb supply and not let the price drop. It is where the stock has stopped going down in the past. A resistance level is where supply absorbs all demand without letting the price increase. It is where the stock has stopped going up in the past. The investor should attempt to buy at a price levels near long-term support and sell near the price range of long-term resistance.

The market technician has many ways to interpret the price dynamics of the market place. However, these techniques are very sophisticated and short-term in nature. For that reason, they do not apply to this investment strategy. But long-term price movements are an integral part of this approach. Low price means low demand and, therefore, low valuation by investors. High price means high demand and, therefore, high valuation by investors.

It is important to remember that it takes time for investor attitudes to change. In other words, the longer it takes to reverse a trend, the greater the amplitude of the following price move is likely to be. Investors become conditioned to their most recent experiences and extrapolate from them into the future. Therefore, it usually takes extensive price erosion to wring out the speculative excesses produced by a dynamic uptrend. When investor sentiment finally swings to the negative side, it is at much lower prices. The accumulation phase may then take an extended period of time, depending on the magnitude of the price drop.

Trend analysis is one of the most important jobs of the market technician. Ideally, his analysis would signal the beginning of an extended uptrend phase of price movement and the stock would be bought. The security would be held until a reversal of the trend was indicated. The stock would then be sold and a profit realized. Then the search for a similar situation would begin if one is not already available. This approach is used to try and maximize the return on capital in the shortest period of time. Look at Exhibit 2.7, "Anatomy of a Price Cycle" to observe the theoretical price dynamics in much more detail.

After an extended downtrend, the price begins to stabilize. This is a period of sideways movement within a narrow range. This marks the beginning of the *accumulation phase* where demand starts to absorb all supply. It will continue over a period of time until increasing demand forces the price higher and higher. After an extended uptrend, the accumulation phase may climax by an almost vertical price movement to the upside. This is the most visible reflection of one-sided emotional enthusiasm by investors. It may also begin the distribution phase.

The *base formation* period will be reflected on a price chart by a time of sideways movement within a narrow range. It will be marked by sharp price movements both up and down. There can be high volume and low price volatility. It can take months or years before this period of neutral price movement is completed.

The second part of the accumulation phase begins as the price breaks out of its neutral pattern and begins an *uptrend*. In order for demand to be satisfied, the price must now increase to bring out more supply of the stock. The movement may be within the borders of a trend channel. This is represented by drawing two parallel lines that confine the price movements. There can be price volatility within the trend channel. During this overall upward advance, the price may increase sharply over a short period of time. These rallies may be followed by periods of sideways movements called consolidations. Occasionally, there may be a sharp drop in price. This is called a reaction. It may happen after the stock has moved up too quickly. Despite these near-term abbreviations, advances generally make higher price levels and reactions do not exceed previous lows. Thus, the uptrend is maintained.

Exhibit 2.7 ***Anatomy of a Price Cycle***

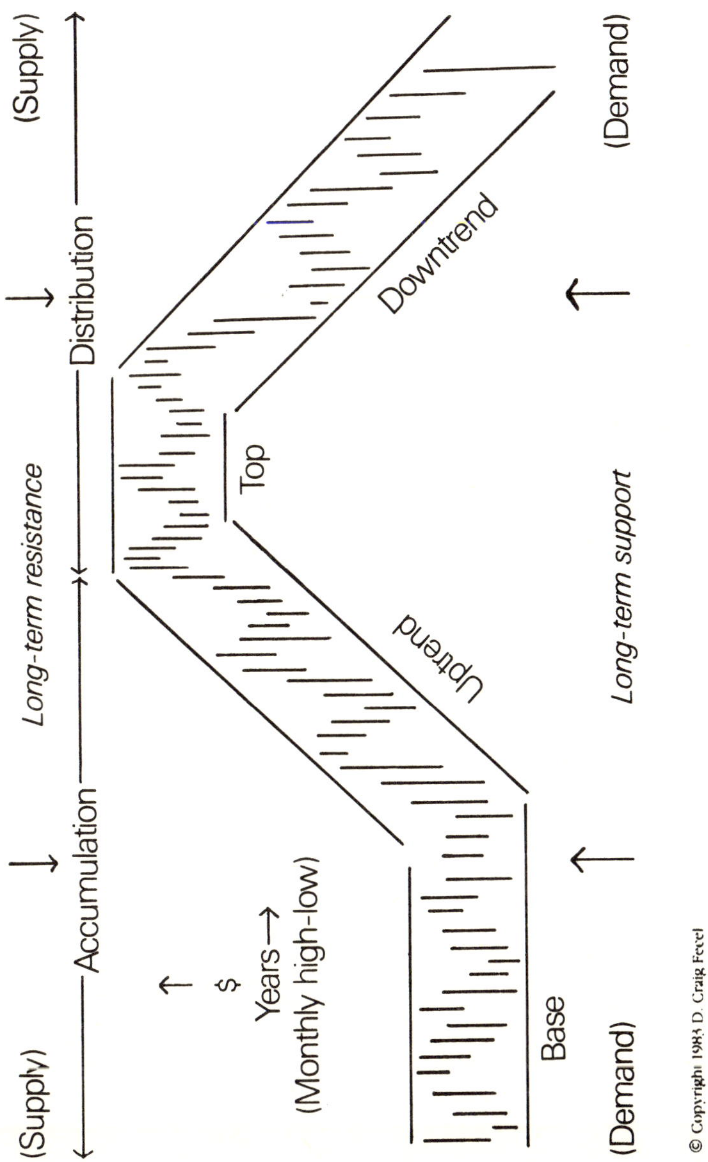

As the uptrend nears completions, the price action may become extremely volatile. Prices may sharply accelerate to the upside only to be followed by slow downside price erosion. Further rally attempts and reactions will change the price trend to a neutral one called a stabilization pattern. This is the beginning of the *distribution phase*.

The sideways action traces a *top formation* on the price chart. It is at this point that fundamentals regarding the company are the most positive. Earnings may be rising dramatically. A dividend increase may be imminent. In general, the outlook for the next several years is very positive. Yet, as the price struggles to the top of its neutral range, it is turned back by supply. Future events have already been discounted in the price. Eventually, supply overcomes demand and the price breaks out of its neutral trading range to the downside.

The second part of the distribution phase is called the *downtrend*. Generally, the price action is just the opposite of an uptrend. There will be periods of slow price erosion, followed by reflex rallies sharply to the upside. After the ensuing consolidations, the downtrend will continue. In general, the highs will be lower and the lows will be lower. Of course, there could be periods of sharp price drops. Ths may be especially true toward the end of the downtrend. It could signal the beginning of the accumulation phase.

The purpose of trend analysis is to participate in the greatest price appreciation in the shortest possible time. The market technician wants to avoid being stuck in a stock that may take a long time in the base formation period of the accumulation phase. He also does not want to be in a stock that is in a downtrend. In general, technical analysis tries to maximize the return on capital by achieving the best gain within a minimum time frame.

Of course, textbook price movement rarely occurs in such an orderly fashion in the real world. The more sophisticated the investors become, the more rapidly the future may be discounted in the price movement. Sharp rises may then be quickly followed by sharp drops or vise versa. On the other hand, the uptrends and downtrends can be very orderly. What often appears to be a top formation may turn out to be the continuation of an uptrend. Of course, the opposite would occur within a downtrend. Occasionally, you will find that a base formation or top formation phase may last several months and at other times it may last many years. So it seems difficult for price movement to be predicted in a predetermined way by the majority.

Let's now become familiar with the 20-year monthly bar chart. This is an essential tool of this investment strategy. Its primary purpose is to identify price levels of long-term demand (support) and long-term resistance (supply). For illustration, we will examine the price movement of Outboard Marine (see Exhibit 2.8, "Accumulation and Distribution").

The chart of the price movement of Outboard Marine spans about 20 years. It begins in 1961 and goes to 1980. There have been no splits or stock dividends. However, the price movement would have been adjusted had there been any. The vertical axis is priced in $10 increments. The horizontal axis is timed in one year increments. Between each year are 12 small vertical lines that seem to run together. These are the high and low price ranges for each month.

It appears that Outboard Marine has gone through three distinct price cycles of accumulation and distribution since the early 1960s. These are detailed in the exhibit and offer some interesting contrasts. The 1963–1968 accumulation phase took six years, whereas, the 1974–1975 accumulation phase took less than 18 months. The distribution phase of 1968–1970 took only 18 months; but, the 1976–1979 phase took four years. The only constant in the price action seemed to be that sharp, vertical movement near long-term support and resistance levels clearly signaled an eventual change of direction.

Exhibit 2.8 *Accumulation and Distribution (Monthly High-Low)*

Outboard Marine

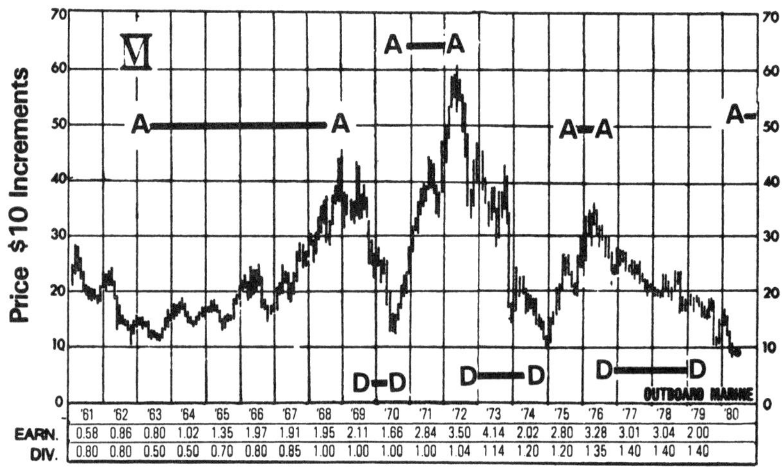

Time
1 Year Increments

Cycle I		
Accumulation Phase	A–A	End 1962 to end 1968
Distribution Phase	D–D	1969 to Mid-1970
Cycle II		
Accumulation Phase	A–A	Mid-1970 to Mid-1972
Distribution Phase	D–D	Mid-1972 to end 1974
Cycle III		
Accumulation Phase	A–A	1975 to Mid-1976
Distribution Phase	D–D	Mid-1976 to end 1979
Cycle IV		
Accumulation Phase	A–	1980 to ?

Courtesy of Moody's Handbook

TECHNICAL SECURITY ANALYSIS

If someone asks you to describe a stock market technician, what would come to mind? Perhaps you would envision a little old man with a green eyeshade on who was stuck away in a back room somewhere. There he would be hunched over his price charts studying various price movements. If this was ever the case, it certainly isn't now.

Actually, technical analysis is the oldest form of security analysis known to man. It has been traced back to the late 1800s and was used before financial statements were available for any type of quantitative analysis. However, in the last 20 years, it has become substantially more sophisticated because the computer has made the accumulation of vast amounts of stock market data easily accessible. Technical security analysis is now considered by many as an important determinant of stock market profitability.

The "bible" of technical analysis was written by two men named Edwards and Magee. In 1948, regarding price, they wrote:

> The market price reflects not only the differing value opinions of many orthodox security appraisers, but also all the hopes and fears and guesses and moods, rational and irrational, of hundreds of potential buyers and sellers, as well as their needs and their resources—in total, factors which defy analysis and for which no statistics are available, but which are nevertheless all synthesized, weighed, and finally expressed in the precise figure at which a buyer and seller get together and make a deal. This is the only figure that counts.

Prices are 100% psychological. That is what the market technician believes. Future earnings, dividends, assets or P/E ratios of a company do not determine the price of a security. Only supply and demand can do that and it is the ultimate reflection of people's feelings regarding the stock.

There are many different reasons why a stock may be bought or sold. A buyer may be concerned with future earnings growth, low asset evaluations, or high current yield. A seller may feel the prospects of future earnings increases have already been reflected in the price of the stock. He may also want to realize a profit or avoid further losses. Of course, he may just need the money.

Each decision maker may also have a different time frame. Some people will be buying or selling for what may happen in the next three months and others may be concerned only with the next three years or longer. But one thing is certain, the only "measure of value" is interpreted within the mind of each investor. This can and does change from time to time.

Stock market price movements are a visible reflection of "people acting like people." Human beings tend to react to similar situations in consistent ways; therefore, human nature remains fairly constant. The fact that people will continue to make the same mistakes in the future that they have made in the past is an important assumption of technical analysis.

Another basic premise is that the stock market and individual stocks tend to act like a barometer rather than a thermometer. That is, they tend to anticipate the future rather than reflect the present. In other words, the stock market is a *discounting mechanism*. The price movements today are reflecting the feelings of investors about the future.

The market technician believes that price movements have momentum and basically follow the laws of physics. That is, once a trend is in place, it will not be reversed without some warning or indication. This will be reflected in certain price and volume patterns which tend to repeat themselves over and over. The ability to correctly analyze these pictures of supply and demand will make it possible to participate in the trend of market prices and to anticipate their change.

It is also important to know how investors as a whole feel about the future. This can be reflected by sentiment indicators of investor psychology. The major underlying assumption of technical analysis is that the majority of investors are wrong at major turning points. So, if one can determine when the majority is very positive about the future or very negative about the future, then it may be possible to anticipate a major change in the direction of prices.

This is also called *contrary thinking*. Once it can be determined that the vast majority of investors anticipate a particular event or events in the future, it may have already been reflected in the price movement of the security. So, for one to invest intelligently, he should think contrary to the majority of investors and do just the opposite, even though the rationale at the time may not be apparent.

The power of money is the driving force of stock price movements. High cash reserves can ignite a rally. Conversely, low cash reserves means that the "fuel" of the upward movement has been exhausted and a correction may become likely. The ability to understand the level of buying power for stocks can be an important tool for the anticipation of a change of direction.

There are three primary sources of demand for stocks. The financial institutions such as retirement funds and mutual funds are by far, the largest. In fact, they now account for about 70% of the volume on the New York Stock Exchange. Private investors play an important role in adding or subtracting money from the marketplace. Investors tend to buy for cash whereas speculators may borrow money and create debit balances in margin accounts. Finally, foreign investors can also be an important source of capital. The market technician can monitor the potential demand or supply from each of these groups.

The level of speculation can indicate potential turning points. Near the top of the price rise, speculators are very aggressive. Buoyed by recent successes, they quest for more and more profits. Margin debt has expanded dramatically and unseasoned new issues are in high demand. The reverse is usually true near price lows. Persistent losses give no reason for enthusiasm. Under these conditions, margin debt contracts as liquidity is rebuilt. A conservative approach to risk avoidance becomes the focus of attention by almost everyone. High levels of speculation tend to identify market peaks; whereas, low levels of speculation are synonymous with market bottoms.

There are specific words used to identify the trend of stock prices. When they are rising, they are said to be in a bull market. Why would that term apply? Well, try to imagine a big bull tossing them upward into the air. When stocks prices are falling, they are said to be in a bear market. Why would that term apply? Again, try to imagine a big bear mauling them to the ground. However, it is rare that all stocks are rising in a bull market or falling in a bear market. There will be times when there will be groups in their own individual bull markets and other groups in their own individual bear markets. The problem comes in differentiating one from the other.

Technical security analysis is an art that uses the application of scientific methodology. There are a vast number of indicators used to determine momentum, sentiment. speculation, and the flow of funds in the marketplace. But sometimes they are at crosscurrents with each other. Like any other profession, successful results require experience, time for study, talent, determination, and discipline. These attributes will not be possessed by most private, part-time investors.

Fundamental security analysis can tell you what company to buy and why to buy it. Technical security analysis can tell you when to buy it. That is, it is primarily a timing tool. However, much of the analysis is geared to forecasting near- and intermediate-term price movements. For that reason, these intricacies are not applicable to this strategy. Let's now examine the magnitude of the effort required if all the many variables that determine future price movements are considered.

DECISION BULL'S-EYE

All investment decisions are based in some part on the ability of the investor to forecast the future and then interpret the events of the future regarding stock price movements. This is an extremely difficult job for even the most highly trained individual. Let's try to group the vast number of complex variables into specific areas of consideration on a step-by-step basis. See Exhibit 2.9, "Investment Target." How hard do you think it will be to hit the decision bull's-eye? It can only be done if you adequately evaluate all of the necessary variables.

Exhibit 2.9 ***Investment Target***

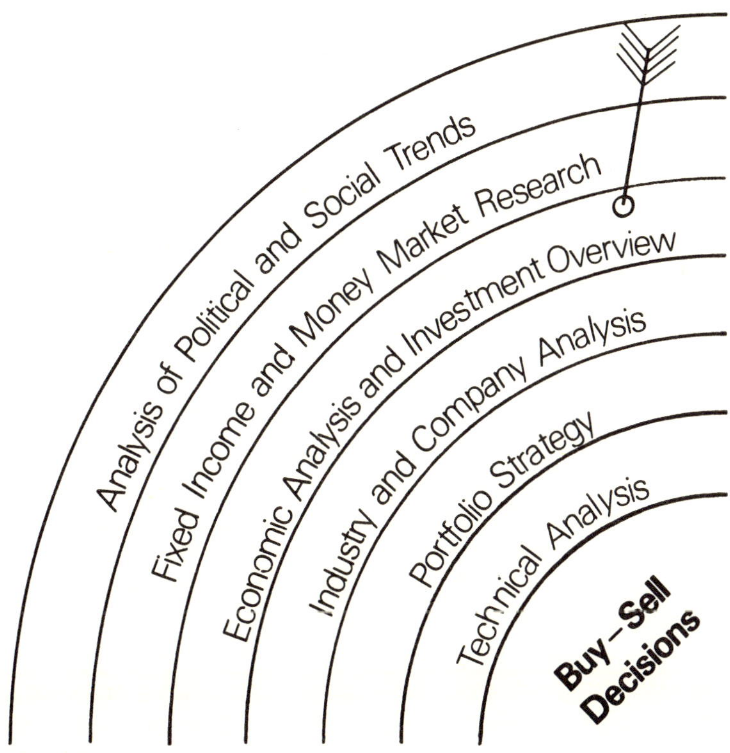

The first place to start would be with an analysis of political and social trends that could affect segments of the economy. Are government policies expansionary or recessionary? Is the mood of the voter more liberal or conservative? Is the government shifting emphasis toward free enterprise or socialism? These are just some of the questions that should be answered.

The direction of interest rates have important consequences for the economy and the stock market. Interpreting government policies may give a clue to interest rates movements. Increasing inflation would mean higher rates while decreasing inflation would mean lower rates. Higher rates may mean that money will flow into fixed-income instruments instead of stocks. A correct prediction regarding the future course of interest rates may give a clearer indication regarding the course of the economy and the stock market.

Now it would be necessary to analyze the economy in order to determine an investment overview. Which segments of the economy will have the greatest utilization of resources? Which industries will have the best growth and profit opportunities? Are there industries that may stagnate under the presumed senario? How and where should the investors' capital be allocated?

Once the industries with the greatest growth potential have been identified, the companies within those industries must be compared. Which one is the leader? Which has the best capital structure? Which company has the highest quality managment? Also, they must be compared as to their value, according to generally accepted methods of fundamental analysis, to determine which of the stocks should be bought.

Now you must develop a portfolio strategy to implement the rational and orderly investment of your money. The word portfolio is a term that simply means the itemized list of securities that will be owned. Has the overall analysis produced any inconsistencies? Is there a common investment theme that should receive special focus? How much risk do you want to assume? How volatile should the portfolio be? How much current yield? What kind of cash reserves do you want to keep? Finally, what overall rate of return would you like to achieve?

Now you can turn to technical security analysis to help you time your decisions. Is the stock market strong, or is it weak? Are your stocks in uptrends or downtrends? Should you buy now or will there be a better opportunity later? Are the majority of investors optismistic or pessimistic? Are there substantial buying power reserves on the sidelines, or are they already committed? Will the actions of your portfolio strategy be similar to the crowd or will they be contrary?

Now that you have carefully answered all of the questions just asked, along with any which suggest themselves, you should have no trouble arriving at buying and selling decisions regarding your portfolio. Of course, this is not just a one-shot deal. All of the complex variables must be reanalyzed and evaluated periodically.

If you are thinking that this process would be a full-time job and beyond the scope of nearly all private, part-time investors, you'd be right. However, this process, along with some variations, is exactly what many professional money managers attempt to go through in running large institutional portfolios. Does it give them the ability to more accurately predict stock price movements? If it doesn't, why doesn't it? More important, can we distill many of these imponderable variables and find a "magic key" that will unlock the door to consistent profits?

A WORKABLE APPROACH

There are two kinds of risk assumed when an equity investment is made. This approach attempts to minimize *price risk* by buying stocks only when they are near 10- or 20-year lows. It also attempts to minimize *business risk* (a company may go out of business), by accumulating only seasoned, high quality companies (mostly New York Stock Exchange). In other words, before you buy a company you want to be sure that it's just out of favor and not going out of business. So the company must have the financial resources to weather a few years of hard times.

The staying power of large companies is often beyond belief. A reduction in earnings or dividends is often overdiscounted in a sharp drop in the price of the stock. In the majority of cases, the decline in earning power is not permanent. Management many be forced to make "painful" adjustments, but a strong asset base will enable the company to endure. Favorable events that were not anticipated often cause a dramatic increase in earnings from depressed levels. The patient investor that accumulates the company's stock at distressed prices is often handsomely rewarded over the long term.

Just remember that in order for a company to make money there must be two basic ingredients. First, it must have assets and second, the assets must be managed properly. If the investor can buy the assets at a substantial discount, then he has reduced his risk in case of insolvency. However, large, seasoned companies rarely go out of business and have their assets valued as worthless. Usually, if a company falls on hard times, somebody will buy the assets for some price. In most cases the assets or stockholder's equity per share is an understated figure. This is because the replacement cost of those assets would be much higher at today's inflated prices.

This strategy is a technical approach to investing that uses 20-year charts of past price history as reference points to buy and sell securities. But it is also a fundamental approach that tries to minimize risk by acquiring the assets of a corporation at a discount to stockholder's equity whenever possible. This technique is built on the following conclusions:

- The majority of investors will always be wrong at major turning points.
- Predicting future stock price movements is a difficult job for even the most highly trained analyst or portfolio manager.

- Long-term profits in the stock market are best realized by attempting to minimize risk, not in trying to maximize gain.

Garfield Drew was a famous market theorist of the mid-twentieth century. Almost 40 years ago he said:

> In fact, simplicity or singleness of approach is a greatly underestimated factor of market success. As soon as the attempt is made to watch a multiplicity of factors, even though each has some element to justify it, one is only too likely to be lost in a maze of contradictory implications... the various factors involved may be so conflicting that the conclusion finally drawn is no better than a snap judgement would have been.

What could be simpler than buying a stock near its historic lows and selling it near historic highs of the last 10 or 20 years? Undervaluation means low price and overvaluation means high price. According to Mr. Drew; even if the investor had time and expertise to do an in-depth financial analysis of a company, his investment decision may not be any "better than a snap judgement." Also, as we shall see in a later chapter, the Random Walk Theory claims that such financial tools as past earnings, P/E ratios, and dividends have not proven useful in predicting future stock price movements.

Cycles are an integral part of human behavior, business, nature, and the universe. The phenomenon of some cycles is easily explainable while others are not. However, the empirical evidence that they do exist has substantial merit. The fact that they are not perfect is what produces the skeptics. With regard to stock cycles, it is because of their imperfection that astute investors can make money from them.

Eventually, many growth stocks become cyclical in price. By understanding the PSYCLE, we can formulate a consistent decision strategy of when to buy and when to sell. The long-term price charts that we will use are not "cut in stone." They are simply the most visible reflection of crowd psychology. In later chapters, we will discuss the price action of stocks such as Federated Department Stores, Ford Motor Company, Sears, Eastman Kodak, Franklin Mint, Outboard Marine, Allis-Chalmers, Milton Bradley, Newmont Mining, and many others. Once the pattern is understood, other opportunities can be discovered.

A prudent investment strategy is to buy quality assets at distressed prices. The investor must then be prepared to hold these assets for an extended period of time until they become overvalued. Then he must sell and look for another undervalued situation. It requires "guts" and cash to buy low, patience to hold, and objectivity to sell high. Of course, past performance is no guarantee of future results. However, using the long-term price charts of cyclical companies seems to be a conservative and disciplined attempt to buy low and sell high. Unfortunately, before an investor will use this approach, he may have to painfully discover that many other investment techniques don't work so well. That was certainly true in my case, as you'll see now.

3

Predictability

MY INVESTMENT WILDERNESS

"I'm a child of a bear market." I used to complain. What does that mean? Well, when I got into the stock brokerage business, it was October 1968, near the end of an 18-year bull market. The stock market in general topped out in May of 1969, the month that I became registered. It then proceeded to go almost straight down for fifteen months. In retrospect, it was just the beginning of an overall massive price drop that lasted through the end of 1974. The Dow Jones Industrial Average was about 1000 when I got into the business. Some fourteen years later, it was trading around 900. That's not exactly a "roaring" bull market. As you can tell, my market timing was not too good. I got in at the exact top.

Why did I go into the brokerage business? Why did I stay in the brokerage business? It is a tale interwoven with greed, fear, frustration, many failures, and, finally, hard-fought success. I wandered for a long time in my "investment wilderness" before I found PSYCLE paradise. My experience is not atypical of many young men and women who charge out into the world to seek their fortune. They march forth into life with high-minded illusions of instant wealth and easy money only to be impaled on the jagged sword of reality.

Mine is anything but a story of overnight accomplishment. Whatever success I've attained has been accompanied by much frustration and pain. So I don't share this part of my life with you as an ego trip. If anything, it's just the opposite. However, by reading some of the experiences that I've had, perhaps they will help you to understand your own motivations. Most important, perhaps they will keep you from getting your "brains blown out" as many times as I did.

I'd worked hard all during my high school and college years, and paid for most of my education. In the summer after I completed my engineering degree and before going to graduate business school, I had a few thousand dollars saved. I thought I should learn something about investing. My father took me down to a brokerage office in my town and there I excitedly bought about 50 shares of a $50 stock. I promptly forgot about it and went off to school. A year later when I checked, the price of the stock was $100. That's right, it had gone up 100%.

Looking back, that is probably the worst thing that could have happened to me in my life. I made money on my first venture into the stock market. In reality, it probably would have been better if I'd lost every nickel I had invested, because I immediately become hooked on the lure of easy money and quick wealth. I tried to duplicate my triumph many times over and lost a great deal of money in the process.

I moved to Houston in 1967 when I finished school and went to work for a major oil company. I was armed with the knowledge of the financial tools that the fundamental analysts use in predicting stock market prices. However, in the markets of the late 1960s that were frothing and bubbling with speculation, they were absolutely useless. Also, it required a great deal of time to go through the financial statements. Sometimes the price of the stock could be changing two or three dollars a day. So I soon discarded fundamental analysis as an approach to serious investing. I discovered something more exciting. It was called technical analysis.

It's a "triple top breakout"! That phase used to be music to my ears. A "triple top breakout" was supposedly one of the most powerful formations in a school of charting called point-and-figure analysis. In my search for an easier way to make money in the stock market, I took a chart course from a man who moved around the country teaching it on weekends. Let's call him Carl. For a couple hundred dollars, you would get a two-day session. It lasted all day Saturday and half a day Sunday. During this time, Carl would show you all the intricacies and secrets of point-and-figure charting. He demonstrated, in retrospect, how to make money by simply following the signals given by the price formations. I attended his course and soon became an expert.

I dutifully spent an incalculable number of hours following various stocks. Every day, I would update my charts on both individual stocks and the market indicators. When I made gains they were considered confirmations of how well the technique worked. When I experienced losses (which were numerous) they were rationalized as a "misinterpretation" of the charts.

Unfortunately, I never did make any money using the technique. In fact, I lost a substantial amount for the reasons I have already discussed. What did not occur to me until later was that Carl, who was a lawyer during the week, was just a "burned-out speculator" teaching a chart course to try to get his money back. After all, if it really did work, why wasn't *he* rich? Why was he beating his brains out flying all over the country on weekends, except for the money? One of the problems was that Carl tended to couch things in terms of positive experiences. And, of course, it was much easier for these charts to work out if the overall market is going straight up as it was during the 1960s.

Of course I had winners using this approach but I also got "whipsawed" a number of times. That is, I would end up having to sell my stock for a loss not only of commissions, but of capital. By *churning* myself in and out of the market in pursuit of this charting approach, my capital continued to be eroded.

During the period from 1967 to 1968, which was the height of my "point-and-figure charting phase," I astutely surmised that the stock market was going down, not up. I came to this conclusion because I was losing money on just about every trade. What was the smart thing to do? Since I felt the overall market was going lower, it didn't pay to be a bull. In order to go with the overall trend of prices, I became a bear.

How do you make money in a down market? You simply go "short." A short sale is just the opposite of a "long" buy. For instance, if you sell short a stock at $25 and it drops to $20, you make five points when you cover. Of course, if it goes up to $30, you lose five points. By selling short, the speculator expects to make money as prices drop.

I started to go short and I made a little money for a while. But, overall, I didn't do so well. Since it was boring to short the slow-moving stocks, I focused my attention upon some of the "high-flyers" of the day. One such group was the computer stocks. In one trade, I shorted 100 shares of Scientific Data Systems at $128. It experienced a "triple bottom breakdown." This was just opposite of a "triple top breakout." It meant the stock should vanish into oblivion.

The stock then dropped quickly to $110. Did I take profits? Of course I didn't. I dutifully waited for the proper "chart formation" before I closed out my position. Unfortunately, it never came. The stock turned around and started going straight upward. It went back to $115, $120, $125, then

$130. At that point I had a loss but I couldn't bring myself to cover the short. I just couldn't stand another loss. I hoped that it would go back down and I could get out even.

Of course that didn't happen. The stock continued to move upward. It hit $135, then $140, $145, and finally $150. At that point, I was beside myself with grief. How could I have let this happen? What went wrong? This was not working out at all as Carl said it would. Finally, sick with fear of further losses, I "pulled the trigger" and took over a $2000 loss. At this point, it was beginning to occur to me that I was not the astute short-term trader that I thought. Although my own ignorance was contributing to my losses, I was not getting much help from my stockbroker, who was a former shoe clerk. Permit me to explain.

The 1960s was a time of easy money for brokerage firms. Because of the extended rise in the stock market since 1950, the public was extremely interested in buying securities. Therefore, it was fairly easy to generate commissions. So, stock brokerage firms expanded and attracted people from all walks of life to be securities salesmen. At one point, the volume was so heavy that the NYSE had to close one day a week to keep up with the paperwork. It was in this environment that I selected my first stockbroker.

Unfortunately, it wasn't done very intelligently. A small brokerage office of a national firm was in the building where I worked. It would be convenient for me to "watch the tape" there. So, I walked into the office one day and told the receptionist that I wanted to open an account. She directed me to the "broker of the day." That's the term for the individual who gets all "walk-ins" and "call-ins." Let's call him Marvin.

The brokerage business has a number of highly reputable firms whose ethics are beyond question. Many stockbrokers are dedicated individuals who try to consider the interests of their customers above anything else. Unfortunately, it was not my luck to make such a good selection. I walked into one of the worst "den of thieves" that ever existed in Houston. Since I was in the office several times a day and because it was small, I got to know everyone pretty well. Let me introduce you to a few of the "boys."

At all brokerage firms, the manager is responsible for supervisory responsibilities. This means he is supposed to be sure that clients are "investing" according to their resources and objectives. This means that there should not be excessive activity (called "churning") in an account. Also, the quality of the securities should not be too speculative. However, in the late 1960s, the regulations were somewhat lax. Firms were drowning in the paperwork of business.

The manager's name was Fats. He was a rather stout individual who would stroll around the office, cigar in hand, urging his brokers to do more business. Needless to say, he was interested in the commissions because he got an override on the profits of the office. One of his rising stars was a 22-year-old named Spike. He was an excellent salesman who could smoothly manipulate hs clients in and out of the market. Another performer was Spuds, whose specialty was potato contracts in the commodities market, hence his name. If you did business with Spuds, you usually ended up owning at least 100,000 pounds of potatoes. He claimed he was particularly adroit at making money for "little old ladies" in the commodities market. Since he had been a used-car salesman before entering the brokerage business, I don't know how he gained his clairvoyance in potatoes.

Of course, all the brokers in the office wanted their clients to make money. The more money in the account, the more commissions that could be generated. However, they thought that if you held a position past settlement date (five business days) it was a long-term investment. There were a few honest and conscientious brokers in the office, but in the environment in which they worked, they too were under intense pressure to generate commissions. I later understood that some of the actions that I observed were illegal, some were fraudulent, and many were unethical.

The Securities and Exchange Commission (SEC) or the NYSE later closed the office for irregularities. The firm went out of business in the hard times of the early 1970s. Fats was censured by the authorities and stripped of his manager's license, but he went to work as a broker for another firm. Occasionally I still see him walking the streets with his cigar in hand.

Most of the rest of the "boys" eventually busted out of the business. Spike is now a high-stakes gambler who "books" a few sports bets on the side. A few years ago, I ran across one of his former clients for whom he lost over $250,000 trading commodities. Spuds vanished into oblivion. The last time I saw another one of the guys, he was tending bar. Another one quit and went to law school; he said he just couldn't stand losing money for his customers. My former broker, Marvin, now gives vivid morning traffic reports on the radio.

With reference to Marvin, he didn't do too much to accelerate my own demise. I made most of my own decisions without any input from him. He dutifully executed my orders. Of course, he consoled me at my low points, but encouraged me in my quest for profits. For a number of years, I was resentful of all the "boys" at the firm. Somehow, I felt they should have guided me better. But, in reality, that wasn't their job. They weren't supposed to take care of me. They probably didn't know any more about what they were doing than I did.

Although I worked very hard in pursuit of my "skill," it was doomed to failure from the first trade. The "whipsaw" movements of stock prices, commissions, interest charges, and market differentials all acted to erode my capital. I got the same rewards that most short-term speculators usually receive: frustration, failure, and financial pain.

When I got out of graduate school, I had a modest inheritance. By the end of 1968, I had managed to lose about two-thirds of it. Interestingly, about one-half of the loss was from commissions. After a hundred or so trades and a substantial drop in my capital, I astutely surmised that point-and-figure charting would not be the bonanza that I originally had anticipated. So I turned my thoughts back to fundamental analysis.

In late 1968 when I got into the brokerage business, my confidence was somewhat shaken, as you can imagine. It was obvious that I wasn't going to make any money using technical analysis. Despite my diligence, I wasn't smart enough to make it work. However, there was another hope on the horizon.

This was the era of the "growth stocks." Forty to 60 times earnings was nothing to pay for a company with "good long-term prospects." New issues were coming out and going up immediately. The public enthusiasm for securities was overwhelming. Of course, this is always the case at the end of a spectacularly long period of rising prices. Well, I decided to mend my ways and find a good, solid, growth company that would appreciate over the long-term.

Let's call the company that I selected DIK Corporation. It was a conglomerate. If you were in everything, how could you keep from making money? The stock was modestly priced at about 40 times earnings. It had earned a dollar, so that put the stock at about $40 a share. It had moved up about 300% or 400% over the last few years, but that was only the beginning because the future looked bright. I was determined not be whipsawed any more by getting in and out of stocks on a short-term basis. So I plunged my remaining capital into DIK with the idea that I was going to stick it out with the stock through thick and thin. Well, unfortunately, all I ever got was thin.

Soon after I bought it, the stock started down, slowly eroding in price to $35, to $25, then to $15. When I astutely "pulled the trigger" on it, the price was $10 a share and the company later went into bankruptcy. Once again, my decision had not achieved the peak of investment brilliance. They say if you give a 21-year-old kid a million dollars he'll probably blow it. I guess that if I'd had a million dollars, I would have blown it too. How do I know? Because I lost nearly all of the money that I had inherited. That's right, I was *wiped out*! I never spent one nickel of that money on a house, a car, a suit of clothes, or a steak dinner. In retrospect, if I would have bought any house in the southwest part of Houston, the appreciation 12 years later would have been over 500%. Of course, I didn't know that at the time.

Needless to say, I was extremely discouraged. Not only had I lost all my money, but what was worse, my ego had been shattered. I was a failure and I had no one to blame but my own greedy self. Of course, I went through a period where I tried to blame my stockbroker, the stock market, and even Carl, the burned-out speculator. However, it didn't make me feel any better. I was laden with guilt. I seriously contemplated suicide.

My despair reached its low point one lonely night in the wee hours of the morning. After a number of drinks, I was especially despondent. I just kept spinning the chamber of a fully loaded .38 police special pondering my failure. How was I ever going to overcome this humiliation? Then it suddenly occurred to me that anyone could kill himself. However, it took "guts" to go on living. I had to face up to my disasters and work through my failures. So I unloaded the gun and went to bed. Somehow, I resolved, I *was* going to make money in the stock market.

Since my own abilities to pick stocks didn't appear to

be great, I decided to find someone who had a good "track record" and then let him manage the money. Of course, I didn't have any of my own money left. But, since I was just getting started in the brokerage business, it seemed like a good way to build and keep a clientele. Fortunately, I found someone right here in Houston.

Ron Greedy (not his real name of course) of Greedy Money Management, Inc. had a sales presentation that could make the mouth of the most skeptical investor water with excitement. It was the most professional presentation that I had ever seen. He showed, with various charts and graphs, the easy way to make money in the stock market. How do you do it? It was simple. All you had to do was own a stock in the industry group that made the biggest percentage gain every year.

For instance, one year it might be aluminum stocks, the next year it could be drug stocks, the following year it might be computer stocks, and so on. All you had to do was to continue to compound your profits into the next top performing group year after year. The finale was a graph that showed that a $1000 investment would have been parlayed into well over $10,000,000 if you had followed this approach over the last 25 years. As you can imagine, at the end of the luncheon almost no ome could eat because they were choked with greed.

Of course, he had designed a secret computer program that would enable him to select these stocks. His objective was to have the client's portfolio loaded with stocks that were in the top ten best performing industry groups every year. For a fee of about 1%of the value of the stocks, he would manage an individual's portfolio. I had several clients who decided to use his money management services. As you may imagine, his results didn't quite parallel what he had shown on his graphs.

In retrospect, what it appeared that he was doing was buying the stocks with the greatest "relative strength." This means buying the stocks that were moving up the most in relation to the rest. He always seemed to own the stocks that had performed the best. Unfortunately, he didn't buy them until they had gone up significantly. In fact, he had an uncanny knack of positioning the stocks very near the peak of their move. After several years of working with Mr. Greedy, I found that his approach was not particularly satisfactory, to say the least.

Six months later, I ran into the president of a small corporation in Houston whose pension plan had been managed by Greedy Money Management, Inc. He told me that Mr. Greedy had "run" the fund into $1 million. I thought that was pretty good until he told me that they used to have $2 million. By then I had already ended my "investment guru" phase.

So I had gone full circle in my search for profits in the stock market. I had tried my hand at both technical security analysis and fundamental security analysis. Either the approaches that I employed didn't work very well, or I wasn't smart enough to use them. The answer didn't matter, the results were the same. My experience with Mr. Greedy and other money managers convinced me that there was no magic "investment guru" who could make profits for me. I was going to have to do it myself. But how was I going to do it?

Well, I got lucky for a change. There was a broker in the office in which I worked that seemed to do very well for his clients. He made money for them over the long term. He didn't go into convulsions when the market dropped like most of the rest of us. He just bought his selected stocks. He didn't get euphoric when the market was hitting new highs. He just sold his stocks, if and when, they reached his price objective. Could it really be that simple? It was for him.

He was kind enough to take me into his confidence and we became friends. In fact, the first four or five stocks I sold for substantial profits I had bought on his recommendations. I have since modified his theory somewhat (I will explore this thoroughly in a later chapter), but the basic approach is the same. In my own opinion, it is the most conservative and consistent way I have ever seen to make money in the stock market and to keep it.

I began to use his strategy to build a clientele. Let me tell you, it was anything but easy. I was young and aggressive, but I didn't have any successes to "hang my hat on." Also, in the early 1970s many investors had had their "brains blown out." The carnage was much greater than indicated by the Dow Jones Industrial Average; it dropped about 45% from 1968 to 1974. In that same period, the value line composite dropped about 87%.

In the 1960s, you were a "hero" if you were a stockbroker. Your advice was eagerly sought at cocktail parties. But in the early 1970s, you were avoided as if you had the plague. By the end of 1974, most people were not eager to buy stocks no matter how cheap they were. They were afraid of further losses.

But I persisted. When I earned a few dollars, I followed my own advice and bought quality stocks at depressed levels. I might add that I had to wait several years for my first success. Unfortunately, I occasionally experimented with other techniques such as options. I won't bore you with the details, but the results were very unsatisfactory. Finally, I learned my lesson on the futility of speculating in the stock market. Meanwhile, I discovered another vehicle for profits; it was called limited partnerships.

As I began to make a little money in the brokerage business, real estate caught my eye. Houston, Texas was the growth capital of the world. And it was my misfortune to have one of my good fraternity brothers in the business of selling real estate syndications. He showed me several investment opportunities that we should be able to sell within a couple of years at a modest 100% profit. A real estate syndication is a limited partnership in which the "little" investor can participate in the wealth to be garnered from real estate.

I was certainly a little investor, but I trusted the judgment of my friend. He worked for a company in Houston called Gold Coast Real Estate. Behind this operation were two investment genuises by the name of Sal and Sam (not their real names of course). The fact that Sal and Sam had been in bankruptcy a couple of times didn't mar their credibility with me, for some reason. My friend Bill told me that they had just fallen on unfortunate circumstances. Anyway, he trusted them completely. The fact that he did not know the score never occurred to me.

I invested in several real estate syndications with him, but only after investigating them very thoroughly over a couple of drinks at the local bar. Then, I would plunge ahead looking for that quick 100% pop. Sometimes the real estate might be going up so fast that we wouldn't even get long-term capital gains on it. That was one of the things we were always worried about. The comforting thing that I found about real estate is that you can make it worth whatever you want it to be. That is, in your own mind. Since there are no daily quotes on real estate, as there are on stocks, you can fantasize your wealth any way that you like.

There are two types of real estate syndications or limited partnerships. They mean the same thing. When a group buys a piece of raw land, they are usually speculating that some "end user" will come along eventually and build on it. An income property is one that may have a building or apartment project on it. It is usually bought for the cash flow and tax benefits, along with appreciation possibilities. The latter is obviously a more conservative investment. The structure of all limited partnerships is nearly the same.

The general partner is the one who puts the deal together. He assumes the risk for any losses. If one of the limited partners drops out, he is responsible for maintaining the payments if the other limited partners don't want to buy the interest. He usually gets a front-end fee, or commission, of at least 8%. It can be much higher depending on "hidden charges." He also usually gets an annual operating fee every year. If and when the property is sold, he gets a percentage of the gains. It can be as much as 10% to 25%. That's not too bad, because he puts up only about 1% of the money.

The investors are called limited partners. They have no risk other than the money that they have put up. They are not liable for any further losses. Usually, they make a small down payment of 10% to 20% and the general partner signs a note for the balance. In most cases, the deals are highly leveraged. As long as the limited partners meet the note payments (margin calls), everything is fine. If the payments stop for any reason, the original owner can foreclose and everyone loses all their money.

Actually, my experience with real estate syndications was not too bad, but I think that I was very lucky. I actually sold one for a profit in one year. Of course, the general partners made almost as much money as the limited partners after their "cut." Then, guess what happened? In 1974, we had a recession and real estate prices collapsed. It turned out to be a blood bath for a number of syndications. Many of the limited partners did not have the staying power to meet the annual payments. The other partners couldn't afford to pick them up so everyone lost all their money.

In all fairness to the boys at Gold Coast Real Estate, they stood up to their obligations whereas many general partners did not. To my knowledge, Gold Coast never let one of their sydnications fold. They either bought out the limited partners or took up their payments. I got my money out of my second deal about eight years after I bought it. It was not exactly a "quick pop." I don't have any idea what my overall return was on my money, but it certainly wasn't spectacular. At that point, however, I "didn't care about the cheese, I just wanted out of the trap."

My adventure in real estate was, at one point, a nightmare. I might have had to declare bankruptcy if it wasn't for a fortuitous turn of events. Let me explain.

As my income started to increase, I decided that I needed a good tax shelter. Fortunately, my friend Bill had just the opportunity. There was a motel on a major freeway in Houston that was near a large development of high-rise office buildings. In fact, it was just a couple of blocks away on the other side of the freeway. But looking into the future, we could see where the land would be needed to put up a skyscraper.

Let's called this motel The Sweetheart Inn. It was in a state of disrepair, thus more opportunity for tax shelter. The plan was simply to buy the property from the owners. They would continue to lease it back from us and continue to operate it. We would get some income and tax shelter from depreciation. Of course, when the time came, we would sell the property to a developer who would erect a large office building. A fairly simple and definite plan of action.

That was also the first time that I heard the term "triple net lease." It meant that the owners would pay us lease money and then pay all the expenses. We didn't have to worry about anything. We would get the benefits of tax shelter against our income, and the appreciation potential from the land. It sounded almost too good to be true. And, in fact, it turned out to be just that: too good to be true.

The sequence of events went something like this. First of all, the Sweetheart people dropped their lease in six months and moved out; that left the limited partnership with the motel to run. Unfortunately, the occupancy rate was not at a high figure. It was about 40%. Also, we found that a few things needed replacing, such as the roof, the air conditioning, and all the television sets. So the general partner asked the limited partners for a special assessment.

This special assessment worked out to be a little over 50% of our original down payment. Guess what? Very few of the limited partners could come up with the additional money. In my own case, I had put all my money into the down payment. I believed that the income from the lease would be enough to meet the payments. I was really strapped for cash.

Fortunately, at about this time, the state security boys were investigating Gold Coast for alleged violations of the law. It seems that a private placement is only supposed to be offered to 33 people or it must be registered with the state. They had probably shown the Sweetheart Inn deal to over 1000 in order to get 33 "mullets" to buy the property. Whether or not they were proven guilty, I don't know. However, they immediately went out of the syndications buisness.

They were also receptive to buying out your percentage if you pressed them. Of course, Sal, who was a great salesman, tried to talk me into staying. He told me about all the profit opportunities I would be missing. He almost convinced me to stay. Fortunately, I was too scared to let my greed get the best of me. Gold Coast Real Estate bought me out over a two-year period and I got my money back. For that, I'll be forever grateful.

My lessons in real estate speculation were much cheaper than those in stock speculation. Unfortunately, school wasn't out yet. My most financially painful and agonizing experience still lay head. I'm going to share it with you.

The year 1976 was an excellent year for me in the brokerage business. Once again, I began to worry about all the taxes that I would owe Uncle Sam. At the time, there was a friend of mine, who was also a stockbroker, who specialized in "tax advantaged investments." Let's call him Bart. He was one of the most positive individuals that I have ever met and he had a solution to my problem. If everything worked out okay, I would get a big tax write-off and make about 300% or 400% on my money. Sound too good to be true? You're right again.

It seemed that there was an oil operator in Louisiana, Jack Magic. It appeared that he had a great track record for finding oil. Some people believed he could even smell it at depths of 10,000 feet. In any case, he was putting together a "package" of five of his best prospects that would be offered as a private placement. He was doing this because he was being sponsored for the first time by an extremely reputable firm and he wanted to make a good showing. If he did so, he would be able to use the firm to raise more money in the future. So far everything sounded plausible.

The prospects were "developmental" wells, not wildcats. That is, they were to be drilled in areas of proven oil reserves. It seemed like a "lead pipe" cinch to hit at least three out of five. This percentage would return the investors at least three or four times their investment. Also, the deal was so good that the general partner wouldn't do it unless he got a 50–50 split with the limited partners. This was so out of line with industry standards that it seemed a great opportunity. Finally, an outside geologist with impeccable credentials had closely examined the prospects and confirmed their potential. How could I lose?

After careful consideration of all the facts, I could see only one problem. The amount of money needed to "buy in" was staggering in terms of my resources. At one stage, I had made a decision not to go ahead. Yet, as the deadline approached, Bart became more and more convincing. Then, one day Bart told me that there was a "little piece" left, but he didn't know if he could get it for me. What did I do? I begged him to get it. Miraculously, he did and then I didn't know if I should feel happy or sad.

I went into the venture knowing that I could lose my entire investment. Of course, I didn't really think that it would happen. Bart believed everything he was telling me. He didn't even make a commission on my participation. But the die was cast. The only thing I could do now was to sweat out the results. Soon, they started drilling the first well.

We hit a monster. Thank goodness! Everyone breathed a sigh of relief. In fact, the well had so much reserves, that it should more than guarantee our original money back. Number two was also a successful well, although not quite as good. Three and four were dry holes and number five was a good well. We hit three out of five, which was great. Now, we waited anxiously for the reserve reports from an independent engineering firm.

Ten to one was the potential return. That is if we could recover all the proven and probable reserves. I was rich! All I had to do is wait for the checks to come rolling in. What was I ever going to do with all the money? When I shared my good fortune with my good friends, they were awed by my success. For a while, I basked in the glory of my brilliance. Unfortunately, my euphoria was short-lived.

Did Mr. Magic hook up the wells so that the limited partners could receive their cash flow? No. He had a different idea. The results looked so good, that he was going to drill more wells to "prove out" the reserves. To my horror, there was nothing legally to be done. We could not stop him. Where would he get the money for further drilling? That was no problem. He borrowed it from the bank by pledging the limited partners' cash flow from the wells.

It seems that all of the wells were "turn key." That means he guaranteed completion to the designated depth. For that, he received a 25% bonus over the cost. For example, if a well cost $500,000, he received an extra $125,000 just for drilling it. Can you see why he was interested in drilling more wells? A rough estimate is that he made over one $1 million just for drilling the wells.

What were the results? Guess. None of them were commercial. Every time a new well was drilled, it reduced the reserves of the original ones. Finally, any cash that would have gone to the limited partners was diverted to service the new loan, which was now greater than the money originally put into the partnership. That meant we were wiped out. We lost every nickel that we had invested. The fact that Uncle Sam would pick up part of the loss was empty consolation at this point.

Needless to say, some of the participants were outraged. It would have been bad enough to have lost all you money on dry holes. But everyone had thought that their net worth had increased dramatically. So, the "come down" seemed very steep. Moreover, we had bragged to close friends about how rich and smart we were. How were we now going to explain suddenly going broke on the deal?

A meeting was called by some of the limited partners to see if they had the grounds for a suit against Mr. Magic. It seems that he had taken money that he had made and bought up a large number of leases of what turned out to be a huge gas field. Best estimates were that he was now worth well over $10 million. A "rags to riches" story. Unfortunately, the limited partners saw none of it.

Sitting around the table with my fellow investors I learned some interesting things. One man was so delighted with his initial riches that he had built his "dream" house which was very expensive. He was now strapped for cash. Two people each had put over $450,000 into various tax shelters in the last several years. Both said that, at this point, they didn't think they would ever get any of their money back. Needless to say, we were not a very happy group.

In an earlier chapter, you may have noted that I seemed negative toward some other forms of investments. Now you know why. I've never personally experienced any success with them. But, there are reasons other than that. I have known investors of all different types over my years in the brokerage business. I tell you from firsthand knowledge that only a very small percentage of them have ever made and kept any money from speculative "investments."

After these depressing adventures, you may not have a high regard for my investment expertise. I can't say that I blame you. But, before you disregard my advice, let's examine a few facts concerning my background: I have a good education. I graduated first in my mechanical engineering class and then went on to attain a master's degree in business. I've worked hard all my life so I am very serious about making money. Although, in retrospect, some of my decisions seem irresponsible, at the time I thought they were rational. What I'm saying is that you can't dismiss my failures through stupidity or bad luck. Because there is much more to it than that.

In my quest for profits, my perception of reality was severely distorted by the greed emotion of my Child Ego State. (I will explain this phenomenon in much more detail in a later chapter). It was because my expectations were unrealistic, that I was eventually destined to suffer intense emotional and financial pain. I found many pitfalls in my investment wilderness, some of them deeper than others.

"What gives this guy the right to advise me about investing?" This is the question that you may be asking yourself right now. Well, the answer is pretty simple. I've personally experienced, or observed, more investment situations than most private, part-time investors could in 25 lifetimes. In addition, I've researched thoroughly and, in a number of cases, actually tried to use many investment approaches. In other words, I've been through the battle for investment survival and have emerged with my capital multiplied many times over. Now I have a questions for you: Will you benefit from my mistakes or will you be doomed to repeat them?

Remember that you will also encounter many "false prophets" in your own investment wilderness. What does that mean? Well, there are a number of highly trained, honest, and dedicated individuals in all areas of investments who sincerely desire to help people make money. Some are very knowledgeable and experienced. However, there are many who have the best of intentions, but don't have any idea of what they are talking about. Of course, there are others who could care less if the investor goes broke; they are just interested in what they will make for themselves. Finally, there are a few who will lie, cheat, or commit fraud to get your money. The problem may be deciding who is who. *Let the buyer beware*! Let's now explore the reality of the stockmarket as perceived by the academicians.

THE RANDOM WALK THEORY

The period from 1950 to 1968 produced one of the longest stock market rises in history. during this time of easy money, many investing techniques, approaches, and theories were proposed as vehicles to consistent profits. Whithin the Wall Street community, arguments would ensue as to what strategies were the *more* profitable. However, some outsiders had a much different point of view.

In the early 1960s the academic community began to apply scientific statistical analysis to various investment strategies in order to determine what approaches, if any, would produce above average profits. The basis of comparison was a portfolio of randomly selected securities that were bought and held over a long period of time. Only if a technique could outperform the basic Buy-and-Hold Strategy (BHS) could it be judged effective.

How could this be accomplished? Here is a simplified explanation. First, get a copy of the *Wall Street Journal* for December 31, 1950. Then take the financial page that lists all the prices of the stocks on the New York Stock Exchange and pin it to a wall. Now, get yourself 20 darts and a handkerchief.

Back up 10 feet and blindfold yourself. Throw all your darts at the page. Retrieve the ones that missed and continue throwing until you have 20 stock selections and their closing prices. You have just selected your "investments" by a random process.

Now, get a *Wall Street Journal* for December 31, 1960 and compare the prices. Then, check your stock guide to determine if there were any splits or stock dividends in order to see if the number of shares had increased. Assume that you put the same amount of money into each initial position. Let's say it was $1000, so that your original portfolio was worth $20,000. Based on the 1960 prices and adjusted for any increases in shares of a position, calculate the closing value of your portfolio.

During that period of time, the Standard and Poor's 500 Stock Index increased about 200%. Let's assume, for argument's sake, that your "dart portfolio" performed in-line and that your ending value was $60,000. Those are pretty good results, aren't they? Most people would be satisfied with that kind of performance, wouldn't they? Before you break your arm by slapping yourself on the back, just remember how you selected the stocks. You did it purely on a random basis without using your intellect or any sophisticated decision technique. You made money simply because you owned stocks in a rising market.

Academicians will now take all available stock market data from that time frame and apply various decision strategies to determine if any approach outperformed the dart portfolio. All information would be used including past earnings and dividends, projected earnings and dividends, and recorded price movements. A technique must do better than the model portfolio for it to be considered effective for use in the future. Both fundamental and technical approaches would be thoroughly analyzed by a computer.

The most famous study of this kind was done by Clive W. T. Granger and Oscar Morgenstern. They published their results in a book, *Predictability of Stock Market Prices*. As you can imagine, the results were not well received by the Wall Street establishment.

They started with four main assertions in economic theory:

1. The market assures the optimal allocation of investible funds—if these search employment in stocks, especially by issue of new stocks;
2. The price movements on the stock market in their aggregate (as represented by various indices) are a *predictor* of subsequent fluctuations in the economy as a whole;
3. The price of a share in the company is a *function* of past earnings, assumed future earnings power, expected continued dividend flows, and other characteristics of the respective enterprise;
4. Future stock prices are predictable in a practically useful manner from their previous, mostly cyclical movements, either individually or in the aggregate.

They concluded that all these beliefs were either untrue or needed to be specified very carefully before having any specific value. A summary of their conclusions, with a few minor deletions, can be found in Exhibit 3.1, "The Random Walk Theory."

Basically, the theory claims that there is no way to predict stock price movements because they vary according to the principle of random walk. As you saw, this means the future is unpredictable according to the past. It does not conclude, as some people believe, that the approaches that embrace fundamental security analysis or technical security

Exhibit 3.1 *The Random Walk Theory*

- Stock market prices vary according to the principle of a random walk; i.e., no useful irregularities of any kind can be specified; the random walk is embedded in long-term movements of various lengths and directions.
- No method exists by means of which profits on the stock market can be assured other than by "inside information" of the specified kind.
- There are virtually no cycles of any ordinary duration in stock market prices, whether in individual stocks or in aggregate indexes, neither seasonal nor any other period. There is only a bare trace of a monthly cycle.
- There are some symmetries in the behavior of prices which in the very short run can be explained as a random walk with barriers. These barriers break down easily but are reformed quickly on different levels.
- There is some evidence of clustering prices; i.e., prices of different stocks are partly interrelated for intermittent periods.
- A small turnover determines the prices of all shares of a given company.
- There is no simple relationship between volume of transactions and price changes.
- Earnings of traded corporations are unpredictable from past records.
- Dividend changes are very difficult to predict from past records.
- Past earnings and dividends are not useful predictors of the future price of a stock.

Source: Clive W. J. Granger and Oskar Morgenstern, *Predictability of Stock Market Prices* (Lexington, Mass.: Heath/Lexington, 1970)

analysis are worthless in terms of making money in the stock market. It just seriously questions the ability of any strategy to outperform a randomly selected portfolio. Yet, there are documented records that show outstanding performance results over certain time intervals. Why is that, you may wonder?

First of all, this can be explained statistically by the nature of the random process. That is, out of a large group of investors, some will do very well and some will do very poorly. Of course, the majority will produce only average results. However, the outstanding performers of one year may not be the same ones in the next year. In other words, performance also can vary in a random manner.

Second, risk is a consideration that is not easy to quantify. In a rising market, a portfolio with a large number of speculative stocks could substantially outperform the averages on the way up, but when prices drop, it may dramatically underperform the market. Increased volatility can increase gains and losses.

The statistical evidence of the Random Walk Theory concludes that almost everything related to the stock market moves in a random manner. This would include past earnings, future earnings, dividends, P/E ratios, and stock prices. Remember that random does not necessarily mean haphazard, but rather it means that the past has no definite correlation with the future and that it is impossible to unravel the cause–effect relationships in stock price movements.

Of course, there are many people, especially on Wall Street, who do not agree with the Random Walk Theory. They believe that they have certain information (or possess special insight) that gives them an important edge in predicting future stock price movements. Surely there are brilliant security analysts, market technicians, portfolio managers, stockbrokers, and private investors who seem to perform much better than their peers. As always, in order for a few to be right, many must be wrong.

It is doubtful whether the validity of the Random Walk Theory will ever be conclusively proven or disproven, but there is a lesson to be learned here. It is one of the cornerstones of my investment strategy: *Predicting future stock price movements is a difficult job for even the most highly trained analyst or portfolio manager.* (The possible reasons will be explored thoroughly in the next chapter.) A corollary is that it will be almost impossible for the private, part-time investor to outperform the stock market using conventional techniques. However, this may not be his biggest worry. For many people, losing money turns out to be a much greater problem than being concerned about relative performance.

The second lesson is probably more important than the first: Mechanical approaches to stock market investing are no guarantee of success. This would include the routine interpretation of certain formations on price charts, using past earnings to predict future earnings, buying stocks with low P/E ratios, then selling them when their P/E ratios are above the market averages, modern portfolio theory which uses the future stream of discounted dividends to determine value, and so on. Mechanical approaches are generally used as a substitute for thinking.

For all the rigorous analysis of the Random Walk Theory, there is an important element that determines future stock prices that would be very difficult to analyze statistically: There is virtually no way for it to correlate the changing moods of investor psychology. The analysis of price formations may change, earnings and dividends may change, P/E ratios may change, interest rates may change, and the "worth" of these and other financial variables in the minds of investors may change. But, there is one constant unchanging phenomenon in the stock market. It will always apply because it is a necessary ingredient for any free auction market to function.

It is another principle of this investment strategy: *The majority of investors will always be wrong at major turning points*. They are the most optimistic and fully invested at the top and they are the most pessimistic and highly liquid at the bottom of any price cycle.

Let's explore this point further because it is critical to the validity of this approach. Academicians may be able to show that many techniques are random when it comes to making money in the stock market. That is, sometimes they work and sometimes they don't. However, to my knowledge, there has never been an instance in which the majority was the most optimistic and fully invested at the bottom. Also, there has never been a time in which the majority has been the most pessimistic and highly liquid at the top. Do you understand what I mean?

Almost by definition, it couldn't happen the way I just discussed. Stock prices must continue to go down until the majority of sellers has been satisfied. Stock prices must continue to go up until the majority of buyers has been satisfied. This means that there is a constant phenomenon in the movement of security prices. It cannot be construed as random because it happens only one way. No matter how sophisticated or enlightened the majority becomes, the stock market always acts to make them wrong at major turning points.

Even though we may understand the unchanging phenomenon of crowd psychology, it certainly doesn't mean that we can easily identify major turning points in stock prices. They will always be somewhat illusive and the identification process will be laden with frustration. However, the PSYCLE will be an important "road map" to help us reach our objective. But can we really make above-average profits by understanding the psychology of a stock cycle? If so, how can the PPTI implement the strategy? Before answering these questions, let's examine the philosophies of two of the most respected individuals in the investment community.

STOCK SELECTION OR MARKET TIMING

John Templeton is one of the most renowned money managers in the world because his investment performance consistently produces a top ranking among the mutual funds. From April 30, 1955 to April 30, 1979 a $10,000 investment in his Templeton Growth Fund would have grown to $243,881. This assumes the reinvestment of all capital gains and dividends. A 2,438% return over 25 years is an excellent example of conservative, consistent capital growth.

Forbes magazine is a widely read investor publication. In 1978, *Forbes* interviewed John Templeton. Here are some direct quotations from that article:

> *Forbes*, which has interviewed them all, considers John Templeton to be one of the handful of true investment greats in a field crowded with mediocrity and bloated reputations.
>
> What separates Templeton from the pack? Just this: He is talking to investors who have the patience and the staying power and—yes, the guts—to stick to a relatively long-term goal.
>
> Templeton is no trader. He says that he holds a typical stock for four years on average. Why four years? No reason, except that is what it seems to take to produce a superior investment record. And there are exceptions along the way.
>
> Buy the world's best bargains, and have patience. It's a simple formula, but Templeton makes it work.
>
> "I look for bargains," Templeton says. "And the time to buy at bargain prices is when the news is so terrible that everyone is selling and driving down prices.
>
> "When I say that a stock is a bargain, I mean that if you hold it throughout an entire market cycle, you're likely to do well with it because you're getting it cheap. It *doesn't* mean we're at a favorable point in the [market] cycle. The only thing I know for sure about bull and bear markets is that *both* will occur.
>
> "Nowhere do I ask if the market is going up or down. Forty years of experience have taught me you can make money without *ever* knowing which way the market is going."

I saw a videotape of Templeton's address to the Empire Club of Canada on November 29, 1979. He seemed to be one of the most unassuming and gracious individuals that you would ever have the pleasure of meeting. There were four ideas that he shared with his audience that seemed significant.

1. He claimed to possess no special insight. His investments are made on a commonsense basis. The financial tools are available from any standard text on security analysis.
2. He admitted that he was right only about two-thirds of the time when he made an investment switch.
3. He said that one of the cornerstones of his investment strategy was flexibility. In other words, he would buy growth stocks, income stocks, or whatever represented the greatest undervaluation to him.
4. If he was fortunate to have a security that did do well over four or five years, he tried not to be mesmerized into believing that it would continue to do as well during the next several years. That is, he may give serious consideration to selling it.

Templeton has his own discipline of buying value at distressed prices. His approach is to accumulate only those stocks that are selling substantially below what he feels they are worth on an intrinsic fundamental basis. He is then prepared to patiently hold his selections until the price more accurately reflects their true value. Then he will sell. This may take up to four or more years.

He also is an advocate of stock selection, not market timing. This means that he does not try to anticipate the general direction of stock market price movements. He also says that "he looks for bargains." "The time to buy a bargain is when the news is so terrible that everyone is selling and driving down prices." Buying good securities when investors don't want them has enabled him to consistently have one of the best track records in the world over the long term.

Robert J. Farrell is one of the best known and most frequently quoted technical security analysts on Wall Street. He has been a market analyst at a very large NYSE firm for more than 20 years and is now vice-president in charge of its market analysis department. Over the years, Farrell has pioneered many innovative approaches in the field of technical security analysis. He has been consistently recognized as one of the most outstanding market analysts by Wall Street professionals.

His firm interviewed him in their investor publication, *Stock Selection, Timing and Techniques*. The following comments are his answer to the question: *What do you consider crucial to successful investing stocks?*

> The most significant key to successful investing is to have a system or discipline and to be consistent. Your system can be geared to a concept, like growth or high yield, or it can be a technical system geared to price influences, but the most important thing is to have a goal and be consistent in reaching toward it. Jumping around getting a tip here and a suggestion there is a random and haphazard key to unsuccessful investing. Probably the most important thing to keep in mind is that those who invest conservatively with modest goals and patience generally do far better than those who buy stocks for quick short-term profits. The conservative investor is often surprised how well his stocks do while the short-term oriented speculator is often disappointed.
>
> It has been my experience in dealing with investors that the people who have been most successful on a consistent basis are those who put the greatest emphasis on stock selection and buy stocks on a value basis when they are out of favor.

Bob Farrell was kind enough to review my investment strategy. On June 22, 1979 he wrote me the following note:

> Dear Craig:
> Your approach obviously works. All you need is the willingness to be contrary and patient. I have my own variations on recognizing sold out stocks, but outside my feelings, your report is quite good. I'm sure it sells.

To have a workable investment approach, you must have a definite rationale of when to buy and when to sell. Preferably, it shouldn't be too complicated. Farrell suggests buying stocks when they are out of favor. How can you tell when a stock is in or out of favor with investors? Well, if they are very negative, then the demand for the shares of the company would be weak. This should be reflected by a low price in relation to past price history. If they are very positive, then the demand for the shares of the company would be strong. This should be reflected by a high price in relation to past price history. Simply stated, an investor should buy when prices are low and sell when prices are high in relation to past price history. This is why our long-term price charts are a necessary tool for this investment approach.

Because the stock market has many internal cycles, Bob Farrell places some emphasis on stock and group selection rather than depending solely on market timing. If anyone could predict the up and down movements of the stock market, it would be Farrell with his expertise, experience, and resources. It is the opinion of many people that his track record has been excellent. Yet, he favors timing the purchase and sale of individual stocks for the average investor. Of course, he feels that overall market timing is important. However, his focus is to try to participate in long-term cycles rather than in short-term trading approaches.

In his analysis, Farrell trys to pinpoint the psychology of the stock market participants. He looks for a thesis that is embraced by the majority. When he finds one, he subjects it to critical scrutiny. He may then formulate his own thesis, which usually will be just the opposite of the opinions held by the consensus. It is this kind of independent thinking that has lead to his success as a market analyst.

When it comes to the stock market, Bob Farrell has developed the process of *contrary opinion* to a fine art. Its rationale is simple. On a stock selection basis, it is an important ingredient of the investment strategy contained in this book.

However, the application of this process to the overall market cycle, is much more complicated. This is the area in which Farrell has gone beyond many of his peers.

Under ordinary circumstances, there will be many conflicting opinions in the marketplace. However, at major turning points, the feelings of investors will become one-sided. When pessimism turns into panic, prices are close to a bottom and it's time to buy. When optimism leads to euphoria, a top is near and it's time to sell. But, why should this be the case you may wonder.

By the time investors develop a consensus, most of the important buying (at tops) or selling (at bottoms) has already taken place. If the majority thinks that prices are going higher, they have already "placed their bets." That means they are relatively fully invested (as a group) and a major source of demand has already been dissipated. Under these circumstances, the only surprise that can have an impact on stock prices is bad news. Good news is expected. If the majority thinks that prices are going lower, chances are they have already sold stocks in anticipation of that event. Now, they are under-invested and highly liquid. The only surprise that will have an impact on stock prices, in this instance, is good news. The worst may have already been anticipated. There is little question that the process works: the difficulty comes in understanding the feelings of the consensus.

Even though the philosophies of John Templeton and Robert Farrell are based on distinctly different approaches to security analysis, it seems they have at least one thing in common. They both emphasize accumulating stocks when they are out of favor with investors. Templeton uses fundamental analysis and Farrell uses technical analysis. Embodied in both approaches is the third principle of this investment strategy: *Long-term profits in the stock market are best realized by attempting to minimize risk, not in trying to maximize gain.*

Remember that there are two types of risk when investing. This strategy is primarily a technical approach that attempts to minimize price risk by focusing only on stocks that are selling near the lows of the last 10 or 20 years. However, it is also a fundamental approach that tries to evaluate the quality of the assets being acquired from a fundamental analysis point of view. In this manner, it hopes to avoid most business risk situations. Besides, when a stock is down in price, usually the fundamental news is the worst. Under those circumstances, it is probable that a more accurate determination of the viability of the company can be made. Does that make sense? Well, let's look at a potential real-life investment situation.

It is the spring of 1978 and a time when a person's fancy may turn to some of the finer things in life. Unfortunately, you're worried because you have $1000 of your hard-earned money to invest and are unsure what to do. You want capital growth, but you don't want "too much" risk. You desire to own a solid, blue chip stock. Your preference is for a company that is part of the Dow Jones Industrial Average (DJIA). Because of your limited capital, you are going to make only one selection.

Now you call your stockbroker and explain your feelings and this is his enthusiastic response:

> Mr. Investor, you should buy Ford Motor Company at $44. Last year they earned $14 per share, which means that the P/E ratio is only about 3. Also, they paid a $3 dividend and indications are that it may be increased to at least $3.50. That would be a yield of almost 8%, which is an incredible current return for a stock of that quality. Wouldn't you agree?

You notice that his voice is quivering with excitement and the volume has increased so that you have to hold the phone away from your ear. Before you can even reply to his last question, he continues:

> Johnny Hotrod, our automotive analyst, *really* likes the stock. He thinks that by 1981 or 1982 the company could make at least $20 a share. He really feels that they could make over $25 per share. A big, famous company like Ford is the kind that the pension funds *love* to buy. As you probably know, the Standard and Poor's 500 Index sold at 15 times earnings throughout the 1960s. So, if Ford sold at 15 times Hotrod's more conservative estimate of $20 per share, that would be a price of $300! This is the kind of investment opportunity that comes along once in a lifetime! Let's take a position in the stock!

While your broker is gasping for breath, you consider the fine points of what he has said. The story sounds good. The quality of the company is beyond question. The P/E ratio is low. Although you're not too sure what that means, it seems conservative. You even like the dividend yield. Surely a company that was earning $14 per share could continue to pay a $3.50 dividend. Finally, the $300 price target is exciting. You even resolve that you'll sell at $250, so that you won't be too greedy. You want to go ahead and buy the stock, but you're still bothered. Why?

Last night you were at a cocktail party. After a few drinks, you were standing in a small group of people that was discussing various aspects of investing. One man said he really like to buy "turn-around" situations and thought that Kennecott Copper was an outstanding value at $22. Although they lost money last year, they have a lot of "assets in the ground." In fact, the stockholder's equity per share was over $50. He also said that the company was selling near a 20-year low in price and he didn't think it would go down much more. Perhaps you should ask your broker how he feels about Kennecott Copper. When you do, the tone of his voice immediately changes.

> Mr. Investor, that stock is too risky for you. They lost a lot of money last year and the yield is less than 3%. Besides, the dividend is shaky and may be eliminated. The price of copper is low and there is currently a large oversupply situation. Every third world country has a copper mine and they can't be choosey about the price they sell it for because they need the money too badly. The stock has been in a down trend for the last four years and it certainly isn't going to go up any time soon. Let's buy Ford, it's more conservative.

Your broker has a long-distance call from New York and he puts you on hold while you ponder his comments. Everything seems so confusing. When he comes back on the line, you can tell that his patience has vanished. Now, he has two calls holding and doesn't seem to care what you buy, as long as you buy something. What'll it be, Mr. Investor? Will you put your $1000 into Ford or Kennecott? You have to decide right now!

Turn to Exhibit 3.2, "Ford or Kennecott" and you can see how well you did. If you bought Ford, you lost 50% of your investment within two years. Don't feel too badly, most people would have done the same thing. It was the easiest and the most rational decision to make. Unfortunately, your remaining $500 is not much of a consolation prize. If you bought Kennecott, you are to be congratulated. Either you have long since learned to do the exact opposite of what your broker tells you to do, or you have been paying attention to the material in this book. Regardless, you made a 100% profit on your money within two years.

Although this little drama may seem amusing, you can be assured that many variations like this one are played daily throughout the country. In 1978, this scenario on Ford, with some minor changes, was actually prophesied by a well-

Exhibit 3.2 *Ford or Kennecott*

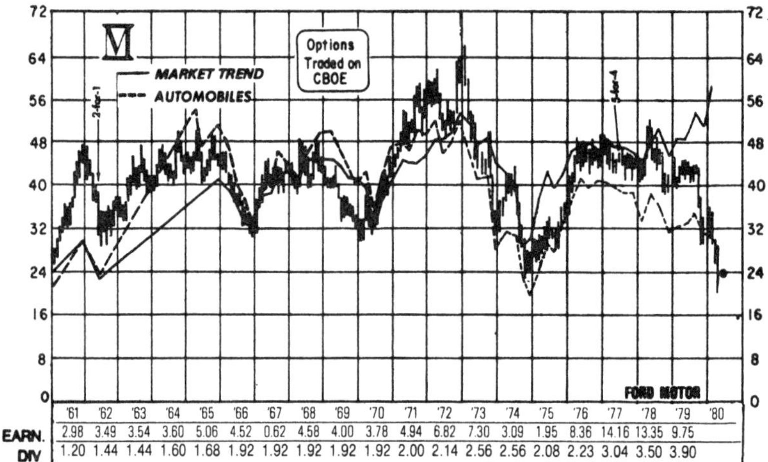

Buy	$ Price	Sell	$ Price	Years	% Profit
1978	44	**1980**	22	2	(50)

respected money manager in a national publication. If you bought Ford, you lost $500. If you bought Kennecott, you made a $1000 profit. That's a 300% difference in performance! It seems to be an extremely high price for trying to be conventional.

There is another point of emphasis that should be considered. Both stocks were in the same overall market environment and both were a part of the DJIA. Yet one went up and one went down. In other words, even if you knew ahead of time that the DJIA would go up about 250 points from 1978 to 1980, you could have lost 50% of your money if you bought Ford. This example underscores the fact that, at times, it can be a "market of stocks" and not a stock market.

Some stock market participants can be divided into two camps. Those who believe strictly in market timing will

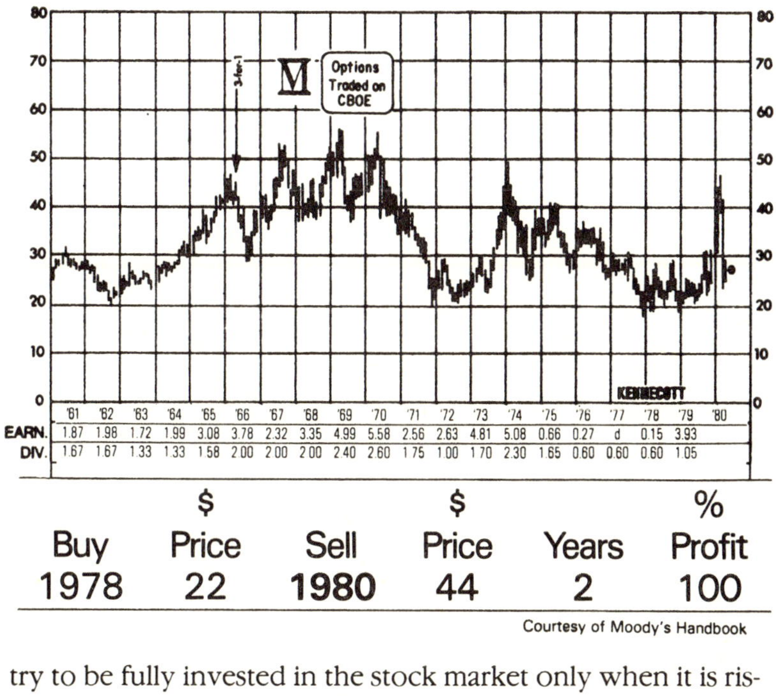

Buy	$ Price	Sell	$ Price	Years	% Profit
1978	22	1980	44	2	100

Courtesy of Moody's Handbook

try to be fully invested in the stock market only when it is rising. When it is going to go down, they would sell all their stocks and sit on the sidelines with cash. The market timers may use various combinations of economic, fundamental, and technical analyses to decide whether the market is going up or going down. Those investors who favor stock selection take an entirely different tack. They do not try to predict what the stock market, in general, is going to do. They are concerned only about selecting stocks that they feel can outperform the market. In other words, in a rising market, these stocks should go up more, and in a declining market they should go down less. Of course, at certain times, many individuals may partially use each technique.

The problem with a strict market timing approach is that the stock market can have different internal cycles. Oftentimes, the market is "two-tier" in nature. This means that there may be segments, or groups of stocks, that are going up, and segments, or groups of stocks, that are going down. Of course, there may be other groups that are doing absolutely nothing. For the past decade, there have been only brief periods when all stocks in the market were in a generally rising pattern or declining pattern.

For the true investor who emphasizes a stock selection approach on a value basis, market timing can be used in a general manner. If the market averages are up and the majority is fully invested because they are optimistic, perhaps he should be more cautious and hold cash reserves. If the market averages are down and the consensus is highly liquid because they are pessimistic, then he can be more aggressive and commit money to buying his selected stocks. However, as a practical matter, this is easier said than done. Now, let's examine the action in the marketplace to see if it can help us understand the psychology of the players.

4

The Player's Problems

All the world's a stage.
And all the men and women merely players
Shakespeare, As You Like It, *Act II, scene 7*

PROFESSIONALS

This certainly applies to the stock market. It is a stage for continuous human drama. The dominant passions are fear and greed. Conflict constantly rages among the players who can be classified into three major groups. The *professionals* operate the theater and act out the dialogue. The *advisers* direct the *investors* who assume the risk of the final outcome. Yet greatest suffering will be that inflicted on the majority, because they are always wrong at important turning points.

The theater for our drama is the New York Stock Exchange. Its trading floor is the stage for the continuous play. The professionals are the only actors allowed on the stage, but they act out the dialogue according to the decisions of the investors. Of course there are other theaters: the American Stock Exchange, the over-the-counter market, and regional exchanges. Yet, with slight variations, the action is the same.

Nearly everyone knows that the New York Stock Exchange occupies a building located on Wall Street in New York City. Behind its magnificent facade there is a large open floor. This is the central marketplace where the common stocks of major U.S. corporations are bought and sold.

There are certain qualifications that a company must meet in order to be listed on the New York Stock Exchange. Some of the minimum requirements are the following: It must be a going concern, it must keep the public informed of its affairs, it must have a demonstrated earning power of at least $2.5 million, it must have over a million shares outstanding, and it must have 2000 holders of at least 100 shares each. In general, most companies begin trading over the counter. Then they may be listed on the American Stock Exchange. When they become large enough, they will usually apply for listing on the New York Stock Exchange. Of the 11,000 companies that are considered to be publicly owned, only about 1550 are traded on the NYSE. In 1981, for example, there were almost 50 million shares traded on an average day.

As a marketplace, the NYSE has several distinctive features. It uses the auction process to arrive at the price of each transaction. This means that an investor may only take as much money out of a stock as someone else is willing to put into it. As each trade takes place, it is reported continuously on a tape so that investors in all parts of the world can follow the prices. Under usual circumstances, both the number of shares and the exact price of the transaction are shown.

Some of the professionals are members of the NYSE. They are the only ones who can buy and sell securities on the floor of the exchange. The majority of the members act only as agents; that is, they buy and sell for the accounts of other people. The *floor brokers* are employees, or partners, of member firms whose primary function is to execute orders sent to the floor by their customers. The *two-dollar brokers* are members who assist other member firms in the execution of orders for a fee when the volume is heavy. Some members can also buy and sell for their own accounts. The *specialist* is a member who is designated by the exchange as responsible for maintaining a fair and orderly market in the stock in which he, or his firm, may specialize. *Floor traders* are members who attempt to profit by buying and selling for their own accounts. At times, when supply and demand are imbalanced, they may provide much needed liquidity. All members are subject to some very strict regulations regarding their particular activities.

Let's examine the market mechanism in action. We will view the process as it pertains to the private investor and to the institutional investor.

Examine Exhibit 4.1, "The Auction Market." Mr. Jones calls his retail broker (RB) with Longhorn Securities in Houston, and instructs him to buy 100 shares of Ford at the market price. His broker will write the order on a ticket with the client's account number. He then takes the ticket to the wire operator who sends the order directly to the Longhorn booth on the perimeter of the NYSE. At the same time, Ms. Smith calls her retail broker (RB) with Hoosier Investment in Indianapolis, and instructs him to sell 100 shares of Ford at the market price. The process is repeated.

A clerk in each of the respective firm's booth removes the wire and hands it to a floor broker. They each walk directly to the post where Ford is traded. There they encounter a crowd (group) of other brokers that is also interested in buying or selling Ford.

The specialist is always present to maintain an orderly market. There will be a large teleray screen that will show the current market for everyone to see. Let's assume the specialist's book shows 700 shares to buy at $19¾ and 2200 shares for sale at $20. The Hoosier broker may offer 100 shares at

Exhibit 4.1 ***The Auction Market***

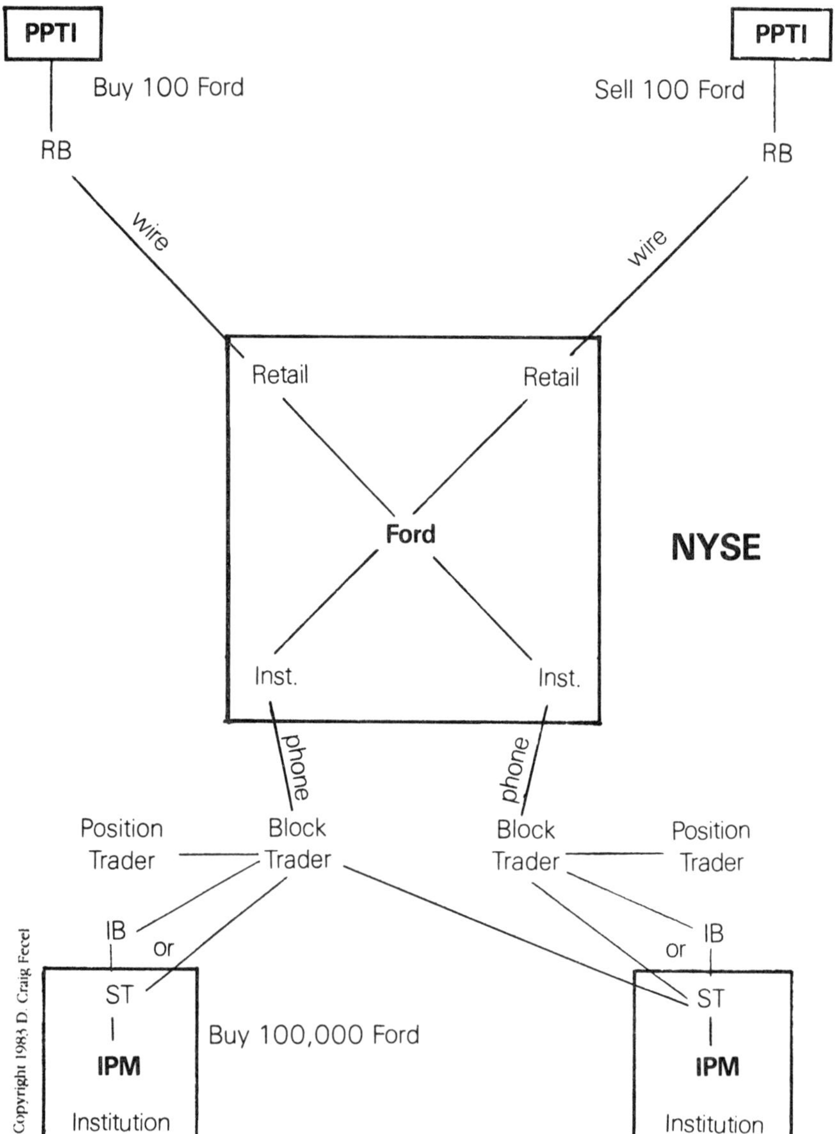

$19⅞. The Longhorn broker thinks that will be the best price that he can get for his customer so he cries "sold." The brokers exchange information and return to their booths to report to their respective clients in Houston and Indianapolis.

Now an employee of the exchange marks a digital readout card and drops it into a slot. A few seconds later the tape prints F 19⅞. If it had been a 700-share trade, it would have looked like this: F 7s. . . 19⅞. If it would have been a 7000-share trade, it would have been printed entirely as F 7000s. . . 19⅞. If the tape is running late due to heavy volume, some of the trades may be abbreviated or deleted. A small trade is easy to execute, but a large one is much more complex.

An institutional portifolio manager (IPM) decides that he wants to buy 100,000 shares of Ford Motor Company. Now the problem is different because the volume in the marketplace would not be enough for him to get an execution in the regular crowd. He must find someone (probably another institution) who is willing to sell all, or a sizable part, of the block of stock that he wants. The portfolio manager could be an employee of a large investment counseling firm, bank, insurance company, or mutual fund. If so, there will be other employees whose job is to get the best execution. They are called security traders. They may go through an institutional broker, or they may deal directly with the block traders of the member firms.

The security trader may call several member firms and ask what merchandise they have for sale. In this case, he may not reveal that he was a buyer of Ford unless a firm has the stock for sale. If he was unable to find any "stock in the Street," he may call the block trader of an institutional firm. Let's assume he calls Instifirm and says that he "may be interested in up to 100,000 Ford at the current market price." The *block trader* works directly by phone with the floor brokers to help them execute large orders. The Instifirm trader would then put the information on a "squawk box" to all the firm's block traders throughout the country. These employees then would call the accounts they handle to see if they might "bring out some stock."

How the trade gets "put up" (on the tape) would depend on the condition of the market and how the stock is acting. The buyer doesn't have to own it all at one time. While this is taking place, an institutional floor broker would be checking the crowd to see if there was a sizable block being offered for sale. In some cases, a *position trader*, who works for the member firm, may short the stock to the institution. That is, he would put the firm's capital on the line in order to get the business.

Ideally, Instifirm would act as a broker and do both sides of the trade. This is called a "cross." Depending on market conditions, Instifirm may end up crossing part of the trade, shorting part of the stock, or buying part of the stock from another firm on the floor. This process is nearly the same for any institutional firm.

Of course, the member firms are concerned with doing as much business as possible on a commission or agency basis. They try to earn these revenues by providing clients with a variety of services and products. This includes research recommendations and efficient executions or orders.

The floor brokers have a very short-term horizon when it comes to their perspective of the stock market. They are concerned with getting the best trade for their client at that instant. Most of them take great pride in trying to beat their fellow floor brokers and the specialist out of eighths and quarters of a point. The other members on the floor have a different problem, because often they must put their own capital at risk.

The specialist is both a broker and marker-maker. That is, he can take orders for possible later execution that the floor broker leaves with him and would be at price limits away from the current market. He records these in his specialist book at the respective prices, but he must also maintain an orderly market. To do this, he must put his capital on the line. For instance, if there is a large imbalance of sellers in a stock, he may have to step in and buy stock for his own account. Conversely, if a stock is rising too fast, he may have to go short. There are very strict rules governing his behavior, but in general, he must act exactly opposite to the current market activity in his stock.

The specialist and the floor trader have been much maligned over the years. They have been accused of market manipulation and, in some cases, fraud. One indication of these charges is the fact that both groups tend to end up with very large short positions at market tops and relatively small short positions at market bottoms. In fact, these are two of the indicators that technical security analysts uses to signal market turning points. The rationale is that they are the informed professionals and can "sense" the direction of the market and profit from it.

Are they really that clairvoyant? Perhaps, but there could be another reason. They could be fortunate victims of the market drama. We will use a little bit of the psychology of a stock cycle to examine this phenomenon. As a price cycle approaches its peak, the buyers become aggresive and the sellers are reluctant. Since the members must act to maintain a liquid market, they are forced to go short to balance supply and demand. At price tops, greed is the predominant emotion and investors tend to buy reactions, because they are bullish. Therefore, the members don't get to cover their shorts. At market bottoms, the sellers are aggressive and the buyers are reluctant. Therefore, the members cover most of their shorts and go long. At bottoms, fear is the predominant emotion and investors tend to sell rallies so the members don't have to short heavily. It seems clear that the probabilities may show that the members are right more often than they are wrong.

This is because they are forced to trade against the emotions of investors.

There is no question that the members have a higher chance of making money trading than the public. Without profits, they couldn't stay in business. One of the main reasons for this is that they don't pay any commissions. So they can trade for quarters and halves of a point. However, they must still put their capital on the line. In volatile markets, they can really get "bagged" pretty badly. One "nightmare" can take away a lot of easy money. At any rate, the concerns of the members focus on the very near-term price fluctuations of the market.

The professionals make their living directly or indirectly from the commission revenues generated by the securities transactions. They are employees of the brokerage firms or the members of the exchanges. Some of the professionals operate the intricacies of the stock market mechanism so that transactions can take place. Some of the professionals try to stimulate the investors to make transactions. When they do this, they take on the role of advisers.

ADVISERS

There are only two ways to make an informed, rational investment decision. The investor can do original research in a particular area, thoroughly analyze the data, and then come to a conclusion. Of course, this is impracatical for most decision-makers. It doesn't matter whether they are an institutional portfolio manager or a private, part-time investor. They don't have the time, talent, resources, or expertise for original research. In the vast majority of cases, they must evaluate the analysis and conclusions of an expert.

There is a perceived correlation between the stock market and the economy by most investors. That is, an expanding economy will produce higher stock prices and a stagnating or a contracting economy may precipitate lower stock prices. The starting point for most fundamental security analysis is a forecast of the economy for the next several years. It would be necessary to project many variables such as interest rates, inflation, and unemployment, to name just a very few. Once that was done, a decision must be made as to the effects this will have on the stock market. Do you think that would be easy? Well let's take an example.

It is January 2, 1978. Your favorite economist, who has a track record of being right 90% of the time, has just made some startling predictions. He says that over the next two years, inflation will be double-digit, interest rates will double, the price of gold will double, and the dollar will be weak. If that weren't enough, he thinks there will be a Middle East crisis that will interrupt oil flow. This is not a forecast that would predict a robust economy.

You have a large stock portfolio, and now you must make some difficult decisions. According to past experiences, if his predictions are correct, a severe market drop would be highly probable. Should you sell everything and go into cash? Of course, this may be the 1-in-10 chance that your economist could be wrong. None of his peers is forecasting such disasters. In fact, they are politely laughing at him behind his back. A number of them are calling for a recession. There are many conflicting opinions.

The stock market has been very weak for the last year. The Dow Jones has dropped about 250 points from around the high of 1000 in 1976. Other market indices have not done as badly. For instance, the NYSE has only dropped from about 58 to 50 and the S&P 500 was off only about 15%. Many market observers are predicting further declines. The institutional cash levels are near historically high levels because the "big boys" are worried about a further slide in prices. Sixty percent of all investment advisers think the market is going lower. Even your stockbroker, who has been determined to "ride this one out." is becoming negative. For the first time in a long while, he is suggesting that you "lighten up" by selling about 50% of your stocks in order to raise cash. Now let's review the situation.

You have a lot of confidence in your economist, but this time he may have "blown a fuse." But if he is right, it should mean the market will continue to drop. Other market participants think that it will go down for a different reason. They see a recession on the horizon. Even your stockbroker is suggesting that you liquidate a large portion of your stocks, "just to be conservative." This really concerns you because the last time he was this bearish was toward the end of 1974.

Let's face it! You are getting pretty tired of the constant erosion of the value of your portfolio. Maybe you should sell now, put the money in high-yielding money market instruments, then buy back later at lower prices. Anyway, you have to make a decision because you can't go on worrying about it. You can sell everything, sell half, or just sit tight. What will it be? You've got to decide right now.

Before we see how well you did, let's examine the role of the economist in predicting future stock market prices. His forecasts affect the decisions of both the investor and the fundamental security analyst. Because of this, it is necessary to understand the total information flow within the investment community.

The vast majority of research available to investors comes from the stock brokerage firms. They use this data as a service to keep their clients informed, and when appropriate, encourage them to make investment decisions. Of course, when this happens, it generates commissions that are their lifeblood revenues.

Because investors are constantly seeking profit opportunities, each brokerage firm tries to hire those analysts and economists with "good track records." It is just common sense. Better information should mean the firm's clients will prosper and this will lead to more new clients and more revenues from existing clients. As well meaning as this logic may be, there are some problems with it.

Examine Exhibit 4.2, "Research Flow." It shows the logistics of getting information from the advisers to the investors. The dark lines indicate where the influence may be the strongest. An adviser is anyone whose job is to transmit recommendations to the investor in order for him to make a buy or sell decision. In most cases, the advisers make money in some way for providing this information to investors. The economists and analysts get salaries (often substantial) from the brokerage firms who use this service to generate commissions. In the case of the private investor, the stockbroker is the medium between the client and the research department. In the case of the institutional portfolio manager, he usually reads the reports himself. The total process is complex, but let's try to understand an overview.

Fundamental security analysis generally requires an economic forecast on which to base decisions. This means the predictions of the economist can influence directly how the analyst feels about the prospects for profits in his industry. Of course, the economist may also take the projections of the industry analyst into account in the evaluation of the economy. Which comes first, "the chicken or the egg"? Sometimes it's hard to tell, hence the arrows showing an exchange of information. However, both groups do come up with recommendations and projections. This input may eventually be used by investors to formulate a decision strategy.

The technical security analysts use internal market dynamics to formulate their recommendations. The retail stockbroker and the private part-time investor tend to rely on this information more than the institutional portfolio manager. The IPM tends to focus on fundamental analysis, but he may occasionally "take a peek at the charts." Of course, after

Exhibit 4.2 *Research Flow*

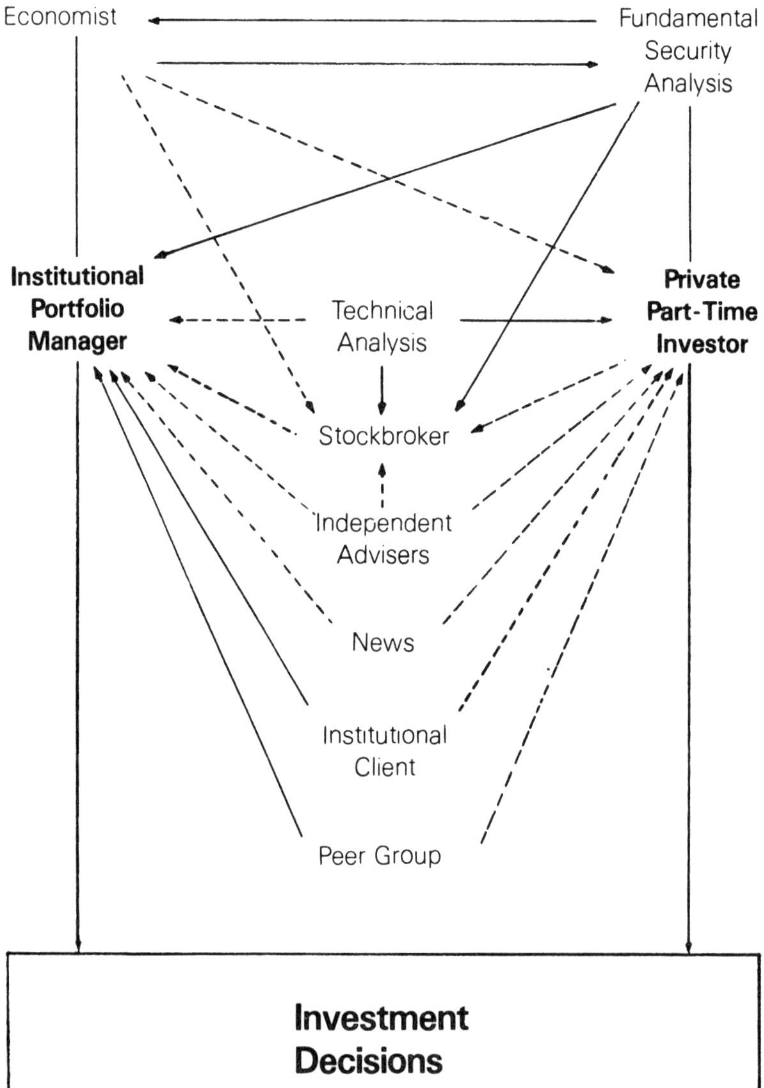

he is caught in a severe market drop, he may become more interested in technical analysis for a while.

Sometimes the stockbroker or the PPTI will have a low opinion of the research of their particular firm. Under these circumstances, they may seek outside counsel from an independent, investment advisory service. There are many different types. However, all have their own special "indicators" that gives them the ability to be in "harmony" with the various forces in the stock market. The stockbroker may use the "guru's" advice to transmit to his client or, in some cases, the PPTI receives the information directly by paying a fee.

The IPM may have other forces with which he may have to contend. Often, he cannot operate in a vacuum. That is, his decisions must be approved by an investment committee at his own firm. He must be able to justify his decisions on a logical basis. Most of the time, they must be put in writing. Of course, he can use recommendations of analysts of the brokerage firms. Unfortunately, no matter how in-depth the research, the desired results may not be obtained.

Let's use Ford Motor Company to illustrate some of the problems of the fundamental security analyst. First of all, when he examined the financial statements, he would see that the world's second largest automobile manufacturer is a huge operation. In 1977, they had sales of $37.86 billion dollars and profits after taxes of $1.67 billion. Nearly 15,000 dealers sell its vehicles throughout the world. The company has a number of subsidiaries outside the U.S. that manufacters and assembles its cars and trucks. It has also diversified into the production of farm equipment, aerospace, castings, communication systems, steel, and glass.

Since forecasting the earnings of the company is the analyst's most important task, he'll have to examine the potential effects of many variables, perhaps more than 100. Ford operates in many different markets in almost 200 separate countries. How will he accurately assess such unknowns as pricing, competition, and the productaive capacity of the company's factories. Because the earnings forecasts are based on a complex number of interrelated assumptions, which are hard to quantify and subject to constant change, there can be some unpleasant surprises for investors.

This could have been the case that many respected automobile analysts may have found themselves in the spring of 1978. The current operating situation did not give cause for alarm. With Ford selling at only three times its highest earnings in history, the 1980 disaster could not have been easy to forecast. Who could have predicted the dramatic increase in oil prices? Who could have known the gas lines would produce panic buying of fuel-efficient cars? Obviously, it was not Ford's management, because they thought Americans wanted the "big car" ride. Unforeseen events made any future predictions absolutely worthless.

But, perhaps that was a fluke. So let's look at an example of a brokerage report issued to its clients in June 1969. The company was Penn Central and its price was $59. The copy is verbatim with no changes (mercifully, this major wire house will remain unnamed; however, it's unlikely that you'd be thanking them for getting you into the stock).

> PENN CENTRAL ($59)
>
> Penn Central is a buy here. We believe the current quotation does not adequately recognize the underlying values in PC's subsidiaries and investments—or the potential inherent in an eventual return of the railroad to profitability.
>
> The many problems resulting from the combination of the Pennsy and Central plunged the merged railroad's operations into the red last year, and will persist through 1969. Yet Penn Central was able to report $3.91 per share in 1968 (and should earn around $4.75 this year) due to its rapidly growing subsidiaries.
>
> These include: Arvida Corporation (59% owned), a major developer of hotels, condominiums and recreational facilities in Florida...Great Southwest (85% owned), engaged in building apartments, homes and industrial parks

> on 125,000 acres in Southern California as well as in Dallas and Atlanta. . . Buckeye Pipe (100% owned), a 7,600-mile oil transportation system, growing and serving major airports.
>
> The especially rapid growth of the land companies (earnings more than doubled in 1968 over 1967, and were up over 100% in the first quarter of this year) has raised Penn Central's equity in its ownership of the stock to over $40 per PC share. In addition, Penn Central's valuable air and property rights in prime downtown sections of the railroad's terminal cities afford further potential for real-estate development.
>
> Penn Central has realigned its management in an all-out effort to end the difficulties besetting the railroad.
>
> Correction of the incompatibility of the two computer systems—a problem which cost PC much lost traffic and customer goodwill—is nearly complete.
>
> And the introduction of modern computerized yards and addition of more unit coal trains, backed by a revitalized marketing staff, should enable PC to pare its railroad losses and eventually move into the black.
>
> In our opinion, PC's management can overcome its problems as well as continue to exploit the many opportunities open to it. Selling at 12.4 times our 1969 estimate, the shares offer exceptional value to the aggressive investor.

In June of 1970, the company collapsed. With $6 billion in assests, Penn Central was bankupt. By then, the stock had already dropped over $50. A few years later, your $5900 investment in 100 shares of stock was worth less than $200. Many institutions owned the stock in their portfolios. The question to be answered is why wouldn't fundamental security analysis have uncovered the company's morass of difficulties ahead of time?

There are many forces working against the fundamental security analyst that may keep him from accurately predicting future stock prices. One of the most important is the influence of random or unpredictable events. An example of this might be the explosive increase in oil prices and interest rates in the late 1970s. Both of these occurrences had a very negative impact on Ford Motor Company. Raw chance influences the outcome of stock price movement more than most analysts might want to admit.

There are problems with the dissemination of information from companies. Because of past abuses, management has to be very sure that everyone has access to the same information at the same time. They also don't want to waste their time with individual appointments with every security analyst on Wall Street. Therefore, management may have periodic meetings and schedule plant visits by all analysts at one time. This means everyone gets the same information, only the interpretation is different. Ferreting out "gems" of unknown data has become increasingly difficult for large companies.

The analyst has another problem concerned with the many dimensions of his job. Besides the rigors of the analysis of the companies that he follows, he must communicate his thoughts to the institutional clients that his firm relies on for commissions. The IPM likes to hear about the company he owns or is thinking of buying "straight from the horse's mouth." This can take the form of a barrage of daily phone calls or trips around the country for personal visits. There are many demands on his time.

Another problem is the time frame of his recommendations. It is usually a six-month-to-two-year forecast. After completing his analysis, he must give an opinion as to whether the stock should be bought, held, or sold. This depends on whether he thinks it will outperform the market, perform in line with the market, or underperform the market. He may be evaluated and paid upon price movements of less than two-year durations.

Many analysts are very astute and accurate when it comes to making a strong purchase recommendation. However, an outright sale opinion may have complications. If the company is an underwriting client of the firm, this means that they couldn't sell any new stock. Also, a sell recommendation by a brokerage firm does not produce a harmonious relationship with the company management and they may lose the business. If they were trying to get their business, they may have just lost their chances. However, there are other reasons why outright sell opinions are rare.

Every client of a brokerage firm is a potential buyer of a stock. Under ordinary circumstances, only a very small percentage will own the shares that may be recommended for sale. This means that the commission potential for a buy opinion is much greater than a sell opinion. In the late 1960s, one portfolio manager decided to closely monitor all the recommendations of the more than 20 brokerage firms that competed for his business. He used a two-year period during which the overall market went up, then down, in a volatile manner. He got 1200 buy recommendations and fewer than 50 sell recommendations. Interestingly, most of the sells would have been profitable, whereas most of the buys wouldn't have made money.

For whatever reasons, the fundamental security analyst is much better able to advise the investor **when** to buy a security. It is much easier to recognize undervaluation than it is to recognize overvaluation. If he becomes cautious about a company, he will usually go to a neutral opinion. When he makes an outright sell recommendation, it is usually because the financial situation of the company has deteriorated badly. However, under most circumstances, fundamental security analysis will not be too helpful when it comes time to sell and take profits.

As in any profession, there are relatively few outstanding individuals who seem to produce much better results than their peers. Common sense dictates that everyone can't be a superanalyst. Unfortunately, there is a much larger number of analysts who produce only average results, the sort that you might get by flipping a coin. Yet most of them are dedicated, hard working, and professional. They try to do extremely difficult job to the best of their abilities. Sadly, they face many problems in trying correctly to advise investors of the direction of stock price movements.

Let's return to our two examples of Ford and Penn Central. The technical security analyst would have argued that, in both cases, the price action of the stock would have indicated impending disaster. The astute investor would have sold his stock before the prices dropped precipitously. Of course he probably lost money, but it wouldn't have been nearly as much as he would have lost by riding the stock all the way down. Yet making decisions based on purely technical analysis has its problems.

As we have seen, the technical security analyst uses indicators of internal market dynamics to predict furture price movements. This applies to the market in general and also to individual security price movements. Yet these indicators are often in conflict with one another. Also, as more people begin to focus on the good results of a particular indicator, it loses its usefulness. Since the market participants are continuously looking for new ways to remedy past failures, an indicator with a "good track record" of predictability becomes more widely followed. When this happens, people begin to anticipate the signals and the indicator loses its effectiveness. Technical security analysis works best when the fewest number of players are relying on it.

When a speculator uses pure technical analysis in the pursuit of profits, he tends to trade more often. This is because he is trying to maximize his return in the shortest period of time. In doing so, he exposes himself to all the forces of expectation loss that can erode his capital. Let's look at a specific example.

One afternoon, after a three martini business lunch, you are sitting in your office trying to complete a report in which you have no interest. You're having a particuly hard time concentrating on what you're doing because you keep worrying about the fact that you haven't been getting along with your wife very well lately. Also, life in general seems to have lost its zest for you. You wonder whether you're going through a "midlife crisis." when you get a welcome respite—a phone call from your stockbroker.

> Mr. Investor, I've been reviewing your stock portfolio and you've got a number of solid blue-chip companies that should grow over the long term. However, we should take a small portion of your capital and try to be more aggressive. If I could show you a way that had a chance to make a 25% return two or three times a year, would you have some money to invest?

You feverishly examine your checkbook and see that you have an extra $1300 that you won't need for a while. So you ask him to explain what he wants to do.

> A stock in an uptrend will usually make higher highs and higher lows as long as its momentum is upward. When it breaks to a new high in price, often it will take a sudden sharp move upward. The trick is to buy it on a "breakout." However, you must be willing to limit your losses in cases it turns out to be a "false breakout." We won't be right everytime, so you must "cut your losses short" if the stock doesn't follow through. We need to preserve most of your capital for the next opportunity.
>
> Sam Trendline is our technical market analyst and he's got a great track record at picking these situations. Skyline Corporation is the leader in the mobile home industry. Our research people really like the stock on a fundamental basis. Sam says the stock just "broke out" of the very powerful "catapult formation" at 12½. Let's buy 100 shares, but we're going to sell out if the stock drops more than 15%. Do you agree?

Turn to Exhibit 4.3, "Skyline Corporation" and you can see how well you did. In January 1980, you bought 100 shares at $12½. Unfortunately, the stock reacts downward

Exhibit 4.3 ***Skyline Corporation Weekly Close Jan 1980 to May 1981***

and you are sold out with a 15% loss. In September, the stock moves to a new high of $13¼. However, after your previous 15% loss and commissions, you have only enough money to buy 75 shares. Again, to your anguish, the stock reacts downward and you are sold out. In February 1981, the stock moves to a new high of $15. By now, you have only enough money to buy 53 shares. What are you going to do? Do you have the "guts" to try it one more time?

You may go on to make a profit on this trade, but you own about half as many shares at a higher price than when you started. Your capital has been eroded almost 45%. You must now have the stock double in price for you just to break even. After taking a beating on the first two trades, it's questionable whether you would go ahead with the third one. Also, your broker probably wouldn't feel like calling you again at this point. Now, you know what it's like to get whipsawed and it's not much fun.

One of the problems with technical analysis is that many participants have unrealistic expectations regarding its uses. The amateur market speculator may view it as a "magic key" to quick profits. A stockbroker may see it as an important source of revenue because of increased customer activity. However, the Random Walk Theory would seriously question the ability of routine or mechanical interpretations of price formations and technical indicators to produce above-average profits. Often, high levels of expectations result in disappointment and frustration.

The most effective use of technical analysis is probably the evaluation of underlying trends or themes in the stock market. Being able to identify when investor opinion forms a consensus is an important tool that may eventually signal a change in the direction of prices. As the players become more sophisticated, the correct use of technical analysis becomes more difficult.

Accurate technical analysis requires accessibility to a large amount of data. Detailed references to market patterns of the past are extremely helpful when one is trying to assess the current market environment. This is an important ingredient of Bob Farrell's success. He has developed computer programs to filter vast amounts of information and display it in meaningful ways. Also, because his firm is so large, he can more precisely identify and monitor the activity in different kinds of accounts. It appears that this combination has given him an important advantage over other technical security analysts.

Most private investors get their investment ideas from their stockbroker. Even if all the firm's research was mailed to them, they wouldn't have time to read and evaluate it. Their access to the research of a brokerage firm is usually "filtered" through their stockbroker one way or another and they end by focusing on the ideas that he likes best.

There was a survey published in the September 1978 edition of *The Stockbroker*, conducted by the Western Opinion Research Center. Out of the 1500 shareholders polled, about 75% indicated that their personal stockbroker motivated their buying activity. The rest were divided among financial publications, investment advisory services, and financial analysts' reports. Of course, some individuals used more than one source. However, there was little question that their stockbroker's recommendations had the most influence.

Being a stockbroker is anything but an easy job. He, or she, earns their livelihood directly from the commissions paid on the security transactions that take place in the accounts of their customers. The more commissions generated, the more money they make. In the relationship between broker and client is a built-in incentive to encourage the buying and selling of stocks. It's just a fact of life. However, the majority of stockbrokers are dedicated professionals who do not consciously violate the trust placed in them by their customers. They will often turn down business that they think may not be in the best interests of their client.

One important requirement for being a stockbroker is that you must have a big ego that is not easily damaged. You must have an opinion, any opinion, as to where the stock market is going. You must also have several stocks that you think will do well. It is necessary to maintain a positive attitude regardless of how wrong you have been in the past. In an up market, it is easy to believe that you are a genius. However, in a down market, it takes nerves of steel to survive.

The basic problem with most stockbrokers is that their level of expectations tends to be too short-term in nature. The faster they can make a profit for a client, the faster they can sell one stock then look for another opportunity. This, of course, produces more commissions. Often the customer is not much help. He has an unrealistic expectation of the return he should receive on his capital. This puts pressure on the broker to try and make the client a "lot of money" in a short period of time. Many people think that they are true investors when, in reality, they are "closet" speculators.

The results are inevitable. An account that does too many transactions will eventually get discouraged with his losses or go broke. Then he must be replaced with a new client. This is one of the biggest problems for the account executive. There is a natural attrition of his client base. Of course, there are other reasons why it happens. People die, they move away, they get out of the market to buy land, or some other broker woos them away. In order to stay in the business, the broker must have a source of new clients. This means that he, or she, must prospect for new business. In order to do this effectively, on a continuous basis, the broker must be a good salesperson.

Most people, including stockbrokers, would rather take a beating than prospect. It is a degrading task that is filled with rejection. It is certainly no fun. That is why there is a very high turnover among stockbrokers. If you have ever sold anything or solicited money for your church or favorite charity, you can understand the feeling. In order to do it, you must be dedicated and believe in what you are trying to accomplish. When an individual first gets into the brokerage business and has a firm conviction that he is going to help people make money, it is easy to be enthusiastic. After the realities of the stockmarket have wiped out a few of his best clients, the unlimited confidence that is needed for prospecting may vanish. Picking up the phone for another dose of rejection becomes laboriously painful.

In most cases, the only way to open a new account is to stimulate the greed motivation of the investor. This is usually done with a good story about a stock. There must be an overwhelming rationale for the skeptical prospect on the other end of the phone to commit his hard-earned money to the investment situation that you propose. In other words, the prospect, or client, must be sold on the idea of risking his capital. In many cases, the successful stockbroker is a much better salesperson than he is a money manager.

There are several problems when it comes to making

recommendations to clients and prospects. The biggest one is finding time to do adequate research. Many firms provide very good information for the broker to communicate to his customers but having time to read and digest it can be burdensome. During market hours, he should be talking to his clients or prospects. Often, they have questions they want answered. The interruptions are continuous. Many a well-intentioned stockbroker takes home a briefcase stuffed with research. Unfortunately, it may never be opened. This may promote physical fitness but not market insight.

Stockbrokers also have the same problem that most investors do. They become emotionally involved with their recommendations. If the stock goes up, it may be hard to recommend a sale. They may feel that they would look bad to the client if it goes higher. If it goes down, it is psychologically hard for everyone to take a loss. It is much easier to hope that everything will work out okay. Often, the story on the company may be so good that it's hard to sell whether it goes up or down. A stockbroker's ego can get in the way of objective investment decisions.

Another problem is that it is much easier to get their clients and prospects to buy what is popular. These are usually the stocks that are moving upward. Invariably, the reason for ownership is overwhelming. These are the stocks that are in the news with optimistic long-term outlooks. Getting in is easy. Getting out with a profit may be much more difficult. Unfortunately, these are not the broker's only problems; his working environment provides some more.

Even a good broker will find many ways to dissipate his time. If you have ever been in a brokerage office, you may have been puzzled by the glazed look on the faces of many of the people sitting behind the desks in a boardroom. No, they are not on drugs, they are merely "watching the tape" as if some divine revelation were to come forth. If you own stocks, tape watching is an exciting way to consume a workday, but it is also counterproductive.

Many stockbrokers are not good administrators. With a large client base, there are always problems and special requests from customers. This is a big source of frustration for them, because they will often put off taking care of something until it is a crisis. Most brokerage firms will not pay enough to hire a competent sales secretary, so they end up having to handle the bookkeeping problems themselves. In addition, they must keep a variety of records and fill out compliance forms on their active accounts. These administrative details sap the energy that could be better focused on helping clients manage their money.

Probably no two stockbrokers have the exact same approach to the business. In the past decade, brokerage firms have developed an array of new products from money market funds to "tax shelters." An individual broker can choose two or three products and try to develop his expertise in that area alone. Some brokers are very aggressive in their stock selection, others are very conservative. Some brokers will hardly ever recommend that their clients buy or sell. Others insist that the client do everything they tell them to do. Everyone seems to have a slightly different method.

All stockbrokers sincerely desire to make money for their clients. They are human beings just like everyone else. They have egos and want to feel like professionals in their chosen occupation. They also have a need to be appreciated and respected by the people with whom they do business. Unfortunately, the very nature of the job may make the realization of these objectives extremely difficult.

We have spent a considerable amount of time discussing how hard it is for most people to predict stock price movements. Unfortunately, many stockbrokers suffer from the same disease. Because they make a living from commissions, their livelihoods, more than anyone else's, may be affected by random price movements. But they continue to search diligently for a way to help their clients make money. Most of them would do almost anything to keep from prospecting.

If a stockbroker, or private investor, becomes disenchanted with the research of his respective brokerage firm, he may seek outside advice. This can be accomplished by subscribing to the service of an independent investment adviser for a fee. They come in many different forms but almost all of them have a recommended list of stocks to be bought and sold.

Each investment adviser has his own particular set of "indicators" that he uses. They may be fundamental, technical or a combination of both. Some rely entirely on mar ket timing, others focus on stock selection. Of course, every one you speak to has a great "track record" of making money in the stock market.

At this writing, one widely followed investment adviser claims near perfect success in calling market tops and bottoms. In a recent interview, someone asked him what stocks he owned. He said that he didn't own any because it would be a conflict of interest. Perhaps that is true, but there could be another reason. He makes $6 million a year selling his service. If, for some reason, it was discovered that he couldn't make money in own account, it would not do much for his image.

The problem with many investment advisers is that their advice can be very speculative. They may suggest unseasoned companies or encourage their clients to move in and out of the market on a wholesale basis. They may even recommend short sales. Their reasoning is that they will be so right in their predictions that their clients won't be really speculating. This defies common sense.

Surely, there may be some excellent investment advisers who consistently do a good job for their clients. However, as a group, they are just as wrong as everyone else at major turning points. See Exhibit 4.4, "Advisory Services." Investors Intelligence is an organization that records the sentiment of all the investment advisory services in the country. If a service is bullish, it thinks the stock market is going up. If it's bearish, it thinks the stock market is going down. Just remember that investment advisers, like everyone else on Wall Street, have a positive bias. They are consistently more optimistic than pessimistic about the stock market.

1974 was the end of a devastating bear market. The New York Stock Exchange Index was under 40 and the DJIA was under 600. At that point over 60% of the investment advisory services thought the market was going down further. The market then rallied for two years and at the top, in 1976, less than 10% of the advisers thought it was going down. Again, there was a drop in the market until early 1978. Then guess what? Over 60% of the advisers felt it was going down.

By the end of 1980, the NYSEI had climbed to the low 70s. On each reaction along the way, the advisers reached levels of bearishness in the mid- to high-50% level. A certain number of the services is always bullish no matter what happens. But when the consensus becomes 55%–60% bearish, most of the price damage may have been done and a bottom is not too far away. So much for outside advice.

Now, let's go back to the advice of your economist. What did you do with your portfolio? If you sold out, you followed the crowd. You also missed a dramatic rise in certain segments of the stock market. Your economist was 100% right about his forecasts, but the stock market didn't go down, it

Exhibit 4.4 ***Advisory Services***

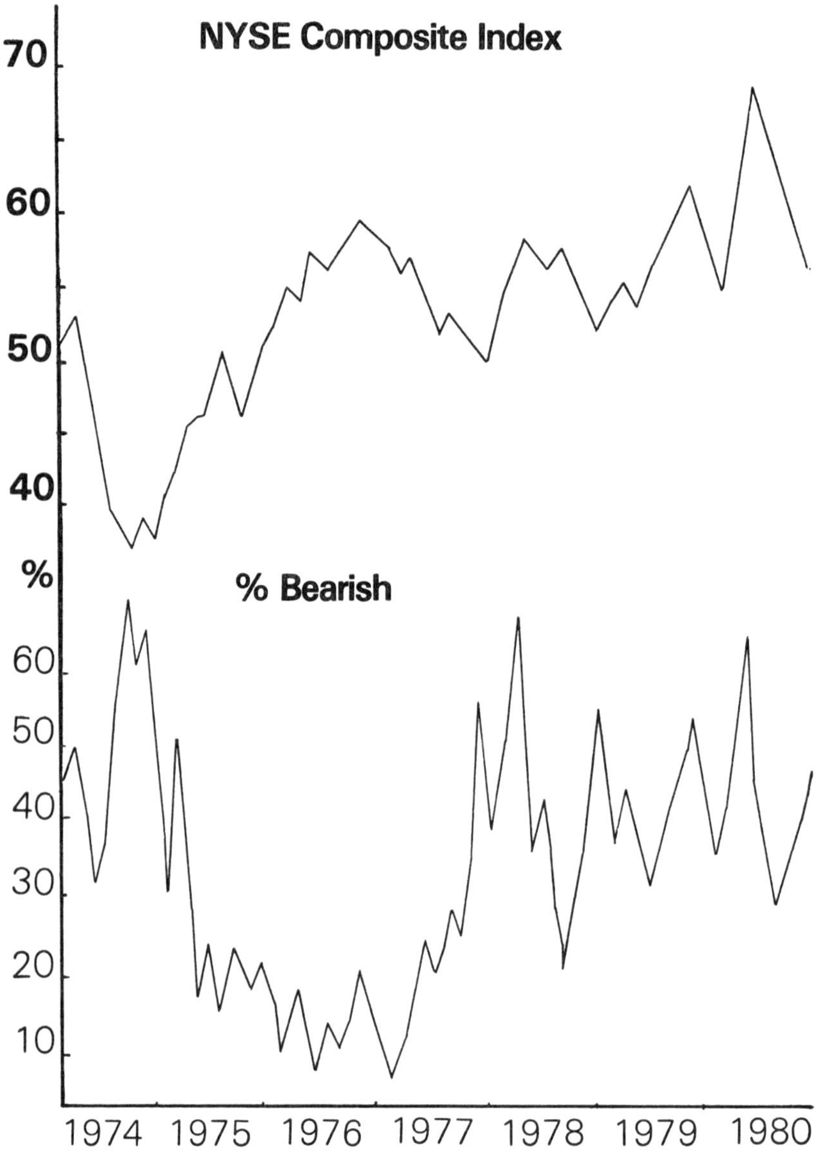

Courtesy of Robert J. Farrell

went up. Of course, it was doubtful if anyone could predict what happened to the economy. Most economists were looking for a recession, falling interest rates, and lower corporate earnings. What actually happened was almost the opposite. One of my favorite sayings in this: If the prediction doesn't get you, sometimes the interpretation will. Now, we are going to see how well the investors, with the abundance of well-meaning advice they receive, fare.

INVESTORS

The most powerful force in the stock market today is the institutional portfolio manager. Stock transactions from banks, trust companies, mutual funds, and insurance companies now account for about 70% of the dollar volume of stocks traded on the NYSE on any given day. Individuals account for the remaining 30% of the dollar volume. Under these circumstances, the highly trained IPM must compete against themselves rather than the public. If you think that it would be hard to beat the market, if you *are* the market, then you'd be exactly right.

Being an institutional portfolio manager can be an extremely rewarding job monetarily. A good IPM can make well over $100,000 a year, depending on where he works. If he has a good track record, he can work anywhere. The reason for this is because the business can be very lucrative. Firms charge a fee of anywhere from a quarter of 1% to 1% of the assets under management. Of course, some may charge much more. It is a business that generally has high fixed costs and low variable costs. So incremental money can be managed very easily and the profits go straight to the bottom line, meaning that it can be split up among the principals. However, there are just a few problems associated with being an IPM.

First of all, the business is extremely competitive. The corporate officers who decide on the money manager will often have unrealistic expectations in terms of performance. They may think of the management of their pension money as a profit center. For instance, a 1% change in the performance of a fund may mean that the contributions for the year can be reduced 15%–20%. Of course, this increases the profits of the corporation. This means that the money managers who are supposed to look for good, long-term investments may be judged on very near-term performance.

Some institutional portfolio managers operate as if there were a loaded gun at their heads. Everyone is measured against the performance of the Standard and Poor's 500 Index. A money manager that underperforms the S&P average by a significant amount for two or three quarters may find himself losing a $50 million portfolio. This does not promote relaxed, long-term thinking. They are given the job of making money grow over the long term, but their performance is judged on a quarterly or semiannual basis. In this kind of environment, objective decision-making may suffer.

Many market observers believe that the performance of a money manager can only be judged over a full market cycle of somewhere between 5 to 10 years. They point out that an investment strategy may take considerable time for the decisions to materialize properly. Oftentimes, a strategy that is good on a long-term basis will not produce very good near-term results. The problem that the portfolio manager has is that he may have a great long-term strategy only to find that his portfolio has been pulled from under him before he has the opportunity for it to be fully implemented.

There is a remarkable phenomenon in the marketplace that shows that time after time, institutions tend to buy the same select group of stocks, usually the "high octane performers" of the moment. This tends to increase your portfolio performance on a near-term basis. As the clients review these portfolios on a quarterly basis, they want to see that they are in the "right stocks." They do not like to see that they are in "dogs" that aren't moving, no matter how great the quality may be. Tremendous pressure can be put on an IPM to change his thinking, especially if he is underperforming the S&P 500 Index.

This can be demonstrated by what happened to a large New York bank in the early 1970s. It had followed a very conservative, value-oriented approach to stock selection. However, they began to lose their largest institutional clients to Morgan Guaranty who had astutely adopted a very successful growth stock philosophy a few years earlier. In late 1972, near the top, they started dumping the sound, lower multiple companies and buying the high multiple growth stocks. Unfortunately, what appeared to be the light at the end of the tunnel turned out instead to be the headlight on a freight train.

As you may imagine, one of the most important things to an institutional portfolio manager is keeping his job. If he has been bagged in stock that has dropped precipitously, he may sell it so that it doesn't show on his record. If he missed a move in a group of stocks that has done well, he may feel compelled to own it as a position in his portfolio. This may lead to "window dressing" before the end of the quarter.

Liquidity is a very big problem when it comes to managing institutional portfolios. Because of the size of the blocks of stock that are bought and sold, the majority of the volume must take place among other institutions. Disposing of large blocks of stock in periods of market weakness can produce catastrophic drops and the rush by the IPM to be in the stocks that are doing well can produce exhilarating price movements to the upside. This phenomenon is an important ingredient of the PSYCLE.

In 1977, Robert J. Farrell made the following observation in *Forbes*.:

> For many years a popular view has been that the individual investor is always wrong, selling at the bottom and buying at tops. Nothing could be further from the truth. Individual investors, whether those trading in odd lots or cash-account round lots, have consistently bought at bottoms and sold at tops. Institutional investors should do as well—in fact, they are the new odd-lotters.

> Since 1919 the biggest odd-lot buying has occurred at major market bottoms, such as 1921, 1938, 1946, 1957, 1962, 1966 and 1970. The glaring exceptions, of course, are 1932 and 1974. But in these cases, the average price of a share of stock on the New York Stock Exchange got so low that odd-lotters could have done their buying in round lots.
>
> We have evidence from our round-lot cash account sample that this is precisely what happened in 1974. This sample showed cash-account round-lot buying—the individual investor—was at its highest level ever in 1974, reaching its peak level near the market low. In fact, a close inspection of our cash account sample shows that individuals bought at every important bottom in the last 12 years and sold at each significant market top. Early in 1976 individual-investor selling was at a new record level and helped retard further market progress after that time.
>
> Institutional investors have assumed the role once relegated to the odd-lotter, that is, sell low, buy high. For years now institutions have had maximum cash levels at market bottoms and least cash levels at market tops. in other words, now that institutions dominate the market, they are the new public.

Exhibit 4.5, "Institutional Cash" illustrates Farrell's comments in detail. He conducts a quarterly institutional survey of the cash levels of large money managers. In late 1976 when the Dow Jones was near the 1000 level, the IPM had a very low percentage of cash to total assests. They were fully invested and expecting higher prices. As the Dow dropped over 250 points, they sold heavily because they feared lower stock prices. As a group, they were fully invested at the top and sold out at the bottom. These statistics would not argue well for their ability to predict future stock prices.

Conversely, according to Farrell, the individual odd-lotter and the round-lot cash account are conservative bargain hunters. They tend to buy heavily when prices are down. Another statistic that Farrell uses is heavy net selling by round-lot cash accounts. They tend to take profits near market

Exhibit 4.5 ***Institutional Cash***

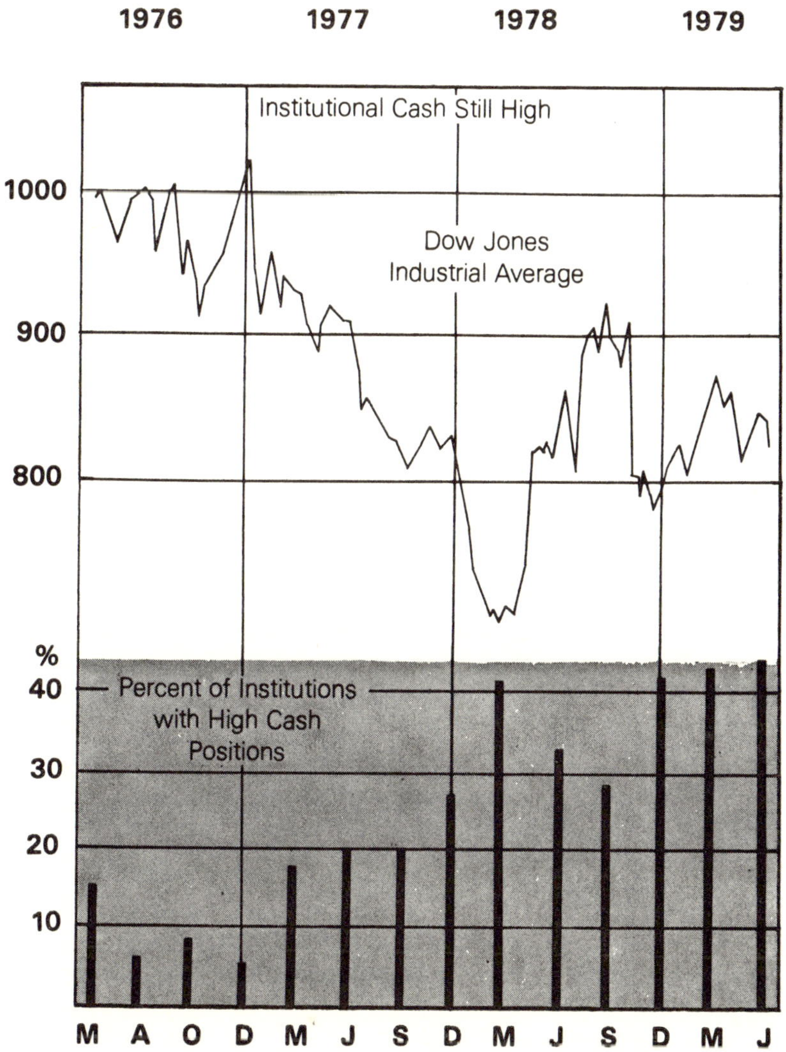

Courtesy of Robert J. Farrell, July 30, 1979

peaks. In other words, the supposedly unsophisticated conservative private investor tends to buy low and sell high.

Unfortunately, the same cannot be said for the margin account trader. He tends to buy as prices move upward and liquidate as prices move downward. This phenomenon occurs for several reasons. First of all, most margin speculators are interested in near-term profits. As prices go up, the value of their portfolio increases and they have more buying power so they tend to use it. As prices drop, they may be forced to liquidate through margin calls and margin debt is reduced. In fact, one good indication that a market bottom is near will be a 25% to 33% reduction of margin debt.

Time is another problem for investors. They simply don't have enough time to allocate to making objective investment decisions. This is especially true for the private, part-time investor. The stress and anxiety that come from just making a living in the cold, cruel world tend to sap most of his creative energies. Usually, the more money that an individual makes in his profession, the harder that he has to work for it. When he does have free time, he may prefer to spend it with his family or in pursuing leisure activities. Somehow, most PPTIs don't ever get around to spending time consistently on rigorous investment analysis. Because they have not thought logically about what exactly they are trying to accomplish, their decisions may tend to be emotional and short-sighted.

MARKET MYOPIA

All the players are subject to a fatal, financial disease: market myopia. One of the reasons for this condition is that it is easy to check a recent price quote in the paper so you can see if you're "right" or "wrong" continuously. This tends to make the investor focus on near-term price movements.

Another reason why they are short-sighted is because price movement tends to be the greatest stimulus to future expectations. The price trends continue until the majority becomes conditioned to believe they will not change. At this point, the player's action will have already reflected their feelings. The stage will then be set for a change of direction. This is not a new phenomenon, as indicated in the following remarks by Charles Dow, coauthor of the Dow Jones Average, in 1901:

> There is always a disposition in people's minds to think that existing conditions will be permanent. While the market is down and dull, it is hard to make people believe that this is the prelude to a period of activity and advance. When prices are up and the country is prosperous, it is always said that while preceding booms have not lasted, there are circumstances connected with this one which make it unlike its predecessors and give assurance of permanency.

Another famous remark made several decades later that seems to validate Mr. Dow's belief is "stocks have reached what looks like a permanently high plateau." The noted Yale economist Irving Fisher said it, but his timing was somewhat off. It was about a 2 weeks before Black Tuesday (October 29, 1929), the worst day ever in stock market history.

A big problem of most players is that they become conditioned to their most recent experiences in the financial markets. They will make decisions in line with current price trends and then rationalize them. They can easily document how an "investment" made in a stock or group of stocks has performed in a superior manner. Or conversely, why a stock or group of stocks should be avoided because they have done so poorly. We will explore this phenomenon in detail in the next chapter. For now, let's call it human nature.

Another problem for everyone is coping with the vast number of variables available for investment decisions. It seems that there is just too much information available to be processed and evaluated properly. Do you remember your high school algebra course? It is a mathematical science designed to help solve problems with interrelated variables. If you passed the course, you could easily solve a problem with one equation and one variable. Two equations with two variables was more difficult. Three equations with three variables was laborious. Now imagine trying to solve 300 equations with 300 variables.

This is the scope of the problems facing the institutional portfolio manager and private investor when making decisions. Turn back to Exhibit 2.9, "Investment Target," to illustrate the dilemma. Do you think anyone could be capable of considering all the variables? Probably not. What happens is they tend to hit one of the bands and make decisions based on two or three key variables they believe are important. The rest are ignored. Almost no one can hit the "decision bull's-eye" consistently.

Still another problem for everyone is that they expect their decisions to work out on a fairly short-term basis, a few weeks or a few years depending on the situation. Advisers are paid and judged on their near-term performance. Investors tend to expect unrealistic returns on their capital and in today's competitive market environment, most of the players emphasize gain over risk.

When it is time to buy, the advisers may give the investors very sound advice but they may be too shell-shocked to listen. A recent erosion of portfolio value does not build confidence. Invariably, the majority is not in a good buying position when distressed opportunities present themselves. The individuals who have buying power are reluctant to use it. The fear motivations that caused them to raise cash are not quickly dispelled.

Almost everyone has a problem when it comes to selling. Unfortunately, the advisers are not nearly as good at predicting when to sell as when to buy and the investors may not be listening too well. Perhaps greed is a stronger emotion than fear or perhaps most people have a bias toward optimism. At any rate, you must sell high in order to buy low. There is an old stock market adage that goes "you can't buy cheap stocks with cheap stocks." Amen.

If you had to summarize all of the problems of all the players into one word, it would be *predictability*. Their ultimate problem is trying to predict the future and then trying to determine how stock prices will react to those events. All the players are engaged in predicting stock price movements in one form or another. Let's see if we can really understand the term.

One thing you would like to know about an investment decision strategy is how often is it right. There is another way to ask this question. Given a large number of decisions, what percentage of the time will you have a successful event? Now reflect for a moment on your own decision-making abilities. Assuming you are highly trained in your own profession, what percentage of the time are you right? Would it be 40% of the time? Is it 50%. Perhaps it is 60%, or slightly more. However, you're probably not right as much of the time as you believe. Few people are. No one is right 100% of the time no matter how expert they are in their profession.

If you know anything about baseball, you know that all the players have a batting average. That is, how many times does he get a hit for the number of times that he gets to the plate. The batting aberage of a very good hitter might be .350. That means that 35% of the time that he steps up to the plate, he has a successful event and gets a hit that puts him on base.

Now, it's very important to understand that every professional, every adviser, every investor, and every decision strategy has a "batting average" regarding the stock market. This means that every decision or decision strategy has a certain *probability* of being right. Let's define "being right" as buying a stock and selling it for a profit, regardless of the time involved. Therefore, you could buy a stock at $10 and sell four years later at $11 and that would be considered a right decision. Obviously, that was not a great return on your investment; however, it would still be considered a successful event. If somehow you could add up all your right decisions and divide them by the number of total decisions, you would have your "investment batting average" (IBA). We will use this term to describe the probability of making a profit on each investment decision.

When assuming financial risk, there is another dimension of the equation that should be understood: How much money do you make when you are right and how much money do you lose when you are wrong. The so-called win expectation (WE) is a more complicated number to generate, so we won't pursue it now. However, many investors tend to take small profits and large losses. Under those circumstances, it is hard to have a large win expectation. If you combine that with even a 50% investment batting average (which may be generous) you can see why it is difficult for many investors to make net profits.

By understanding the PSYCLE, you'll be forced to invest contrary to the crowd. Therefore, your investment batting average should be a very high percentage and most profits will be substantial. It has been well within my experience over the last decade to be right over 8 out of 10 times. That means you should have an investment batting average of better than 80% with this approach.

Your win expectation should be close to 100%. Some gains will happen within two or three years and some will take longer. Most of the time when you're right, it'll be in a big way. Occasionally there may be a disaster. But, because you will have spread your your risks, the loss can be taken in stride. The overall rate of return on your capital should be quite positive.

All successful stock market participants have a common attribute: They are independent thinkers regardless of their discipline or technique. However, their biggest problem may be "sticking to their guns" when months or years go by and their course of action appears to be incorrect. So they must work especially hard at being rational and continue to fight the temptation to be caught up in the current fads of the crowd.

A free auction market always functions to make the majority wrong near important turning points. Greed is the predominant emotion at market tops and most of the players are focusing on maximizing gain. Fear is the predominante emotion at market bottoms and most of the players are worried about avoiding further risk. Now let's investigate the psychological dynamics that produce this phenomenon.

5

All Markets are the Same

When I was a child, I spake as a child,
I understood as a child, I thought as a child;
but when I became a man,
I put away childish things.
— I Corinthians 13:11

PERSONALITY MODEL

Let's think about this famous quotation from St. Paul in the Bible. What does it mean to you personally? Have you "put away the childish things" in your life? If so, you may not be having much fun. On the other hand, have you had a recent outburst of anger toward your spouse or one of your children over some small incident? Later, you may have felt guilty because you threw a temper tantrum like a two-year-old. If we are truly adults, why do we sometimes act like children?

Let's face it. Many of us don't fully understand our own emotions and behavior patterns. Certainly we are, at times, confounded and confused by our irrational actions toward someone whom we are supposed to love. On the other hand, how can the well-intentioned things that we do be seemingly unappreciated by those people whom we desperately want to like and admire us? Why is it so difficult for us to accept compliments and praise from our friends? Why do we work so hard to make money? Why might we be destroying our health with cigarettes, alcohol, or drugs? Why is it so hard to say to a precious son or daughter, "I love you"? Even though each of us has complex feelings, there is now a relatively simple way that we can psychoanalyze our own behavior.

Most of us don't think that we're mixed-up enough to go to a trained psychiatrist. If we did, we might find an individual who operated within the theoretical framework of Freudian psychiatry. Even though we are fairly well-educated, we may not understand the basic concepts or terminology. Also, in our fast-paced world, we may not have the patience to stay with the procedure. We need something that will fit within our daily experiences, is simple to understand, and that can be used immediately to effectively improve our lives. Fortunately there is such a process and it is called Transactional Analysis.

You bought this book to help you make money in the stock market, not to help solve your personal problems, isn't that right? Well, remember that stock prices are 100% psychological. Until you have some understanding of the feelings and emotions that motivate the other players, you can't be objective about your own investment decisions. And the more that you understand your own internal motivations, the more rational you can be in a crisis. The best way to accomplish this is through a structured arrangement of data, principles, and terms representing an individual's personality. We will use this so-called personality model as a standard frame of reference for the communication of analysis, ideas, and feelings.

The analysis of human behavior is a very complex subject. The TA personality model is an attempt to identify and understand the illusive process of interpersonal and internal transactions. It is not perfect and is subject to different interpretations. To my knowledge, it has never been applied to the psychodynamics of stock market players. Although this writer is not a trained psychiatrist, I've spent a great deal of time researching the current thinking of experts on psychoanalysis and Transactional Analysis; but the interpretation of human behavior, regarding the players, is based on my own personal feelings, experiences, observations and perceptions.

There may be some psychiatrists who will not agree with my interpretation of the TA personality model. That's okay. They've probably never made any money in the stock market. There will also be a number of stock market players who will not agree with my investment approach. That's okay, too. The "acid test" of anything is whether or not it works. In this case, the use of the Transactional Analysis personality model should help you to better understand the behavior (including your own) of the players and enable you to consistently make money in the stock market. If it can do that, then it should be considered a valid interpretation.

Do you have a big ego? Are you egotistical? We've all heard these terms used in different ways, but do we really know what they mean? The dictionary defines ego, from the psychoanalyst's point of view, as the conscious aspect of the psyche that develops through contact with the external world and protects the organism by resolving conflicts between the id and the superego so as to conform best with reality. After that definition, you may understand why Freud won't be of much help to us.

Actually, the vast majority of people don't have just one ego state; rather, they have three distinctly different ego states. This has been supported by continuous psychological observation. Eric Berne, the originator of Transactional Analysis, puts it this way:

> In more practical terms, it (an ego state) is a system of feelings accompanied by a related set of behavior patterns.

> Each individual seems to have available a limited repertoire of such ego states, which are not roles but psychological. This repertoire can be sorted into the following categories: (1) ego states which resemble those of parental figures, (2) ego states which are autonomously directed toward objective appraisal of reality, and (3) those which represent archaic relics, still-active ego states which were fixated in early childhood... Colloquially, their exhibitions are called Parent, Adult and Child...

See Exhibit 5.1, "Ego State Structure" to better understand our model.

Each of us has a brain that is far more marvelous than any computer yet designed by Man. Everything that we experience in life is recorded in microscopic electrochemical elements called neurons. Our brain contains about 100 billion such places to store information. If that weren't enough, each neuron can have several thousand connections. It is believed that there are about 100 trillion such neural connections that record information, access past data, and process current reality with previously learned knowledge. This is what produces our actions and reactions to the world in which we live.

Of course, we are all born with the instincts that provide for the survival of our species. These functions would include sex drive, child rearing, aggression, territorial prerogatives, and fear. However, Man's higher brain functions take place in the cerebral cortex, which is only a couple of million years old. This is where we can read, write, create, imagine, and think. It is what makes us different from all the other creatures on earth. We have the ability to change and to create our own destinies.

At birth, our neuron cells are empty. The pathways that are there to connect them are blank. As we live and grow, our brain creates additional neural pathways to perform its functions. As we emerge from the womb, our brain contains

Exhibit 5.1

EGO STATE STRUCTURE

Ego States **Emotions**

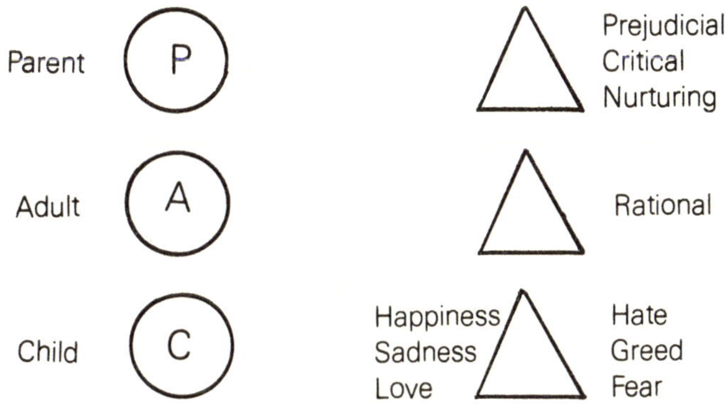

TRANSACTIONAL ANALYSIS

Wife **Husband**

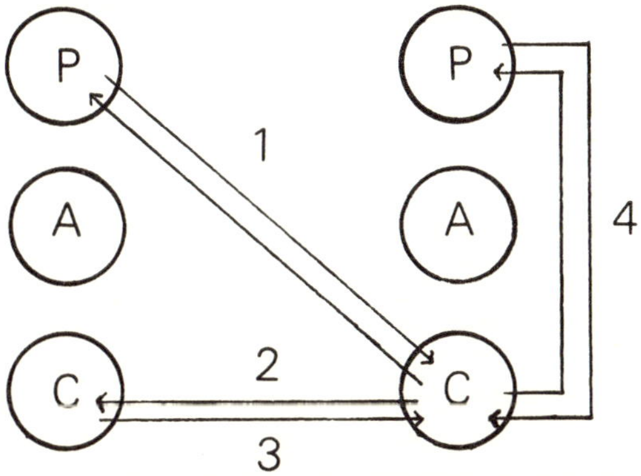

Source Eric Berne, *Games People Play* (New York: Ballantine, 1964)

no information or knowledge; it only possesses instincts. However, at that instant, it begins to gather and store data. All of our thoughts, feelings, and behaviors will be *learned* from our experiences in life.

Now begins the creation of two of the ego states that will eventually determine our individual personality. The Parent Ego State is primarily a vast recording of past data from external sources. The Child Ego State is a recording of the feelings that were produced internally as life was experienced. Later, the Adult Ego State will be formed to think, evaluate probabilities, and make decisions in a rational manner. Now, let's examine more clearly the Parent, Adult, and Child within each of us.

The Parent Ego State basically is made up of a vast amount of data recorded before the age of six. These data come primarily from our interactions with our parents. There is no scientific evidence of instinctual *abilities* for raising children in either primates or humans. So each successive generation must learn how to be parents from their parents. As the individual grows and matures, the Parent Ego State is also updated from other man-made value systems. This includes religious dogma, one's social environment, and the laws necessary to govern society. Our Parent Ego State forms what is called our conscience. That is, what we come to initially believe as "right" and "wrong." It also provides much repetitive "how-to" information for the large number of tasks that we routinely perform. The Parent also tries to keep us from hurting ourselves. For instance, your Parent automatically acts to keep you from touching a hot stove. Without the vast store of data to call upon from our Parent, we would have to start all over each time we were confronted with a decision.

As effortless as our Parent can make our lives, it can also be a source of misery. All data recorded in our Parent is taken in without editing. That is, it is recorded verbatim as if it were the truth. This is especially true in our early, formative years. The Parent has no facitity for evaluation. All external information becomes a "tape" that can be replayed at any time later in life. It can never be erased.

The Child Ego State reacts to external events by producing internal events. Since a little child has no vocabulary during the formative stages of his first few years of life, he reacts by *feeling*. When you are frustrated, anxious or afraid you are experiencing the emotions of the helpless Child. When you are carefree, happy and full of life, you are like the uninhibited little person who may be laughing and playing with a new puppy. The important thing to understand is that when you are feeling anything you are probably in your Child Ego State. Your Child can be happy, sad, afraid or mad. He isn't rational. He is emotional.

At about one year of age, the Adult Ego State begins to form. It is a very small part of the personality for the first few years of life. It is easily dominated by the whims and wishes of the Child or the rigid dictates from the Parent. As the individual grows and matures, the Adult assumes a larger part of his personalilty. Full potency is probably not reached until adolescence.

The function of the Adult Ego State is to process present incoming data and past recorded data. A healthy Adult Ego State will challenge its validity. In *Games People Play*, Eric Berne says,

> The Adult is necessary for survival. It processes data and computes probabilities which are essential for dealing effectively with the outside world... Another task of the Adult is to regulate the activities of the Parent and the Child, and to mediate objectively between them.

In other words, the Adult is our computer mechanism that tries to keep us in touch with reality.

You can have a good idea of which ego state that you are communicating from by your behavior patterns. Of course, this would also be true of anyone that is attempting to communicate with you. Facial expressions, voice tone and body gestures can give an important clue to an individual's ego state.

Transactional Analysis is used to understand the communication between different ego states. These can be with another person (external) or within oneself (internal). Berne defines this basic scientific unit thus:

> The unit of social intercourse is called a transaction. If two or more people encounter each other in a social aggregation, sooner or later one of them will speak, or give some other indication of acknowledging the presence of others. This is called the *transactional stimulus*. Another person will then say or do something which is in some way related to the stimulus, and that is called the *transactional response*. Simple transaction analysis is concerned with diagnosing which ego state implemented the transactional stimulus, and which one executed the transactional response.

Let's now look at a few examples.

If someone said to you, "your ears are too big," how would you respond? It may depend on how old you were at the time and who said it. If you were two years old and one of your parents said it, then you would take it in as reality. For the rest of your life, every time you looked into the mirror, the Parent tape might replay "your ears are too big." This tape may produce a self-conciousness that could affect your social life. If you were eight years old and one of your playground buddies said it, you may respond by saying "your nose looks like an elephant's." Of course, if it made you mad enough, you may punch *him* in the nose. Your Child Ego State does not like to receive this kind of transaction.

Regardless of who said it, or when they said it, the transaction was Parent to Child. Let's say that you are 23 years old and the girl you love says "your ears are too big." What do you do now? If you slapped her face you responded from your angry Child Ego State. If you were not insecure about the size of your ears, you might say "Yes, but don't you think they give my face a lot of character?" If you were concerned about them, you might say, "I've been thinking about plastic surgery." In the last two examples, you responded from your Adult Ego State.

Behavior patterns are fairly definite in each ego state. The Parent can be nurturing but it usually tends to be stern, prejudicial, or critical. If you are talking to someone with a scowl on your face, wagging your finger at them, you are probably admonishing them for something they should be doing, or have already done. In this case, you are "coming on" from your Parent. If you are at a football game cheering and rooting for your team, you are in your Child. If you are screaming at your spouse for something she did to you, the Child in you is in control. When you are having lunch with an associate discussing a business deal, your rational Adult is charge. The majority of time, people transact from their Adult with other than family members.

Refer back to Exhibit 5.1, "Ego State Structure," so that we can discuss a few examples. Let's suppose that you come home about 2:00 A.M. one night. You've been out having dinner and drinks with a business associate. While you're getting undressed, your wife wakes up and says in a hostile tone "Where have you been so late?" If you respond in a soft manner, "Honey, I was out trying to close the Mammoth Corporation deal," you had a complementary Parent–Child transaction as in No. 1. If you responded in an angry outburst, "I was out trying to make a living, you ungrateful wench," you responded from your Child to her Child. A fight will probably ensue as in No. 2. Later, when tempers have cooled and you're holding and cuddling each other, your transactions will also be from your Child Ego States. However, No. 3 will be happier and more affectionate. So much for external transactions. Let's now examine internal transactions.

Have you ever heard the voices in your head? Of course you have, but you may not have understood what they were. According to our model, they were transactional stimuli from your various ego states. For instance, do you remember the last time you felt guilty or the last time you were mad at yourself? Those feelings represented internal Parent–Child transactions.

Let's suppose that you're playing a heated tennis game and you hit an important shot into the net. You say to yourself with your teeth gritted: "You idiot! How could you be so stupid?" That's a Parent–Child transaction represented by No. 4. A few shots later, when you miss an overhead, you throw your racquet down and shout a few profanities. You're obviously "coming on" from your Child. These are not the actions of a mature, sensible adult.

What causes the Adult to lose control to the Parent or Child? When you "climb" up into your Parent you are righteous and powerful. As you admonish someone else for their faults or nurture them at a time of weakness, you don't have to worry about your own personal inadequacies. You will "drop" into your Child Ego State any time a transaction produces a childlike feeling within you. So anything that makes you feel happy, sad, afraid, inadequate or mad will "plunge" you, at least temporarily, into your Child. In general, moments of stress, anxiety or excitement will produce a shift from the Adult to the Parent or Child.

Now, let's use our P-A-C personality model to help us understand the psychological motivations of stock market participants. Psychiatrists can find only two reasons that motivate behavior. The only justification why anybody does anything is to *gain something* or to *avoid losing something*. At extremes, these motivations can manifest themselves in the respective emotions of *greed* and *fear*. We will use these terms, regarding the stock market, to reflect any desire to gain or to avoid loss, no matter how intensive it may be. People make investment decisions based on two primary emotions of the Child Ego State. They buy motivated by greed and sell motivated by fear. We will now explore these feelings in more depth.

If you are going to invest in a stock, what exactly are you doing? You are trading something that you already have (money) in hopes of gaining something of greater value. You may want a profit in the form of capital gains or income from dividends. Even though you may not be obsessed with a desire for excessive wealth, you still anticipate a considerable gain. Your Child Ego State is dreaming of future rewards. The emotion that you are experiencing is *greed*.

What happens when you sell a stock? Well, if you thought it would continue going up, you wouldn't sell. Your primary motivation is still greed. You would sell only if you anticipated a loss of what you already possessed in terms of market value. Your primary motivation would thus have shifted to *fear*. This is an unpleasant and powerful sensation, brought on by the anticipation of danger. Most people do not consider selling until they are keenly worried about loss.

What about the rational-thinking Adult? Don't we use objectivity in making investment decisions? Well, we may think that we do. Yet, as we observed, in moments of stress or anxiety, the Child Ego State may seize control of our thinking. When this happens, our perception of reality may be severely distorted by fear or greed.

There is an element of our Adult Ego State (Exhibit 5.2) that believes a person is in perfect touch with reality. We will label this character Mr. Macho. After using the internal computer of the mind to process data, estimate probabilities, and think about the decision, Macho will arrive at a conclusion that he believes is correct. Unfortunately, Macho has the same problems in predicting future stock price movements as everyone else.

Have you ever watched the behavior of a little child for any length of time? If you have, you may have concluded that the child focuses on instant gratification. The child wants what he wants, when he wants it. If he wants to play with a toy, he wants to do it *now*. If he wants to eat, he wants to do it *now*. If he wants something enough, he may scream, cry, or

Exhibit 5.2 ***Child-Adult Transactions***

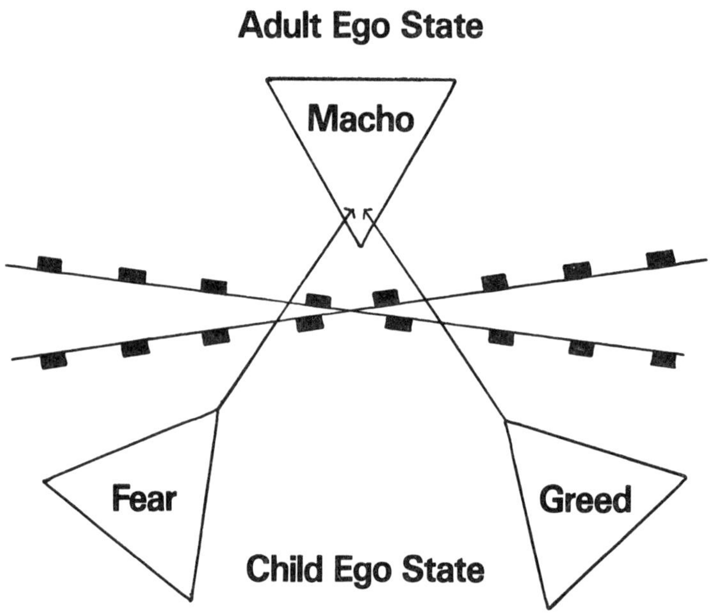

sulk. This is because the Child within us has a minimal conception of time, or the future.

The Child Ego State is one of the reasons why price movement is the greatest stimulus to investor sentiment. The more rapidly that prices move upward, the more the greedy Child anticipates further gains. The more precipitously that prices fall, the more the fearful Child anticipates further losses. It is for this reason that the majority of investors are most optimistic at the top and most pessimistic at the bottom of any price cycle.

The rational, objective Mr. Macho also plays a part in the decision-making process. Upward price movement reinforces his positive expectations. So he becomes even more convinced that he is "right." Downward price movement reinforces whatever negative expectations that he has and now he begins to question the validity of his decision.

Now superimpose the respective transactions of Greed or Fear on the Child Ego State. The result produces the perfect environment for investor euphoria at the top and investor panic at the bottom of every price cycle.

The emotions that keep Mr. Macho from being objective are Fear and Greed. They distort his perception of reality. Even if he rationally considers selling as a price peak approaches, Greed is at his side assuring him that there are more profits to come. Even if he considers holding on as prices fall into a trough, Fear is imploring him to sell to avoid further losses.

Remember that every decision made in a financial market has only a *probability* of success. Usually the higher the risk, the lower the probability. Also, the higher the risk the more likely that a loss might be suffered, up to a total wipeout. So the losers automatically have to stop playing until they can get another bankroll. But what about the winners? They have a different problem.

Few winners are capable of taking their money and quitting. Mr. Macho's decisions are being reinforced. Greed is demanding more profits. So the winner usually will keep on playing with his initial capital and his profits. At least, until the probabilities catch up with him. Then he will be wiped out too. Greed makes it very difficult for most people to quit while they are ahead. Yet, as we shall see, fear and greed are only the outward manifestations of a greater psychic need.

YOUR HUNGRY CHILD

Today we live in a modern, cosmopolitan society. In this environment, what do you believe is the greatest motivator of human behavior? Think for a minute. Some of the things that you might think of are food, shelter, clothing, sex, money, recognition, or self-realization. Assuming your basic living requirements are being met, what will motivate your behavior?

The Freudian model is based on the belief that sex is the greatest motivator of human behavior. Certainly, the human sex drive can be a powerful force, but is it the most powerful? Many modern psychologists say no. As important as Freud's original work is as a base for modern psychiatry, it has been subsequently both expanded and modified. Disciples have built upon the work of the Master.

A new school of psychiatry believes that *feelings of inferiority* are the most universal motivation in man's struggle to succeed. Thomas A. Harris underscores this point in his book, *I'm OK—You're OK*, in which he states that Adler broke with Freud over this concept. Adler believed that all children experience a feeling of inferiority to the adults in their life. This is because of the child's small size and helplessness. Dr. Harris puts this concept thus:

> I believe the evidence points to the overwhelming accumulations of NOT OK feelings in the child, making logical (on the basis of the evidence *he* has) his NOT OK conclusion about himself. In explaining Transactional Analysis to patients and non-patients, I have found a generally *that's it!* response to the explanation of the origin and existence of the NOT OK Child. I believe that acknowledging the NOT OK Child in each of us is the sympathetic, thus curative, way games can be analyzed. Considering the universality of games, the universality of the I'M NOT OK is a reasonable deduction.

Eric Berne in *Transactional Analysis* puts it another way. He believes that each human being has a very strong desire to be touched, recognized, and to structure time. Berne labels these cravings as stimulus-hunger, recognition-hunger, and structure-hunger. These feelings can only originate in our Child Ego State, so our primary motivations and behavior patterns come from our *Hungry Child* (author's term). He does not desire food to live, he desperately needs stroking.

The psychological stroke, or simply a *stroke*, is the fundamental unit of social interaction. It can take many different forms. It could be a physical stroke as you might give an infant or your spouse in a tender moment. It could be a verbal compliment such as "you did a great job on that report." It could also be a special nod of approval. Whatever shape it takes, it implies recognition of another human's worth.

When two people exchange strokes, social intercourse has taken place. Berne believed that a person's hunger for strokes will determine how he structures his time. For instance, he may spend hours, or even days playing psychological games.

The games that Dr. Berne discusses are defined as "a series of transactions with a gimmick." They are played as a desperate attempt to gain strokes. Even though they may reinforce old habit patterns of inferiority, they are played because they take up time and prove again that archaic opinions are correct. Unfortunately, psychological games also prevent honest, intimate, and open relationships among players.

If you could interview objectively the Child Ego States of many high achievers, you probably would discover deep seated feelings of inferiority. It may prevent them from forming intimate, interpersonal relationships. Moreover, the Hungry Child within many of us does not accept the fact that he is truly accepted and loved by his parents. Therefore, an important way to attempt to get strokes is through accomplishment.

If you now believe that everyone has a Hungry Child that needs strokes, your perception of reality may change. It could become much easier for you to be well liked by your friends and acquaintances. You can now be on the lookout for opportunities to give strokes to the people in your profession, personal and family life. It's a reasonable assumption that the more strokes that you give, the more strokes that you are likely to receive in return.

Positive strokes are the "grease" that make the machinery of social relationships turn much easier for everyone. The positive stroke must fit the reality of the situation. It must be done with honesty and candor. It should make the other person feel alive and important, and give him a sense of well-being. When you give someone else a positive stroke, it makes them feel good about themselves. If someone else makes you feel good about yourself, you natuarally tend to like him more. Positive strokes can be very subtle. Just listening attentively to someone else can be a positive stroke. So can sending someone a two-line thank-you note or giving another person a big smile. Few people get all the positive strokes they crave.

Performance and accomplishment give your Hungry Child the ability to fantasize strokes if none are forthcoming from other people. But if the successes are short-lived, the feelings of inferiority soon return. Your Hungry Child may live with all the trappings of financial prosperity, but he is still anxious and unhappy. He can't enjoy the present because he is replaying past failures or focusing on future expectations. He loses the pleasure of the moment. The only way to be objective about your investments is to be aware of your own internal motivations. It is likely then that your investment decisions will be rational ones.

When you invest in the stock market, it must be understood that your Hungry Child views profits purely as a way to keep score. When you buy a stock that goes up, its rise reaffirms one's self-worth. The Hungry Child in you does not want you to sell a stock that's still going up because he is going to lose his source of strokes. He does not want the old feelings of inadequacy to return. He will manipulate your Adult side with every conceivable rationalization. The faster the stock is rising, the more sensational the strokes. It makes him feel like a winner. This phenomenon explains why almost no one thinks about selling as a price peak approaches.

Just the opposite happens when a stock starts to drop. Now, instead of positive strokes, he is getting negative ones. This accelerates the return of the old feelings of inadequacy. He begins to feel like a loser. By getting rid of the stock, he removes the source of irritation. This explains why people often sell stocks at levels far below their purchase price.

What would make your Hungry Child want to sell a stock that was just "moving sideways"? That is, a stock without any real profit or loss. A "dead" stock does not produce instant gratification. It is *the thrill of risk* that enables your Hungry Child to fantasize about the future. While he believes that there is a way to make more money, or to achieve greater recognition, he can banish feeling inadequate in the "now."

There is only one way for an investor to gain control of the fear and greed behavior pattern of his Hungry Child. He must strengthen his Adult ego state through awareness of his own interconflicts. Naturally, this is much easier said than done. Yet just being aware of Greed or Fear will make his decisions more objective.

CROWD PSYCHOLOGY

In 1895, a Frenchman named Gustave LeBon published a book titled *The Crowd*. The term is now used any time it is felt that investor sentiment has become a consensus. LeBon believed that a group of people form a crowd when

> ...the sentiment and ideas of all the persons in the gathering take one and the same direction, and their conscious (individual) personality vanishes. A collective mind is formed doubtless but presenting very clearly defined characteristics. The gathering has then become...a psychologic crowd.

All of us have seen western movies where the good guy is in jail. He has been wrongly accused of murdering one of the town's popular figures. Outside is a group of drunk, irate townspeople that want quick, frontier-style justice. That is, they want to lynch him. The bad guy is outside whipping everyone into a frenzy. Soon, they begin charging the jail and threatening to burn it down with their torches. All they can think about is getting the hero out and hanging him. They are devoid of all reason.

A psychological crowd has many similarities. However, it does not have to be in one physical location. Investors can be spread throughout the entire United States or world, for that matter. But their thinking is usually the same. LeBon explains:

> A Crowd thinks in images, and the image itself calls up a series of other images, having no logical connection with the first... These image-like ideas are not connected by any logical bond or analogy or succession and may take each other's place like the slides of a magic lantern... Crowds being only capable of thinking in images are only to be impressed by images.

Let's now use our Parent-Adult-Child personality illustration to attempt to understand the phenomenon of crowd psychology. First, do you think your Hungry Child is happiest alone or with other people? Actually, he feels much more comfortable when he is with a group of people who think exactly as he does. If he becomes aware that a large group of investors are thinking in one way, he has an irresistible urge to rationalize his thoughts to conform. This is especially true if price movement reinforces the concept.

Feelings of inferiority are the motivating force behind all speculative manias. The term mania is here used to describe extreme excesses in a financial market that may engulf a group of investors, or a whole nation of them. Relentless upward price movement consistently produces an exaggerated sense of well-being and euphoria. Invariably, the greater the financial excesses are, the greater the crash in prices that will be.

All investing manias have several commonalities. They generally begin in periods of a prosperous economy. They start out as reasonable investments. The participants can point to years (perhaps decades) of past history in which the "investment" was a superior performer to other ones. There are many stories of instant riches and overnight wealth. A new reality is created to justify higher and higher prices. Finally, the excessive use of credit produces an exhilarating and rapid price rise as the peak approaches. Let's examine two historical examples.

Would you trade a bar of gold for a tulip bulb? It doesn't sound too logical, does it? Well, that was equivalent to what was happening in Holland in 1636. Many tulips became worth more than their weight in gold. We will use the description of "Tulipomania" in Charles MacKay's *Extraordinary Popular Delusions* to follow the events of the speculative mania that developed in tulip bulbs.

Tulips had found their way into Holland in the early 1600s. They were very beautiful and the environment seemed just right for their cultivation. Owning tulip bulbs became very fashionable. The nobility of Europe seemed to have an insatiable appetite for the bulbs, expecially the rarer varieties. The Dutch became the principal suppliers of the bulb. By 1625, the demand had been rising steadily.

In 1633, prices began to accelerate upward. In Amsterdam, one resident made almost $100,000 from his garden in less than half a year. MacKay says that people began to abandon ordinary work in favor of speculation in tulip bulbs. "Nobles, citizens, farmers, mechanics, seamen, footmen, maid servants, even chimney sweeps and old clotheswomen dabbled in tulips. People of all grades converted their property into cash, and invested in flowers." Bulbs were traded in taverns and on the sidewalks. Rumors swept through towns about foreign orders that would move prices higher. Everyone believed that prices could only go up.

A call option market developed not unlike the option market in stocks. This permitted the investor to put down only a small amount of the purchase price. Prices soared to unbelievable heights. One rare tulip bulb was exchanged for more than ten acres of prime land. In 1637, prices peaked and then collapsed. Several months later, most tulip bulbs were about as valuable as onions. Holland was plunged into an extended depression. The aftermath was grim. Let's examine a mania that is a little closer to home.

The 1920s were a time of confidence and prosperity in America. There were abundant savings and cheap credit. The Consumer Price Index was almost flat. There were good times without inflation. Under those circumstances, corporations made increasing profits and paid increasing dividends. Stock prices had been in a generally rising trend for a number of years.

In 1927, the Dow Jones Industrial Average increased about 25% from 155 to 195. With the bull market in full force, stocks could be bought on razor-thin margins of 10%. The brokers were eager to lend the rest. In fact, borrowings for stock went from about $3.6 billion in the summer of 1927 to a peak of $8½ billion in September 1929. In 1928, the market took off like a rocket as the public rushed in. The Dow topped out at 381 in September 1929. Much of the final rise had been fueled by credit.

Nearly everyone who was anyone was caught up in the euphoria. Fredrick Lewis Allen described it accurately in his history of the 1920s, *Only Yesterday*:

> The rich man's chauffeur drove with his ear laid back to catch the news of an impending move in Bethlehem Steel; he held 50 shares himself on a 20-point margin. The window cleaner at the broker's office paused to watch the ticker, for he was thinking of converting his laboriously accumulated savings into a few shares of Simmons... Across the dinner table, one heard fantastic stories of sudden fortunes: A young banker who had put every dollar of his small capital into Niles-Bement-Pond and was fixed for life; a widow had been able to buy a large country house with her winnings on Kennecott. Thousands speculated—and won, too—without the slightest knowledge of the nature of the company upon whose fortunes they were relying...

Although the initial panic in the stock market was severe, it was just the beginning. On Black Tuesday, October 29, 1929, it was usual to have stocks drop 15% to 40%. There were intermediate rallies, but stocks were at the beginning of a devastating three-year bear market. Prices eroded until July 8,

1932, when the Dow hit its low of 41.22. At the bottom, few people had any cash left to buy stocks or bonds. Did the Crash cause the Depression of the 1930s? That's a matter of conjecture. The numerous failures of banks were primarily due to the excessive use of credit in many different areas. American industry had overexpanded, so some contraction was due. However, the disruption of credit and financial markets certainly made it more severe.

In both cases, when these financial markets reached the mania stages, prices were trading on the "Greater Fool Theory." This theory holds that the buyer knows that he is overpaying, but he believes that a greater fool will come along and take it off his hands for even more. He feels that way because he has been conditioned by relentless upward price movements. He may suspect that it can't go on forever, but he doesn't think it is going to stop *now*.

Can there be another mania that could enjulf us? Perhaps. But it won't be exactly like the ones of the past. It will be something different, something unique. Yet, it should have all the ingredients that we discussed earlier. Could the United States be in the midst of an impending crash right now?

If someone told you that the price of your house could drop 50% over the next few years, you may feel the urge to burn him at the stake for heresy. Yet almost no one believes that housing prices can go down. Everyone feels a similar surety at the height of any mania.

Excessive use of credit usually fuels an acceleration of prices near the peak. According to Federal Reserve Board statistics, the 1960s saw mortgage debt for family dwellings double from about $135 billion to $270 billion. However, in the 1970s it almost quadrupled to approximately $1 trillion. This alone accounts in part for the dramatic increase in housing prices.

Most people buy a house on margin. Yes, the term is correct. They put a small percentage down and mortgage the rest. This figure is usually 10% to 20%. The purchaser has margin calls every month. They are called mortgage payments. As long as he meets the margin calls, everything is fine.

Under ordinary circumstances, deciding to buy a house is a sound investment. Yet the escalating prices of the 1970s forced "panic buying" by many people before it was "too late." They bought bigger houses than they needed, or were forced to pay far higher prices than they could afford if times got a little tough. Many speculators also entered the market. It is common, in some areas, for someone to own 10 or 20 houses as "investments." They are often bought with a negative cash flow. The speculators are counting on inflation to bail them out. Another form of the "Greater Fool Theory."

The housing bulls argued convincingly for higher prices, but there were some sobering facts around for those who cared to find them. First, the baby boom of the 1940s and 1950s had a lot to do with the family formations of the 1960s and 1970s. The last baby of that group was born 25 years ago. Since housing sales are based primarily on credit, can mortgage debt continue to expand at its present rate? History would argue against it. Also, with 15%-to-16% mortgage money, the inflation hedge concept goes out the window. In housing, prices have gone up as much as 300%, or even more. Is this a commodity that will go up forever? Probably not.

This is not necessarily a prediction of a crash in housing prices. It is merely an attempt to draw an analogy with past manias. Even a small drop in housing prices could produce a negative psychology in the country. This is because about two-thirds of American families own their own homes. As prices rose in the 1970s, a house was considered an ever increasing "nest egg" of wealth. So the consumer spent his money freely. If housing prices started to drop, people could become cautious about spending and begin saving more of their income. This could beget further economic dislocations. Some home owners could lose their jobs and be unable to make their mortgage payments. This would tend to increase the supply of houses, reducing prices. The downward spiral could be as painful as the upward spiral was exhilarating.

MINIMANIAS

All markets are the same. They are created by people trading goods, services, commodities, real estate, stocks, or cash. Greed motivates the buyer, who tries to make money. Fear motivates the seller who tries not to lose money. Each time a trade takes place, the participants must have opposing viewpoints. It therefore can be said that prices in financial markets are entirely psychological.

LeBon said that the crowd focuses upon images. Another way to say the same thing is to point out that the majority embraces an *investment thesis*. The underlying theme of this thesis must be very simple to understand. The profit potential should be enormous. The assumptions used to support the thesis should have a wide range of latitude in order to keep it vague and to maintain its mystique. It must also be reinforced by upward price movement. Under these circumstances, future expectations can rise to incredible heights.

Each up cycle in the stock market must have its leaders. Generally this is a select group of companies that are favored by the players. As the prices climb higher and higher, the rationalizations, or theses, for continued performance become crystal clear. These stocks will generally be bid up to unrealistic levels in price on the belief that spectacular future earnings growth is virtually assured.

Turn to Exhibit 5.3, "Investment Theses." There you will find six former "high flyers" grouped according to their price ranges. The vertical lines are the yearly high–low price range. The year listed at the bottom is the year in which the stock reached its high. Each chart shows between 5 and 10 years of price history. In every case, a spectacular rise is

Exhibit 5.3 ***Investment Theses (Yearly high–low)***

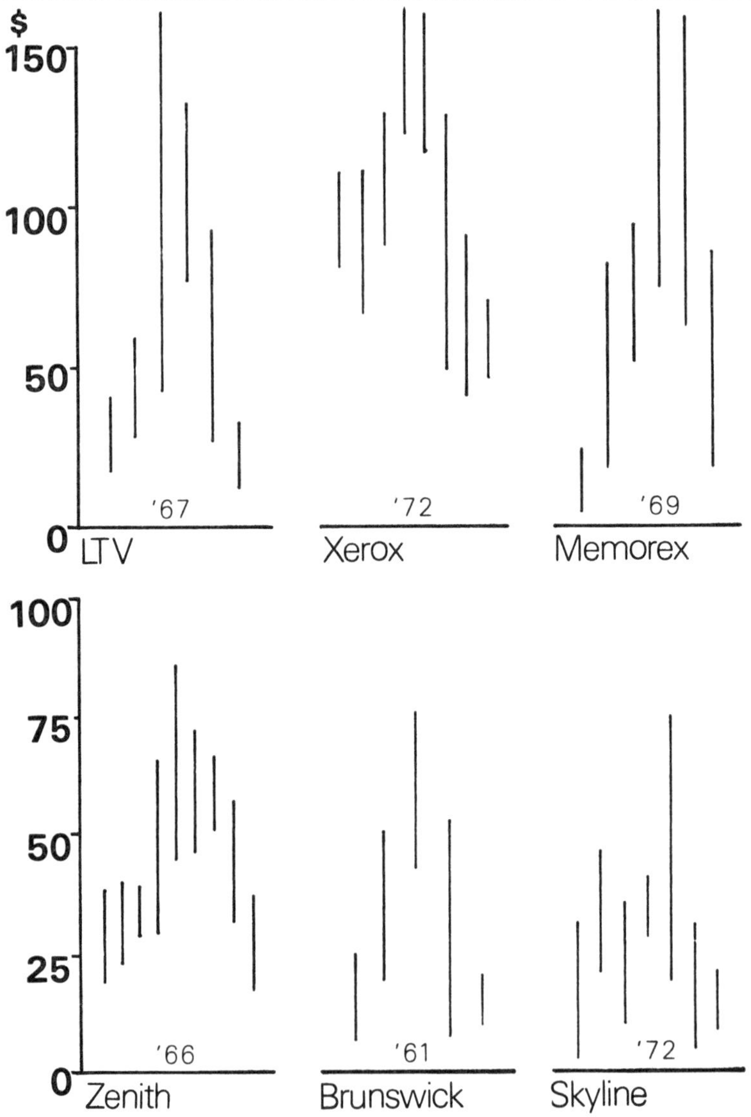

eventually followed by a frightening drop. Let's try to examine each thesis in general terms.

Have you ever been bowling? Most of us have. In the late 1950s the invention of automatic pinsetters made the sport very popular. Bowling alleys became much more profitable and they spread rapidly. Brunswick and other bowling-related stocks shot up in price. In 1961, the stock sold at 31 times earnings. To justify that projected growth rate, there would eventually have to be more bowling alleys than gas stations.

Do you have a color television? You probably do. Almost no one watches black-and-white anymore. What do you think happened to the stocks of the companies that made TVs when color sets came in? They boomed. Zenith went up almost 300%. Unfortunately, no one was thinking about the Japanese. If you had bought 100 shares for $7500 in 1966, you could have traded them for a color TV 14 years later. In 1980, your investment would have been worth about $1000. It's an expensive way to buy a television set.

How much does 1 + 1 equal? If you said 3, then you understand the conglomerate game of financial synergism. That means that the whole is worth more than the sum of its parts. The justice department frowns on mergers in the same industry, but what's wrong with an aircraft maker buying a sporting goods firm? James Ling was the king of the conglomerate makers. With dazzling acumen, he merged low P/E ratio companies into his high P/E conglomerate. The result was instant earnings growth. Unfortunately, when the music stopped, all he had was a big mess, and LTV Corporation dropped out of sight.

Computers are the wave of the future. So investors believed in the late 1960s. They bought almost any company that was even closely related to that industry. They were right.

Almost every corporation uses computers very heavily today. But unfortunately, they don't use Memorex computers. The stock dropped from around $170 to $2.

Everyone needs a place to live, right? What's better than a house you can take with you? Especially if it can be made much cheaper in a factory. The answer was mobile homes. The same companies also made a variety of recreational and travel vehicles. Skyline was the leader of the industry and went from $14 to $74 within two years. When oil prices skyrocketed, five years of earnings growth stopped and the stock went back to $10.

One of the most disastrous minimanias was that of the "one decision" growth stocks. The thesis was powerful. Its idea was that there are a few very large companies that had demonstrated proven earnings growth records over a long period of time. They were well-managed and could exploit new market opportunities. They should continue to grow well into the future so the stocks could be bought and held forever. They never needed to be sold. Therefore, the only decision required was the buy decision.

The players chose about 50 stocks that took on an aura of near-religious mysticism. They were considered sacred bastions of strength during the bear market of the late 1960s. By the end of 1972, the stock market had rebounded to about 1000 on the Dow from its 1970 lows of around 550. However, the only real participants were the "nifty fifty." Most other stocks recovered only modestly. In early 1973, the market began a sickening drop. But one by one, then they too fell. The percentage drop was from 60% to 95% for each company. A painful development.

Xerox was one of the most sacred of the glamour growth stocks. It had long term "earnings visibility." In a nutshell, this means that the players believed that a certain earnings-per-share growth rate could be projected into the future ad infinitum. In fact, this writer had a personal experience related to this stock that was typical of the consensus view of that time.

In the early 1970s, there was a group of young "gunslingers" in Houston who set up a money management firm. They were successful in attracting a relatively large amount of pension and private money. They accomplished this by working through stockbrokers as a source of referrals. Since they were aggressive, the commissions the brokers received were lucrative. As you might imagine, they were highly recommended. Their strategy was to play the "hot stocks" of that time.

One dreary day in November 1972, I was in the office of Jimmy Perfect (not his real name, of course), one of the partners of the firm whom I knew personally. The purpose of the call was to beg for some business, but what happened was entirely unexpected.

As I walked into his office, he looked up from a paper that he was absorbed in reading. He had a euphoric smile on his face. Before I could even say hello, he launched into a monologue. "Boy, I'm going to buy this Xerox in *size*." (Even though he was my age, he liked to affectionately call me "boy." It was a matter of his ego.) He excitedly jumped from his desk and waved a forty-page, institutional research report on Xerox in my face. "Boy, the earnings on this stock are going to double! The dividends on this stock are going to double and the price of Xerox is going to double!" he shouted. Then he broke into uncontrollable laughter. When he stopped, he walked over to my chair, where I was listening to his words. He carefully put each of his hands on the arms of the chair and leaned down so that his nose was almost touching mine. Then he whispered, ". . .and Boy, we're (meaning his clients) going to get a big piece of the cheese (profits)." Then his face became wreathed in a euphoric smile.

Well, as they say, "Two out of three ain't bad." By 1979, Xerox's earnings had doubled and the dividends had doubled. Unfortunately, the stock was still down 66% from its high. The drop began several months after my visit to see Jimmy. When the "glamours" went down the tubes, his clients went with them. A money management firm goes out of business without any money to manage. I run into Jimmy occasionally, when I see him wandering the streets of Houston. Yet every time I see that euphoric grin on his face, I wonder what disaster might be lurking just around the corner. I notice that he doesn't call me "Boy" any longer.

Now let's look at a more recent minimania. It's the "inflation hedge" thesis. The late 1960s and 1970s were times of high inflation because of persistent deficit spending by the government. During such periods, "tangible assets" generally appreciate in price as we have already discussed. The common stocks of natural resource companies who have "assets in the ground" can also participate. As the price of the commodity—gold, silver, or oil—appreciates, the worth of the company is believed to increase.

Examine Exhibit 5.4, "Assets in the Ground." There you will see the Psychology of a Stock cYCLE in action. What is shown is the 1979 low to 1980 high in price range. The percentage gain in less than a 24-month period was dramatic. It illustrates an important phenomenon of the PSYCLE: Prices tend to go higher than anyone imagines possible but when the "bubble bursts," they go down farther than anyone can comprehend. The 1980 high to the August 1982 low is also shown. As you can see, the corresponding drop in prices was also scary. It's very hard to make and keep money chasing the favorites.

The year 1979 marked the end of a decade of growing economic and political crises. In November of that year,

Exhibit 5.4 *Assets in the Ground*

	1979 Low–1980 High	1980 High–August 1982 Low
Natural Resources **($/sh)**		
Asarco	14– 58* (+314%)	58– 17 (–71%)
Homestake Mining	20– 88 (+340%)	88– 17 (–80%)
Newmont	22– 67 (+190%)	67– 28 (–67%)
Phelps Dodge	21– 48 (+128%)	48– 18 (–63%)
Santa Fe Industries	10– 36 (+260%)	36– 13 (–64%)
Oil **($/sh)**		
Gulf Oil	23– 54 (+134%)	54– 24 (–55%)
Louisiana Land and Exploration	22– 64 (+190%)	64– 20 (–69%)
Standard Oil of Ohio	20– 91 (+455%)	91– 27 (–70%)
Oil Services **($/sh)**		
Halliburton	30– 86 (+186%)	86– 21 (–76%)
Schlumberger	27– 87 (+222%)	87– 30 (–66%)
Precious Metals **($/oz.)**		
Silver	8– 49 (+512%)	49– 5 (–90%)
Gold	220–850 (+286%)	850–300 (–65%)

*In some cases, prices are rounded approximations.

radical Iranians took over the United States embassy in Tehran. They held the 50 American hostages for an inordinate length of time. International tensions increased as the crisis dragged on and on. Precious metals became a safe "haven" form both inflation and chaos. Under these conditions, prices skyrocketed. As shown in the exhibit, gold was up about 286% and silver was up about 500%. Everyone from the Arab oil sheiks to dishwashers were caught up in the "inflation hedge" minimania.

Let's take a moment to focus on the silver debacle because, in retrospect, it was disastrously absurd. A billionaire Texas family began to accelerate their holdings of silver bullion. In the summer of 1979, silver shot above $10 an ounce and began a breathtaking rise to about $49 an ounce in January 1980. As the price rose, people lined up to sell everything form silver teaspoons to tea sets. The smelters were working day and night. It is an economic reality for supply to increase as price increases. Somehow, the silver bulls did not consider this in their calculations.

When the silver market broke, the aftermath was grim. As silver prices plummeted back to earth, the commodity speculators couldn't get out. This was because the contracts were "locked down the limit" every day. Unsecured debits at the brokerage firms mounted. Rumors of insolvency swept the financial community. The stock market panicked and prices crashed.

Well, the "big boys" settled their debts like gentlemen, and the crisis passed. However, rough estimates guess that Texas wealth dropped well over a billion dollars. Many other speculators were also ruined. One doctor, client of a stockbroker friend of mine, had caught "silver fever" just as prices peaked. As they fell, he had to liquidate his stock portfolio at distressed levels to meet his commodity margin calls. A lifetime of patient equity accumlulation was wiped out in a month. The result of speculation for many people is financial pain.

As precious metals and even copper soared in price, so did the mining companies that had "assets in the ground." As oil prices increased, the price of the shares of oil companies increased for the same reasons. Always the reasoning is that the "wasting asset" cannot be replenished. History and economics would argue against that thesis. As prices increased, supply increased and demand decreased. In 1981, oil and gasoline were running over the tops of storage tanks. It's funny how that works.

The thesis for buying oil service companies was a derivative of the "assets in the ground" minimania. The rationale was that because oil was at such high prices and would always be needed, the services of these companies would also be needed ad infinitum. Therefore, high earnings multiples could be justified. They assumed the mystique of "one decision" stocks. But like their "brothers" before them, they also dropped dramatically from their highs. Will it never change?

On November 20, 1980 in the "Heard on the Street" section of the *Wall Street Journal* was an article that clearly demonstrated that the news is always positive at the top. It was headlined "Fundamental Positives of Oil and Gas Industry Expand Daily and Analysts See No Adversities." It was filled with quotes by industry analysts discussing why everything looked great. One analyst even said, "I must admit that things look almost too good to be true." Unfortunately, he was the only one that was right. The article turned out to be the "kiss of death" for energy related stocks. At the time, most of the stocks were experiencing sharp, upward price movements. Within two weeks of the article, prices began to drop. The theory of contrary opinion tells us that when "everybody" is certain of something, "everybody is usually wrong. That's one truth that doesn't seem to change in the stock market.

In actuality, I was selling the stocks whenever I could pry clients and potential clients out of them. Of course, it wasn't easy. Asking people in Houston, Texas to sell their

Exhibit 5.5 ***Bonds vs. Gold***

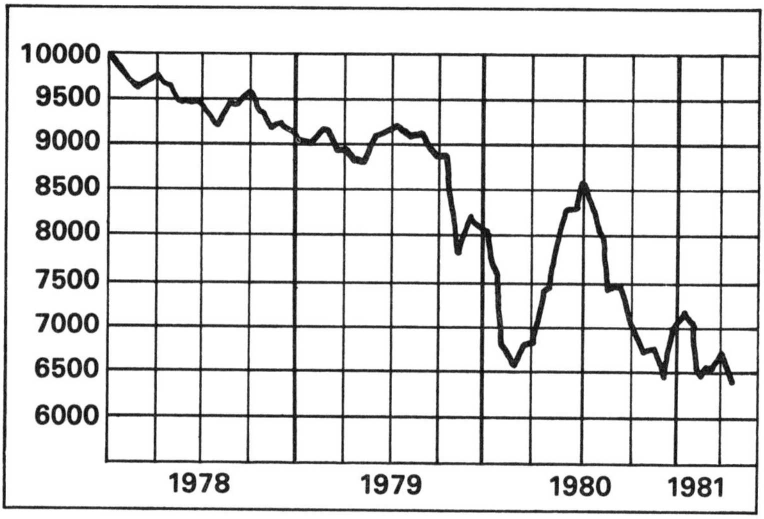

Treasury Bonds

rising oil stocks is tantamount to treason. Many sold, but some did not. One incident stands out in my mind.

A client of mine had 4000 shares of a Houston-based energy company. He had worked for the company all his life and most of his net worth was tied up in that one stock. For months, I did everything, including begging, to get him to sell even 1000 or 2000 shares in the $70's. Although he wholeheartedly agreed with my approach, he said it didn't apply to energy stocks. He told me about increased demand and earnings and how bright the future was for the company. He said I just didn't understand the energy business. Unfortunately, that was the only thing he was right about. When the stock dropped to about $44, he called and asked, "What should *we* do with the stock now?" Fear and greed does manage to keep

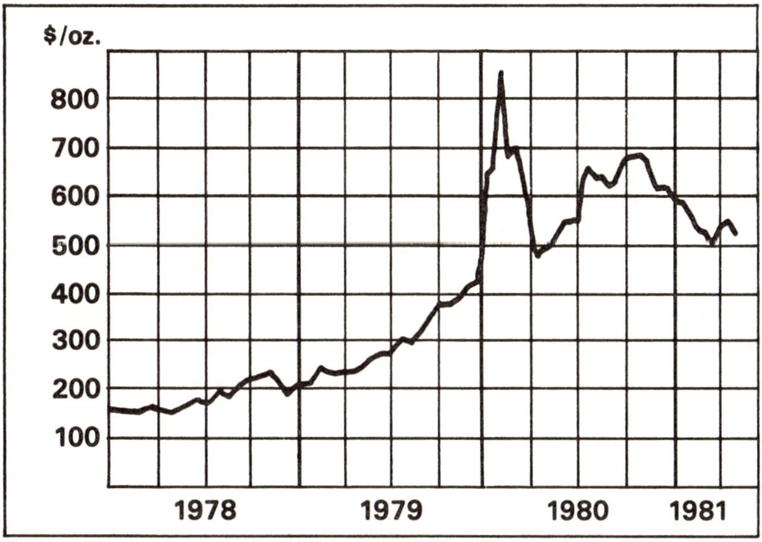

Gold

All markets tend to reach important trend reversals when prices reflect accelerating fear or greed. Both bonds and gold showed classic climactic trend reversals in 1980. Bonds appear to be forming a major cyclical bottom. Gold has completed a cyclical peak. These interpretations of the markets favor a disinflationary bias in 1981–82.

Courtesy of Moody's Handbook

---

human nature fairly constant (See Exhibit 5.5. above). These charts appeared as illustrations in an interview with Bob Farrell, published in *Barron's* in 1981.

> All markets tend to reach important trend reversals when prices reflect accelerating fear or greed. Both bonds and gold showed classic climactic trend reversals in 1980. Bonds appear to be forming a major cyclical bottom. Gold has completed a cyclical peak. These interpretations of the markets favor a disinflationary bias in 1981–1982.

In the next chapter, we will explore the Psychology of a Stock cYCLE in detail. However, as Farrell says in *Barron's*, "All markets are the same." In January 1980, bonds were in the *capitulation* phase. That is, prices broke sharply as sellers became aggressive and buyers reluctant. Just the opposite happened in gold. It was in the *conviction* phase. The buyers became aggressive and the sellers reluctant, so prices shot upward. The correct strategy would have been to sell gold and buy bonds.

Of course, almost nobody would have seriously considered doing that. Here's why. The individual who bought gold in the first place was probably worried about economic chaos. He probably felt that bonds would be worthless because of inflation. The upward price movement of gold and the downward price movement of bonds was confirming his thinking. Now you might see why it's so hard, emotionally, to sell what is "in favor" and buy what is "out of favor."

Nothing lasts forever, almost everything goes in cycles and prices are purely psychological. If you remember this little saying of mine, it should be much easier for you to make and keep money in the stock market. Now, let's try to understand how cycles may affect both financial markets and even our very lives.

6

Cycles

NATURE

Do you know that 15 or 20 billion years ago a very large explosion occurred? It involved all of the energy and matter in our known universe. This phenomenon is called The Big Bang. It is the most widely accepted theory on how the universe began, and it is the earliest event about which scientists have any record.

Since the Big Bang, all of the matter in the universe has been moving away from the center of the explosion at an incredible rate of speed. Will it continue forever? Some scientists believe so. Others take a different point of view. They believe that there is enough matter in the universe so that the force of gravity will eventually slow and then stop the expansion. At that point, a contraction will begin until all of the matter and energy is, once again, condensed into one spot. Then another Big Bang will occur. This will continue for infinity.

If the so-called "closed universe" interpretation of the Big Bang theory is correct, then it is the ultimate cycle. In fact, the dictionary defines the word cycle as *a completed round of events or phenomena in which there is a final return to the original state.* Of course, many individuals cannot comprehend this. If they could, they would not believe it or simply dismiss it as irrelevant. However, the forces that produce the cycles in the universe may have a far greater effect on our lives here on earth than most people realize.

The basic building blocks of all matter throughout the universe are exactly the same. Everything is made up of atoms. They are so minuscule that they can't be seen by even the most powerful microscope. You probably remember from chemistry class that an atom is composed of a nucleus surrounded by orbiting electrons. Each atom has the same number of electrons as protons, therefore, it has a neutral charge. Every chemical element has been given an atomic number depending on the number of protons and electrons it has. Hydrogen, the simplest element, has one proton and one electron; therefore, its atomic number is 1. Gold, a much heavier element, has an atomic number of 79. Atomic theory states that the heavier atoms can be formed only by combining the lighter atoms by fusion, a process we will discuss in more detail shortly.

The nucleus is composed of both protons, which are positively charged, and neutrons, which are neutral. However, it is the very strong nuclear forces of the neutron that keep the nucleus from flying apart. This is because the like positive forces of the protons tend to repel each other. The neutrons are the "glue" that keeps the atom intact.

The number of electrons that each element possesses determines its chemical properties. That is, they give iron its hardness and gold its glitter. Since atoms are made up primarily of empty space, you might wonder what keeps your hand from passing through the door handle of your car when you try to open it. The negative charge of the atoms in your hand repels the negative charge of the atoms in the iron of the door handle. This is the force that allows you to open the door. What does all this chemistry have to do with making money in the stock market? More than you might think.

The stars and their accompanying planets are the results of the gravitational collapse of interstellar gases and dust. For instance, the interior of our sun has a temperature of tens of millions of degrees. The light and heat that we receive on earth is produced by the process of fusion. This takes place when two lighter atoms collide with such force that the positive repulsion of the protons are overcome by the nuclear force of the neutrons and a heavier atom is formed. Energy is released in the process. Carl Sagan, in his fascinating book *Cosmos*, explains:

> All the elements of the Earth except hydrogen and some helium have been cooked by a kind of stellar alchemy billions of years ago in stars, some of which are today inconspicuous white dwarfs on the other side of the Milky Way Galaxy. The nitrogen in our DNA, the calcium in our teeth, the iron in our blood, the carbon in our apple pies were made in the interiors of collapsing stars. We are made of starstuff.

The way that the cycles in the universe affect us here on earth may be beyond the comprehension of our frail, human minds to accept. Yet, the scientific evidence is there for anyone who cares to examine it. The very atoms that compose the matter of our bodies were once cooked inside a star. At some point, billions of years from now, they may be again. Even the matter of our sun is in its second or third cycle, Sagan clarifies:

> The origin and evolution of life are connected in the most intimate way with the origin and evolution of the stars. First: The very matter of which we are composed, the atoms that make life possible, were generated long ago and far away in giant red stars. The relative abundance of the chemical elements found in the Cosmos matches the relative abundance of atoms generated in stars so well as to leave little doubt that red giants and supernovae are the

> ovens and crucibles in which matter has been forged. The Sun is a second- or third-generation star. All the matter in it, all the matter you see around you has been through one or two previous cycles of stellar alchemy.

Sagan goes on to say that he believes that events from deep space may affect us here on earth. "We are, almost all of us, solar-powered. Finally, the hereditary changes called mutations provide the raw material for evolution. Mutations, from which nature selects its new inventory of life forms, are produced in part by cosmic rays—high-energy particles ejected almost at the speed of light in supernova explosions. The evolution of life on Earth is driven in part by the spectacular deaths of distant, massive suns." (See Exhibit 6.1.)

Right now your Child Ego State may be screaming, "No! No! I'm special! I'm unique! I don't accept that!" Don't worry, that's a natural reaction. Man, by his very nature, still wants to believe that the universe revolves around the earth. Worse, he may feel it revolves around himself.

The planet earth is an infinitesimal speck in a vast cosmic ocean. The space between stars is so vast that it must be measured in terms of light-years. A beam of light travels 186,000 miles in a second, so, in a year, it would travel about 6 trillion miles. It takes eight light-minutes to get to the sun. It is approximately 30,000 light-years to the center of our galaxy. The nearest spiral galaxy called M31, which is a large cluster of stars, is almost 2 million light-years away. The space between the stars is enormous.

Our sun is only one of 400 billion such stars in our Milky Way Galaxy. Each sun probably has its own planetary system. There are estimated to be over 100 billion such galaxies in the universe. Everywhere the building blocks are available for life. Only the proper conditions are needed.

There are other cycles that are a part of our lives that we can more easily acknowledge. The earth revolves in a 24-hour cycle. Further, it revolves around our sun in a

Exhibit 6.1 ***Relative Distances in Space***

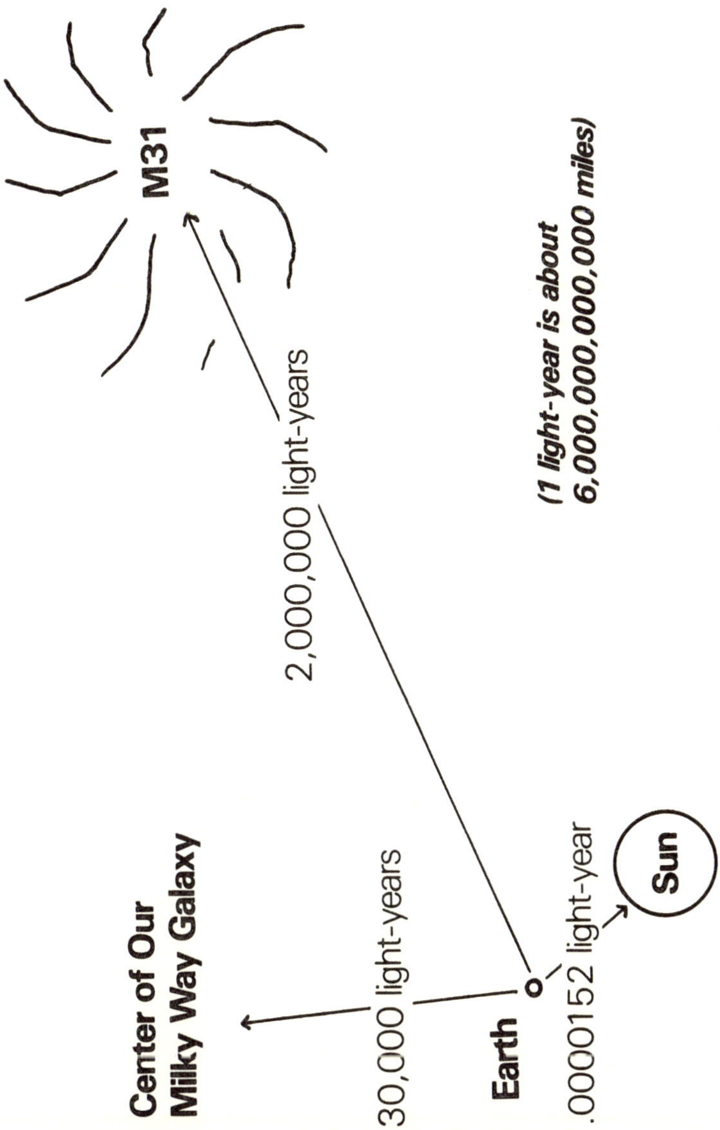

Source: Carl Sagan, *Cosmos* (New York: Random House, 1980)

365-day cycle. Our sun revolves around the center of the Milky Way Galaxy in a cycle that takes about 250 million years. All of this can be calculated with a scientific accuracy that is awesome.

One of the most comprehensive studies of cycles has been done by Edward R. Dewey, who was president of the Foundation for the Study of Cycles when he published his thought-provoking book, *Cycles: The Mysterious Forces That Trigger Events*. In this book, he details the many different and varied cycles found on earth. His conclusion is that there are outside forces of unknown origin that produce the cycles in nature.

> We can now theorize that *something somewhere* acts on the electromagnetic field in which the earth is immersed and that this field affects the chemistry of our bodies to make us alternately optimistic or pessimistic, energetic or slothful, warlike or pacific.

His proof of that conclusion is that all cycles of the same period or wavelength rise and fall at about the same time. He continues:

> We now have hundreds of well-authenticated cycles and thousands of allegations of other cycles to be restudied and reevaluated. Periods group at certain definite wavelengths. Things that have the same wavelength turn at about the same time. Cycles keep on coming true after discovery, and when distorted return to their former timing. Cycles go back continuously for hundreds and thousands of years; in fact, they have left their imprint on rock strata that are millions of years old.

In one notable example, Dewey illustrates 37 cycles of approximately 9.6 years in duration. They encompass such diverse entities as rabbit abundance in North America, tree ring widths in Arizona, and cotton price fluctuations in North America. Since they move up and down simultaneously, he concludes that the same forces must affect the changes.

The findings and conclusions of Edward Dewey would be hard for many people to accept. Some cycles are easily explainable. They are the ones that people tend to call coincidences because they don't understand them. It is possible that Man in all his magnificence is as ignorant about cycles today as he was 300 years ago about germs.

The word cycle implies a returning to the origin. In order to fully understand a cycle, it should be graphed in a mathematical way. Turn to Exhibit 6.2, "The Anatomy of a Cycle." In the top portion you will see a symmetrical cycle or wave. Time is the horizontal axis. The period, or *wavelength,* is the time it takes for the completion of one cycle. The amplitude is the value from the low point to the high point of the cycle.

The word cycle also implies a rhythm or continuous repetition. The middle of the exhibit shows a continuous and rhythmic cycle. The bottom cycle has a negative correlation with the one above it. That means it bottoms when the other one tops and vice versa. This is an important phenomenon that can take place in the stock market between different individual stocks.

Of course, not all cycles are symmetrical. There can be fluctuation within a long-term, or secular trend, as shown at the bottom of the exhibit "Secular Uptrend." It would be just the opposite if the secular trend was down.

Cycles will not always be represented in terms of absolute values such as price. Often they will be standardized to reflect a percentage deviation from an average value or mean. The objective here is not to make one an expert on cycles, but to acknowledge their existence. Almost everything in Nature has some fluctuations to it.

When one uses the term cycle, it usually implies rhythm, that is, a repetition in a continuous or harmonious manner. A rhythmic cycle implies predictability. This means one should have the ability to determine when the cycle will

Exhibit 6.2 *The Anatomy of a Cycle*

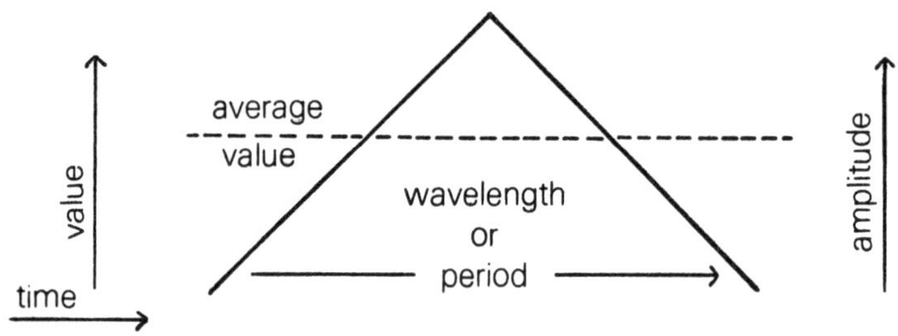

Symmetrical Cycle or Wave

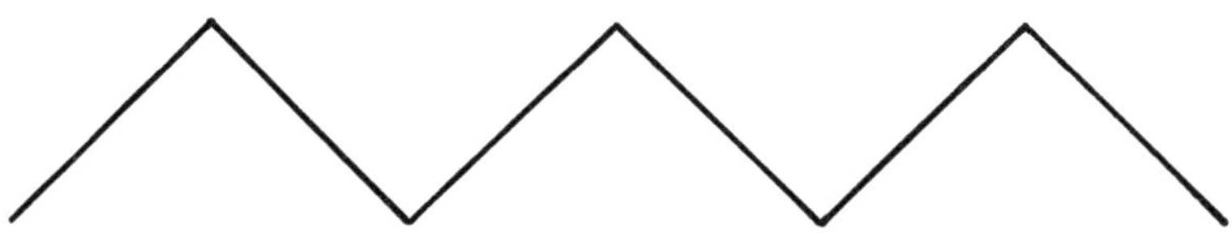

Symmetrical and Rhythmic

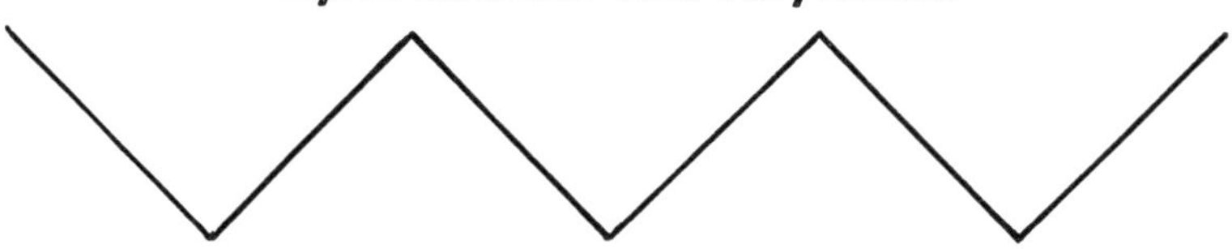

Negative Correlation

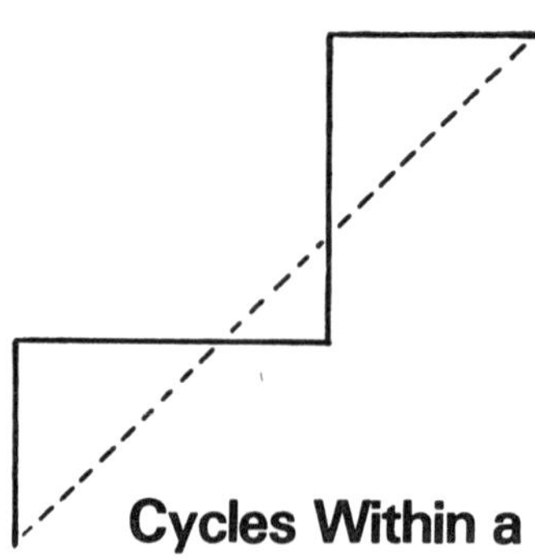

Cycles Within a Secular Uptrend

peak and when it will trough ahead of time. That conclusion may be questionable when it comes to predicting stock price movements.

Even the most uninformed observer would acknowledge that stock prices can fluctuate dramatically over time. Are they movements in price cycles or are they just random coincidences? This author's conclusion is that, yes, the cycles are there, but they are not perfect. That is, the wavelengths will not always be the same. Turn back to Exhibit 2.8, "Accumulation and Distribution," and you will observe different time periods and amplitudes of each cycle. However, because stock price movements are purely psychological, we can identify the characteristics of the bottoms and the tops of a stock cycle. Therefore, we can make more objective and informed decisions. We shall now see how the capitalistic business cycle is also greatly influenced by the psychology of individuals. Just remember that no cycle is perfect and it will make understanding them much easier.

BUSINESS

Statistical evidence would argue that the United States is the victim of a 54-year economic cycle. This is the theory of the Russian Nikolai D. Kondratieff in an article, *The Long Waves in Economic Life*. Of course, his conclusion applied to all capitalistic countries. With limited data, he postulated the economic cycle as a self-correcting process that lasted a little over half a century. His analysis showed that a 32-year expansion phase would be followed by a 22-year liquidation phase. Since his Communist masters did not like to hear that the decadent capitalists could perpetuate themselves forever, they banished him to Siberia where he died.

Examine Exhibit 6.3, "The Kondratieff Wave." There you will see the actual movement of wholesale commodity prices since 1800. Overlying the actual movement is the Idealized Kondratieff Wave. Before dying, he observed

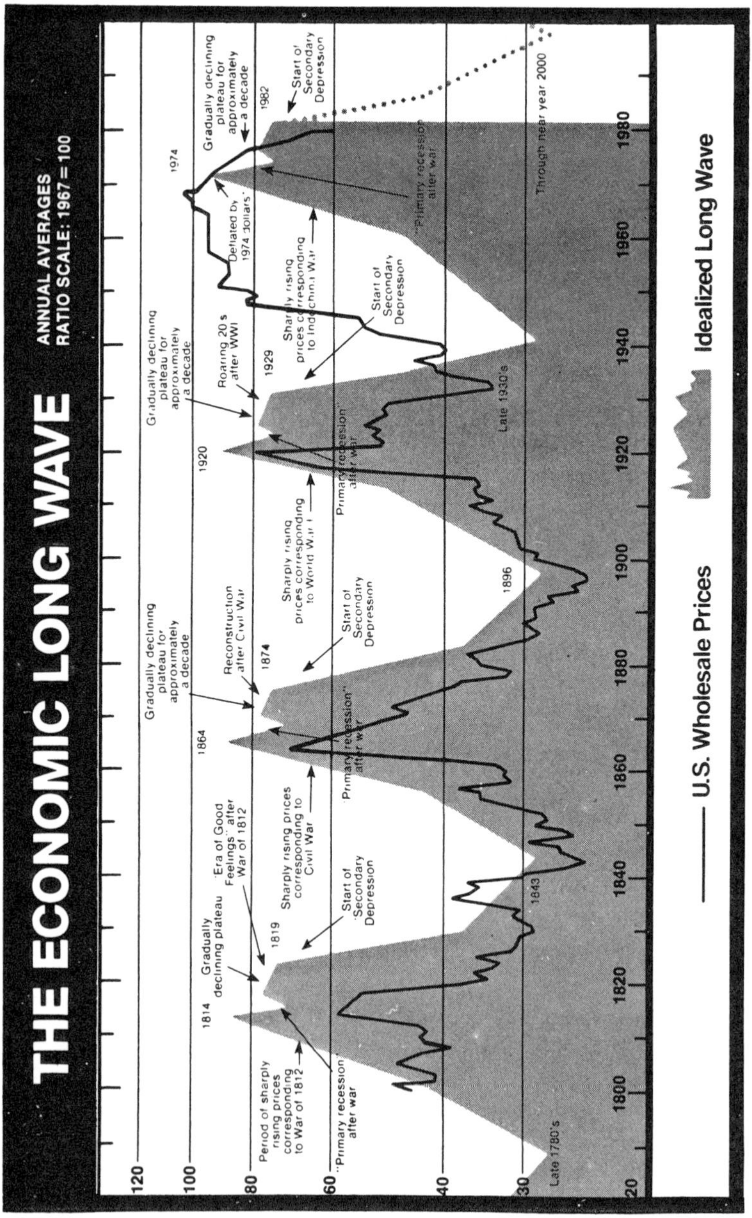

Courtesy International Moneyline

inflationary peaks in commodity prices in 1812, 1866, and 1920. His theory correctly predicted the depression of the 1930s and the expansion of the 1950s, 1960s, and 1970s.

Kondratieff noted that wars tend to identify the highs and lows of the inflation cycle. The war economy generated by the "trough" wars occurs at a time when the stimulation will tend to produce a recovery. The "peak" wars tend to come along in the later stages of the expansion. Because the people have been used to "good times," the government prints money to pay for the war. This produces a sharp rise in wholesale prices. By the way, if you doubt the existence of cycles, you might notice that the average time between each war is roughly 20 to 30 years. Let's examine these wars more specifically.

Table 6.1 ***War Cycles***

	"Trough" War	"Peak" War
Cycle I	Revolutionary War (1775-1783)	War of 1812 (181-1815)
Cycle	Mexican War (1846-1848)	Civil War (1861-1865)
Cycle III	Spanish-American War (1898)	World War I (1915-1919)
Cycle IV	World War II (1941-1945)	Vietnam War 1966-1974)
	Korean War (1950-1952)	

After each peak war, wholesale prices are supposed to drop modestly. For about 10 years after peak wars, positive feelings and price stability are supposed to occur. The "Era of Good Feelings" came after the War of 1812. Reconstruction came after the Civil War. Of course, we all know about the Roaring Twenties after World War I. History has not yet labeled the time after the Vietnam War.

For lack of a better name, let's call the period after the Vietnam War the "Soaring Seventies." Because, instead of prices going down, they skyrocketed. The increases were fueled by continued deficit spending by the government. Under usual circumstances, this would have stopped after the War, but, unfortunately, we had turned into a Welfare State. Transfer payments were out of control.

Another factor continued the economic boom longer than it should have. Residential housing prices had an accelerating upward movement. Under these conditions, people increasingly saw the equity in their house as an ever-growing "nest egg." They were less inclined to save and even took on additional debt. Such a course couldn't continue forever. Nevertheless, many people were relatively happy in the Soaring Seventies because the value of their houses and other tangible assets were increasing all the time. That's what they thought anyway.

During the plateau period after the peak war, the stock market usually does pretty well. We are all familiar with the rise in the 1920s that preceded the Crash. If one believes the Kondratrieff Wave, the economy could begin a secondary liquidation phase in the mid-1980s. This would be followed by a long period of deflation. Is the Kondratrieff wave a real cycle or just a random coincidence? Let's look at it from another point of view to see if we can come to a more accurate judgment.

A more understandable explanation may be one of *psychological conditioning*. Man tends to be conditioned by his most recent experience. If these experiences persist long enough, he may incorporate them into his subconscious value system, and he will then judge the world in the light of that value system. Becauses of this phenomenon, the rate of long-term interest rates may be the best indication of where we are in a business cycle. See Exhibit 6.4, "The 54-Year Business Cycle." At the top, you would expect high interest rates as everyone uses debt to exploit opportunities. At that point, since the assumption of more risk has proved generally rewarding, you could expect very aggressive behavior. Positive

Exhibit 6.4 ***The 54-Year Business Cycle***

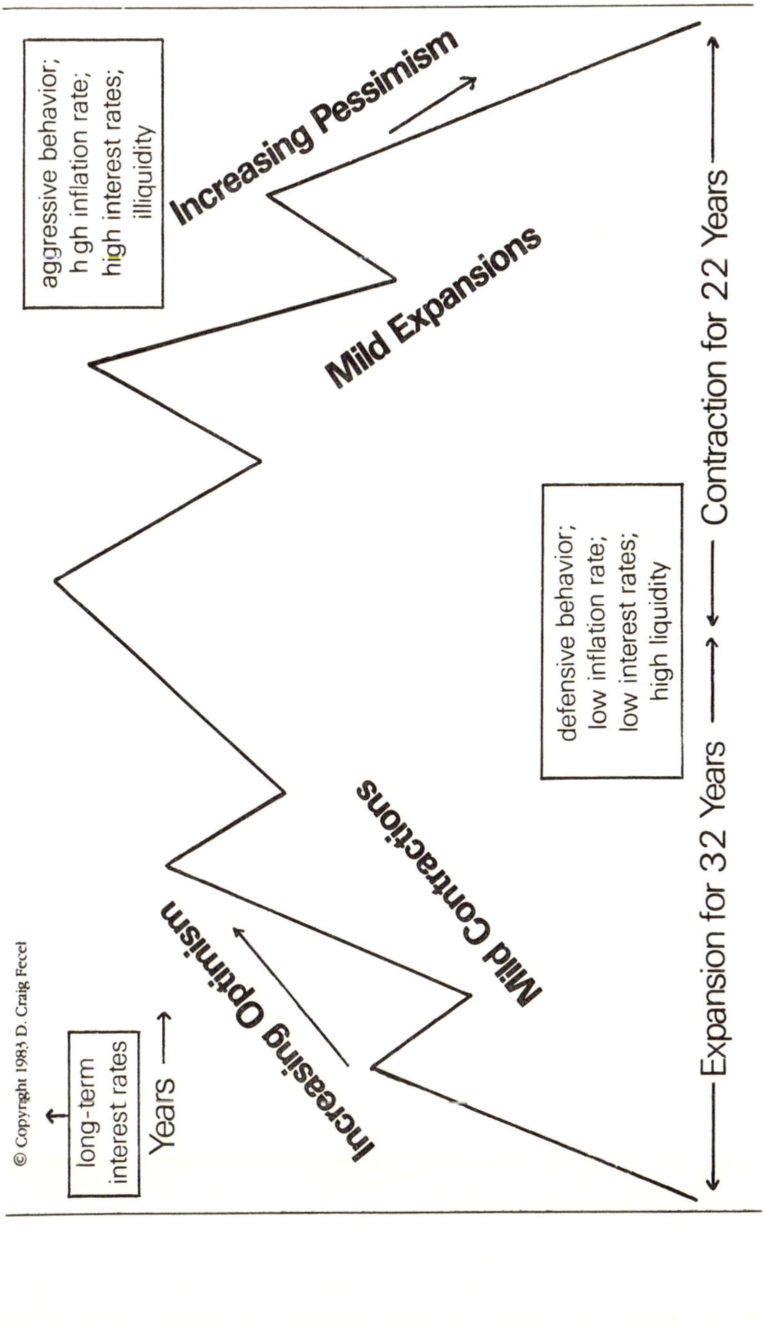

experiences increase the level of confidence and encourage more risk taking. Inflation is running rampant as limited resources are used in marginal opportunities. Now the supply of goods and services has become greater than the demand. This usually occurs at a time when the cost of doing business is the highest.

At a top, such as in 1929, people were conditioned to "good times." Their focus was on the pursuit of pleasure. For a while, the profits in both business and the stock market had been easy. Under those circumstances, more and more marginal opportunities had been pursued. Speculation had increased because everyone wanted their "piece of the pie."

During the previous 30 years, they had been conditioned to believe that after a contraction in the economy, it would then expand. As time went on, people's behavior had become more aggressive. They had adopted a standard of living that did not include much saving. Both consumers and businessmen took on additional debt as they desired to benefit from a growing economy. In 1930, when the pendulum started to swing the other way, the economy was illiquid; that is, debt was excessive and there were not enough monetary reserves to fuel another expansion. Therefore, a liquidation of excesses had to take place. The new generation of risk-takers that had been accustomed to good times would now have their behavior changed. This could be done only through conditioning by painful experiences.

In the liquidation phase, the economic contractions are sharp and brutal whereas the expansions are relatively mild. People become more pessimistic and their behavior becomes defensive. Businessmen respond to deteriorating business conditions by reducing capital expenditures, inventories, and laying off workers. As unemployment spreads, even the people with jobs curtail their spending. The contraction then feeds on itself. The world appears to be a much more risky place to live. Conservatism becomes the byword.

That was the situation in the late 1940s. People had lived through the depression of the 1930s. Then the United States had been involved in World War II. Prices had doubled because of the debt raised to finance the war economy. Uncertainty prevailed. Would the U.S. be plunged into another depression? The painful experiences of the past two decades had altered people's value system.

After a number of years, the liquidation had run its course. But the years of uncertain times had greatly modified behavior. People were defensive. Speculative investments were avoided. Interest rates were very low because the demand for money was low compared to liquidity. The cost of capital was low. Also, labor was much more cooperative. People were glad to have a job and were much more likely to put in a full day's work. Therefore, productivity was high. This was the solid base on which our recent long-term, economic expansion was built.

You may question whether interest rates are a good example of the measure of the psychyology of the business cycle, but let's look at the most recent expansion phase. In 1949, the coupon on high-quality bonds was 2¾% despite the high inflation caused by the war. In the early 1980s it was about 16%. In the late 1940s buyers were eager to "lock up" 2¾% because rates had been on a downtrend. In the early 1980s, buyers skeptically purchased the 16% bonds because rates had been increasing. As always, price conditioning determines psychology. We will now examine this phenomenon with relationship to stock price movements.

THE STOCK MARKET

In order to understand the cycles that take place in the stock market, let's examine part of the transcript of an interview with Bob Farrell that was published on March 1, 1982 in

Barron's. Afterward, we'll examine an important exhibit from that same article. Then without trying to be presumptuous, we will summarize the lessons to be learned.

> *Barron's:* Bob, when you were last here, in April of '81, you were bearish for an indeterminate short term and bullish for the long term. Your timing was just a little off, but you certainly called last year's market. So the question is, How do you feel now?
>
> *Farrell:* The stock market is in a bear trend that has not reached bottom, but the likelihood is that we will reach bottom in 1982. A year ago, I must admit, I thought we were going to reach a bottom in late '81 down around 850. But it isn't so much the exact target—it's what you should do—how to react to current conditions. For example if we have a top, we should sell, get defensive and get into cash, which was the strategy that worked in 1981.
>
> *Q.* And worked very well...
>
> *A.* When you get to the bottom, or what you think is the bottom, then you ask if things have occurred that would lead you to think that it is a major bottom and that a new bull market should start.
>
> *Q.* How can you tell?
>
> *A.* I take a fairly simple approach. There's only one constant in the market, and that is people. Economics change, politics change, everything changes but the actions and emotions of people.
>
> *Q.* You're saying you're a student of human nature?
>
> *A.* Well, if there's any way to describe what I do it's more accurate to say I'm a student of human behavior than just that I'm a market technician who looks at charts.
>
> *Q.* In other words, psychological influence is very important in the market, in your view.
>
> *A.* It's crucial. If you look back at the '78 bottom, after a decline in the Dow from 1000 in '76 to 750 at the low, fairly rational, intelligent money managers said: "I don't want to buy stocks anymore, I want to have a high cash position." Then, two years later, after the market had zigzagged its way up to 950, those same people—fairly intelligent people—said, "I love stocks; you gotta get your cash back in; the long term is great." On a rational basis,

you'd expect people to get more bullish as stock prices go down and more bearish as they go up. In actual fact, we do the opposite. So what I'm waiting for, before turning bullish, is for the people who really liked stocks at 950 to 1000 to turn around and start trying to convince me they're awful at 750 or some lower level.

Q. But somebody obviously hasn't liked stocks much lately, from 1000 all the way down to the low 800s. Isn't that a sign of bearishness?

A. There's a difference between the trend in the price and the attitude. What still troubles me about current opinion is that, essentially, investors still lack perception of risk. I mean, the main difference between early '81 and early '82 is only that expectations on how far the market's going up have been scaled down. A year ago, there were all kinds of projections of big, new highs—1200, 1300. Lately, the feeling has been, "Well, the market's not going up very much; it'll be in a trading range until interest rates come down. I'm going to ride this one out because there's not much risk; I'm bullish about the long term; we just have some problems to get through and when they disappear, the market will go onward and upward." That says to me that we really haven't had the capitulation stage; that is, the stage where people are focusing on how far down the market's going rather than the potential on the upside.

Q. What you're saying is that investors are still way down deep bullish?

A. Yes, there's still more fear of missing the turn than there is about real downside risk...

Q. So you're convinced that people have to be shocked into disenchantment with stocks before the market turns bullish?

A. I'm playing the one constant, which is that people will get discouraged at a good bottom. In fact, analysts are still predicting that earnings will be up significantly this year. When you see comments that everybody's bearish, you should be bullish. But if everybody's really bearish, why haven't institutional cash levels been raised more? There's been a good return available from cash equivalents; it's been an attractive alternative, after all. So why hasn't more margin debt been liquidated?

> *Q.* But didn't margin debt come down almost $1 billion in January, Bob?
>
> *A.* Yes, but it's not a significant decline compared with other historical periods. And the actions people have taken so far haven't reflected expectations of a lot of bad things happening. Essentially, this ride-it-out philosophy just is not the psychology you see at the bottom of a market.

As we discussed in earlier chapters, there are many complex and constantly changing variables when it comes to predicting stock price movements. Farrell believes that there is only one constant in the stock market and that is human nature: *The majority will always be wrong at important turning points*. That is, they will be optimistic and fully invested at the top and they will be sold out and pessimistic at the bottom. This phenomenon will never change regardless of the sophistication of the players.

Bob Farrell's chart of the S&P Composite Average (Exhibit 6.5) tells the story. At the bottom in 1978 when the gin debt had been liquidated and institutional cash was high, the consensus was to keep high cash reserves and sell stocks because there was a recession coming. But the recession fooled people for three years. At the top in November 1980, most of the bears had turned bullish. Institutional cash was low and margin debt had almost doubled. Now the consensus had changed to a very posititve secular case for the 1980s. Under these conditions, you should buy reactions and don't worry about a recession. That's when the market started into a downtrend.

Farrell does not pretend to be able to call stock market turns with pin point accuracy. However, his message is pretty clear. When the majority is defensive and scared, it may be time to be aggressive and buy stocks. When the majority is optimistic and fully invested, it is probably time to become conservative and sell some stocks to build cash. As we have discussed, acting contrary to the crowd is hard for most people to do. That's why it will almost always work.

Exhibit 6.5 *Farrell's Chart of the S&P Composite Average*

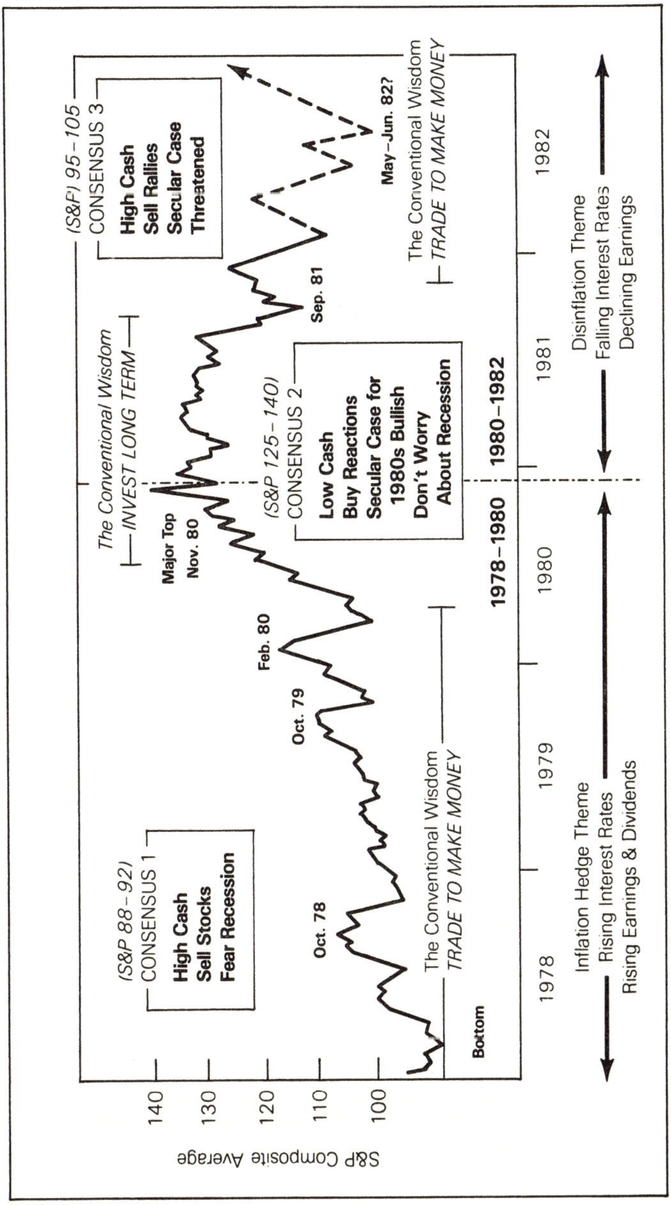

Courtesy of Barron's

Farrell's chart also highlights another interesting phenomenon: market themes. In early 1980, the price of gold skyrocketed to around $850 per ounce. That accelerating price move to the upside was probably the death knell for the end of the "hard asset" inflation hedge theme. Two years later, gold had dropped to the low $300s. Many stocks that were inflation hedge beneficiaries also had precipitous price drops. In the early 1980s, the stock market may be saying that stocks which favor a disinflation theme will be the best performers for a while.

One of the most dominant cycles in the stock market is shown by Farrell's chart: the so-called Presidential Election Year Cycle. It shows that there is a tendency for the stock market to do well for the two years just prior to the election. It also shows that in the two years after the election, the stock market performance is disappointing. Although it doesn't *always* happen like this, the exact high was around the November 1980 election.

In the initial phase of a bull market, the players feel they must *trade to make money*. Farrell's chart highlights the rationale. Notice that the reactions in October 1978, October 1979, and February 1980 were very sharp and violent. People were nervous and quick to sell. This is the sign of a healthy market.

As the top approached, most players wanted to *invest long term*. There were buyers on price weakness. Therefore, the reactions were shallow. You will also notice that at the high on the S&P 500 index it went up over 10 points in a very short period of time. One-sided optimism was again reflected by vertical price movement after an extended uptrend.

Few of us have Bob Farrell's expertise and objectivity when it comes to predicting the stock market, so for most people, the emphasis should be on stock selection. It *is* a market of stocks. Sometimes the cycles will have a negative correlation. Therefore, we must be able to take advantage of the individual pricing opportunity, regardless of overall market action.

INDIVIDUAL STOCKS

The life cycle of a corporation is, in some ways, analogous to the human life cycle (Exhibit 6.6). Unfortunately for a corporation, the infant mortality rate is very high. The major cause of most small business failures is that they are undercapitalized. They don't have enough cash to operate comfortably in the initial start-up phase which may take several years.

Once the business has stabilized into a going concern, it may enter a rapid growth period. The demand for money and resources becomes very high. It is sometime during this adolescent period that the company will go public (if it can) to raise capital for further expansion.

At some time during its adulthood, the corporation may enter a period of strong earnings growth. This could be due to technological innovation in its industry. For example, computers changed IBM, jets changed National Airlines, and color television changed Zenith. Investors may become very excited about the prospects for the company. They may bid up the price of the stock and dramatically expand the price/earnings ratio. A company with a bright outlook may sell at 50 times earnings or more. Invariably, the price of the company outruns—or discounts—its prospects. Should earnings become erratic or the P/E ratio contract because the company is entering a mature phase, the price of the stock can drop precipitously.

As the market for the products matures, the company may have to undergo a dramatic change or metamorphosis. It may reach a phase where its earnings are more influenced by the economy than new market opportunities. It becomes a so-called cyclical stock. Of course, not all corporations follow this general model.

Under these circumstances, the best approach is to buy

Exhibit 6.6 *The Life Cycle of a Corporation*

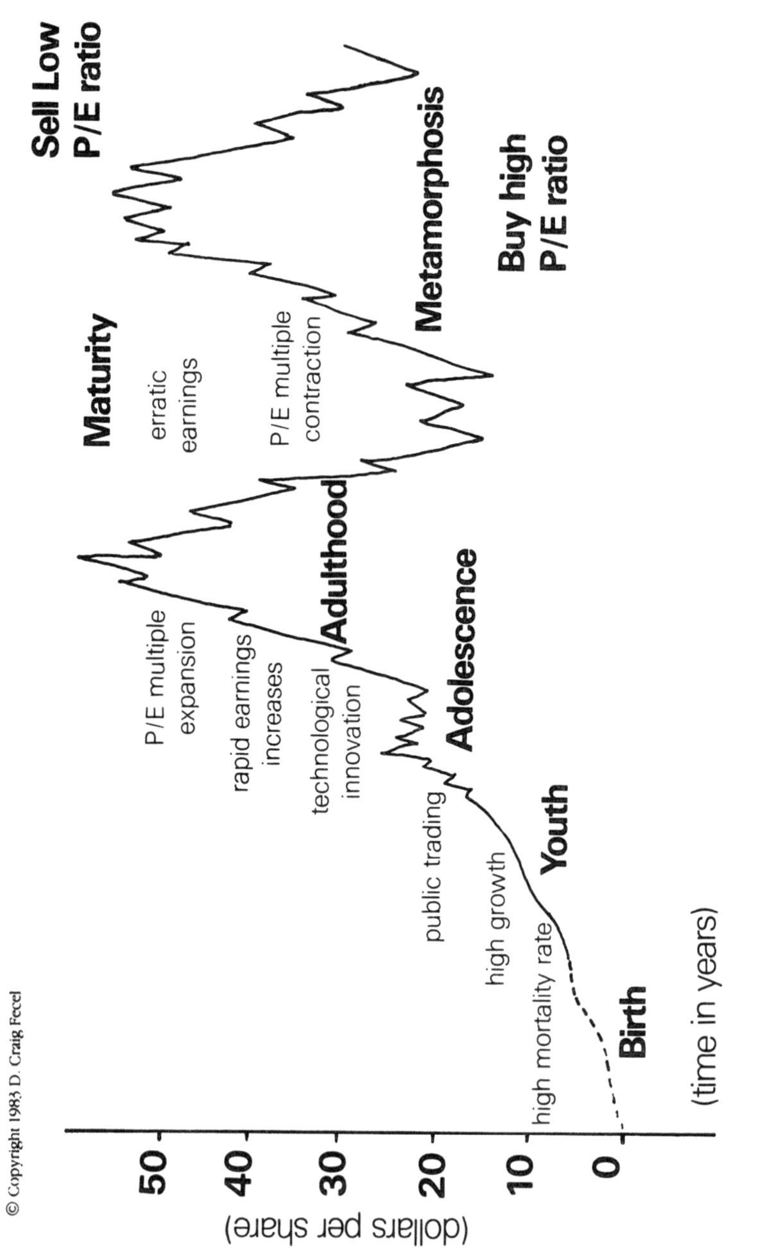

when the stock is down in price due to lack of earnings. At this point, the P/E ratio will be high. The best time to sell will be when the stock is up in price and the earnings are good. Then the P/E ratio may be low. At the top of the price cycle many investors will perceive a new era of growth. That means they will try to turn a cyclical stock back into a growth stock.

There are events that naturally affect the life cycle of a corporation. Competition is one of the most important. As other entrepreneurs see opportunities for profit potential, they will try to exploit them. Markets may become saturated. Patents that provided an important edge can become obsolete by innovation. There are other pitfalls.

Management may become complacent in its success. Although they undoubtedly worked very hard in the formative years of building the company, they now may be ready to reap the fruits of their labor. They also may become more conservative. A lack of new opportunities may slow their growth. The aggressive innovators that could run a $50 million company may be ineffective at running a $500 million company. The needed management styles and systems are completely different. Unforeseen events can play havoc with management plans for the future. High interest rates or a depressed equity market may reduce access to badly needed expansion capital. A severe recession could alter the demand for products. This may force production cutbacks and the firing of needed key personnel. The government may decide to interfere in the industry by placing restrictive controls on it. Finally, a totally unexpected event, such as an oil embargo can disrupt the most carefully laid future plans.

Now let's examine a stock that definitely has been cyclical for more than half a century: Allis-Chalmers. Exhibit 6.7 shows the yearly high–low price action since the late 1920s. (The chart has been adjusted for splits). Notice that the stock has cycled from the low teens to the low thirties six times. Note also that the cycle is not perfect. We could have paid $14 and seen the stock drop below $10 on several occasions and we could have sold in the low thirties only to see the stock

Exhibit 6.7 ***Allis-Chalmers Corp. (yearly high–low price chart)***

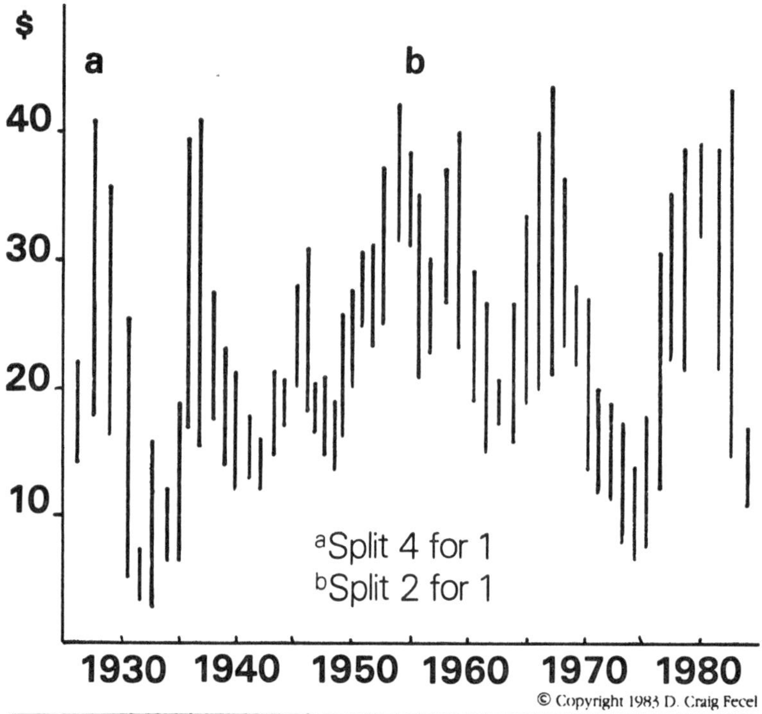

climb to $40 on a few occasions. But, our overall results would have been much better than those of the individual who bought the stock in 1928 for $14 and had a small paper loss in early 1982.

Few stocks, however, have the long-term cyclicality of Allis-Chalmers. What this strategy attempts is to find growth stocks that have turned cyclical in price. In some cases, we will also try to exploit depressed opportunities when we believe the stocks may be in the process of turning cyclical in price. In both situations, however, we will only buy the stock when it is in an area of long-term price support. We will then be prepared to sell if and when it approaches an area of long-term resistance. (In the next chapter we will discuss the exact implementation of this strategy in detail.)

To be sure, there will be times when the direction of the overall stock market will have important influences on individual price cycles. However, there also will be times when some stocks will approach their highs at the same time others approach their lows. Under those circumstances, you can sell high and buy low in a fairly short period of time.

Let's examine two actual examples in early 1980 (Exhibit 6.8 "Negative Correlation"). When silver was over $40 an ounce, mining stocks boomed. Eastman Kodak, the biggest user of silver in the world, collapsed below $50. What should we do? Sell Phelps Dodge and buy Eastman Kodak, of course. When oil prices were going through the roof, along with oil stocks, the tire stocks were breaking down. Why? Because they use a lot of petroleum for their products. Even though it didn't make much sense, we sold Gulf Oil in the mid-forties and bought Goodyear in the low teens. Two years later we were substantially better off.

These examples in no way imply that every exchange will be this fortuitous, but these trades were actually made in my accounts. However, each bull market will usually have new leadership. Occasionally, we'll be lucky (preparation meeting opportunity) and our stocks will be the chosen ones. But we must be willing to sell high so that we can buy low. It's worth repeating to say that "you can't buy cheap stocks with cheap stocks."

In order for us to have made these timely switches, there must have been someone willing to buy our Phelps Dodge and sell us their Eastman Kodak. The same would be true for Gulf Oil and Goodyear. Of course, they are probably different individuals. The point is simply that the consensus didn't do a very good job of prodicting stock price movements. Let's see if we can figure out why they always have problems.

Exhibit 6.8A *Negative Correlation*

Phelps Dodge

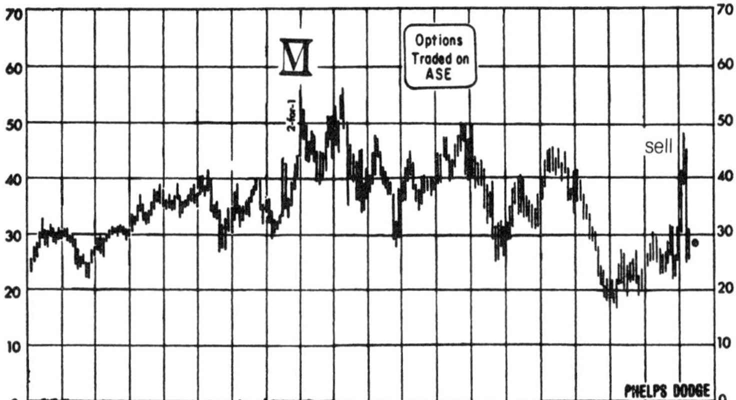

	'61	'62	'63	'64	'65	'66	'67	'68	'69	'70	'71	'72	'73	'74	'75	'76	'77	'78	'79	'80
EARN.	1.88	1.91	1.92	2.72	3.29	4.05	2.52	3.17	4.43	5.36	3.62	4.01	5.31	5.47	2.26	2.11	0.73	1.16	5.06	
DIV.	1.50	1.50	1.50	1.55	2.00	2.13	1.70	1.75	1.95	2.10	2.10	2.10	2.18	2.20	2.20	2.20	1.80	0.60	1.20	

Eastman Kodak

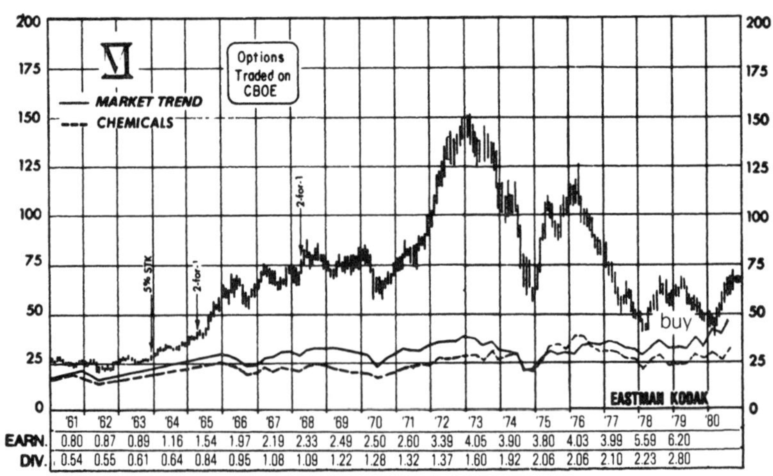

	'61	'62	'63	'64	'65	'66	'67	'68	'69	'70	'71	'72	'73	'74	'75	'76	'77	'78	'79	'80
EARN.	0.80	0.87	0.89	1.16	1.54	1.97	2.19	2.33	2.49	2.50	2.60	3.39	4.05	3.90	3.80	4.03	3.99	5.59	6.20	
DIV.	0.54	0.55	0.61	0.64	0.84	0.95	1.08	1.09	1.22	1.28	1.32	1.37	1.60	1.92	2.06	2.06	2.10	2.23	2.80	

Courtesy of Moody's Handbook

Exhibit 6.8B *Negative Correlation*

Gulf Oil

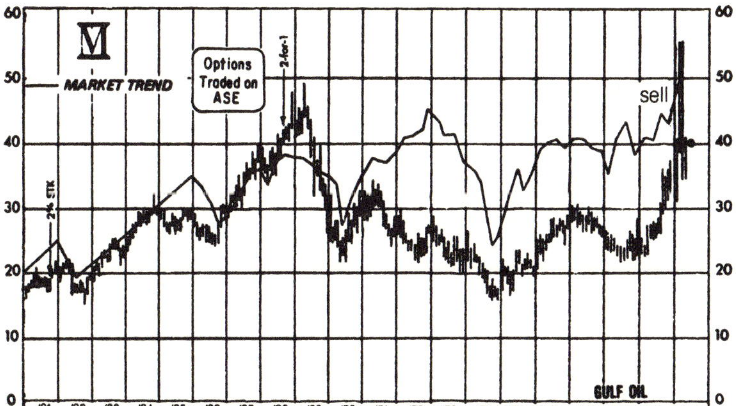

	'61	'62	'63	'64	'65	'66	'67	'68	'69	'70	'71	'72	'73	'74	'75	'76	'77	'78	'79	'80
EARN.	1.61	1.64	1.78	1.91	2.06	2.44	2.74	3.02	2.94	2.65	2.70	2.15	4.06	5.47	3.60	4.19	3.86	4.06	6.78	
DIV.	0.55	0.73	0.80	0.85	0.93	1.05	1.25	1.40	1.50	1.50	1.50	1.50	1.50	1.58	1.70	1.73	1.85	1.90	2.06	

Goodyear Tire & Rubber

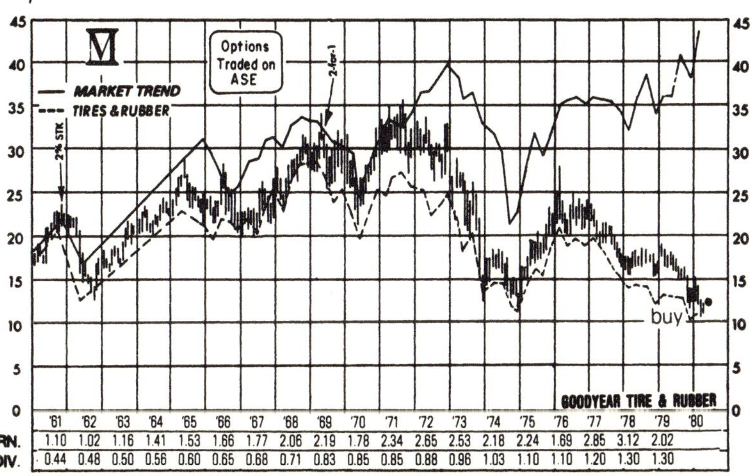

	'61	'62	'63	'64	'65	'66	'67	'68	'69	'70	'71	'72	'73	'74	'75	'76	'77	'78	'79	'80
EARN.	1.10	1.02	1.16	1.41	1.53	1.66	1.77	2.06	2.19	1.78	2.34	2.65	2.53	2.18	2.24	1.69	2.85	3.12	2.02	
DIV.	0.44	0.48	0.50	0.56	0.60	0.65	0.68	0.71	0.83	0.85	0.85	0.88	0.96	1.03	1.10	1.10	1.20	1.30	1.30	

Courtesy of Moody's Handbook

PSYCHOLOGY

Why aren't more people making money in the stock market? Because, as we have seen people buy motivated by greed and sell motivated by fear. So, we must learn to buy when we're afraid and sell when we feel euphoric. The only way we can do that is if we understand the PSYCLE (pronounced Psyc'ill). The term is appropriate because the majority of investors are *psychologically sick* with greed at the top and fear at the bottom of every price cycle.

Hopefully, by now, you believe that the price of a stock is determined purely by the psychology of all the players, many of whom are very long term owners who will hold the stock regardless of the price movement. Others are speculators who want trading profits. Some believe themselves true investors, but they will buy only "good fundamentals." Of course, there is the bargain hunter who hopes to buy value at distressed prices and eventually profit from a "turnaround situation." Also, there are many other types of players with different motives. However, everyone's behavior tends to change as the price of the stock moves up and down. Please turn to Exhibit 6.9 "The PSYCLE." There you can see each distinct phase illustrated.

At the bottom of the price cycle, the predominant emotion is fear. Not only are some investors afraid that the stock will go lower, some may be afraid that the company may go out of business altogether. The focus of the majority is upon avoiding losses, not upon seeking gains.

After a stock has come down from its highs, it is viewed with *contempt* by investors. Those who bought it cheaply, only to ride it up and then back down again, are unhappy. They are kicking themselves because they didn't sell. Those who bought it at much higher prices now have a big loss. They are angry for making a bad decision. Yet, because they are human, they want to blame someone besides themselves. The company's management or their stockbroker is a good choice.

Exhibit 6.9 *The PSYCLE*

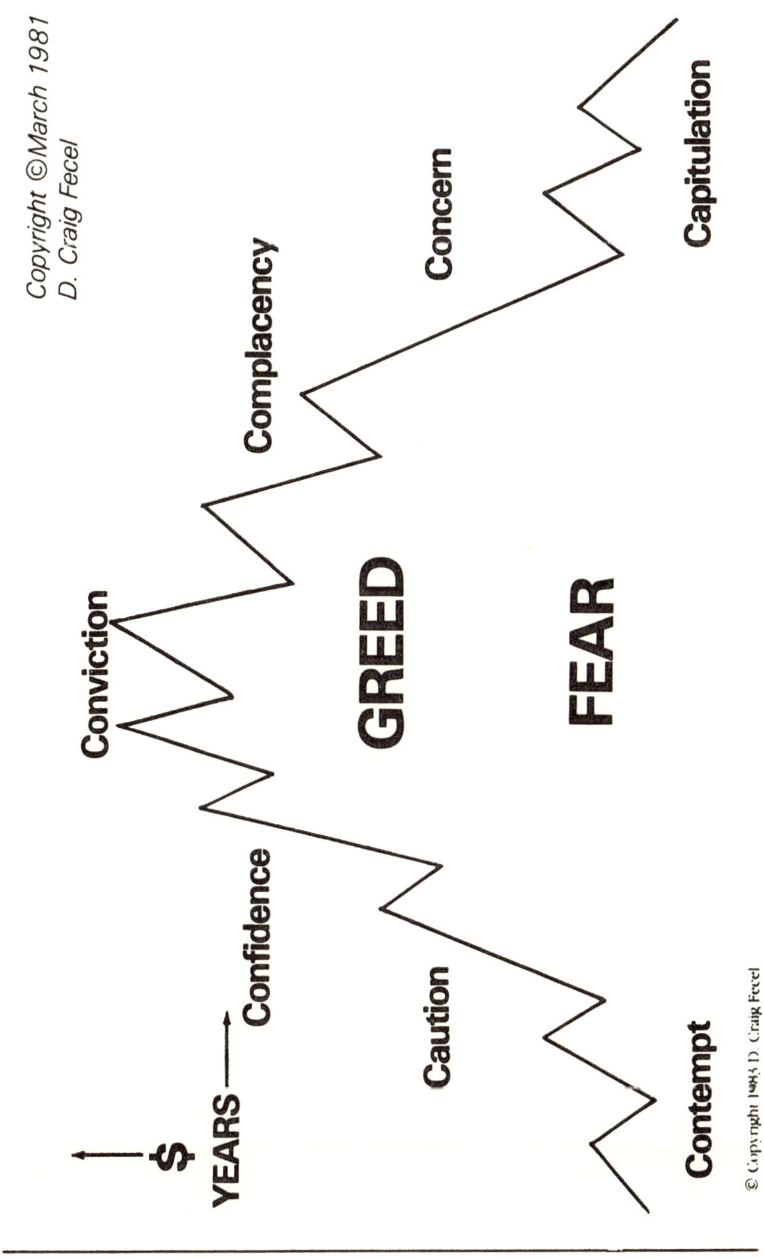

Potential buyers also view the stock with disdain. This is because news, in terms of earnings, is usually bad. The fundamental outlook for the company, in the foreseeable future, is highly suspect. They are fearful that the stock may go down further in price. They certainly don't see any prospects for it going up any time soon. The consensus reality is very negative.

The price action now becomes erratic. It is during this period when the price movement stops going down and begins to go sideways. It is a time for base building in terms of the stock market technician. That is, supply and demand tend to even out within a price range.

There are a number of fits and starts as the stock tries to rally out of its base. However, the price retreats because of a supply of sellers. This price movement does not go unnoticed by speculators. They perceive that the way to make money in the stock is to trade. That means it should be bought when it pulls back toward the low end of its base and sold when it reaches the high end. They may even go short at that time and cover at lower prices. For a while, this strategy may work and reinforce the thinking of the speculators.

It is during this period that many of the owners of the stock who bought higher prices finally get disgusted and sell. This means that potential overhead supply is being worked off. The longer this process takes, the more dramatic the uptrend can be. However, the contempt phase can last for months or years; no one really knows how long.

As the stock begins to move out of its base trading range, *caution* is prevalent because investors are still motivated by fear. They have seen the stock attempt to rally before, only to be disappointed. Some old investors who bought the stock at higher prices now go ahead and sell. They have been waiting to get out even, but they are afraid the stock may return to its former lows.

This phase of the uptrend may be laced with sharp reactions. This is becauses investors are not really committed to the long term; therefore, they are quick to sell on any disappointments. So the price may move ahead grudgingly to the upside only to give up its hard-fought gains very quickly. This is a healthy sign of the beginning of an uptrend because it keeps people on edge.

The news in terms of earnings and future prospects for the company remains gloomy. The stock must climb a wall of worry. In the early stages of the price advance, there must be many problems and even a few potential disasters around so the majority will remain cautious and uncommitted. However, their buying will be welcomed at much higher prices. Even though many potential buyers remain skeptical, bargain-hunters appear as the stock pulls back. During this phase, the most bullish behavior the stock can have is to go up slowly and pull back sharply.

As the price of the stock continues to move upward, *confidence* in the continued uptrend becomes more apparent. At this point, the primary motivation of fear begins turning into greed. Instead of worrying about how much they may lose, investors begin thinking about profits. In other words, instead of worrying about risk, they begin to focus on reward.

Another subtle change takes place at this point. Instead of being nervous about near-term reactions, investors begin to focus on the long term. When prices were lower, they may have sold for a three- or four-point profit. Now they begin to increase their position size and profit objectives. They may be intent on making a "killing" on this one.

The reason for this behavior is fairly simple. Rember that price movement is the primary stimulus for investor expectations. Therefore, as prices continue to appreciate, positive feelings are reinforced and greed motivates buy decisions. The news is now getting much better. Many potential sellers have already been "washed out." Others continue to hold becauses the price is now going up. The upward movement becomes a little more volatile and the reactions are shallow. This is because new investors are buying "at the market." They earnestly want to participate in the future price appreciation. This phase is the prelude to the most exciting part of the uptrend.

At the top of the price move, enthusiasm is at its apex. The *conviction* of the majority is that the price can only go higher. After all, haven't they been conditioned to a dynamic uptrend? At this point, the sellers back away and the buyers become very aggressive. Often this is reflected in an almost vertical price movement to the upside. This invariably means that the consensus of investors has become one-sided. It is this imbalance of supply and demand, reflected by an accelerating price movement, that can be the most visible reflection of one-sided "crowd psychology" at major turning points.

Greed is now the predominant emotion. Most of the players now focus only on future gains. Many people feel euphoric. Some of the players who sold too soon stop kicking themselves for getting out and plunge back into the stock. Those who had thought nervously about selling the stock at lower prices, now forget about it altogether. At this point, investors excxitingly check the paper every day to see how much money they've made. They may even be disappointed if it's only one or two points. This is when they begin to realize just how brilliant they are. Anyway, almost no one is thinking about selling because they feel the stock will be higher soon.

Of course, trend reversals are only confirmed in the retrospect. A sharp, upward movement certainly doesn't mean that the stock will turn around and go straight down. That would be somewhat rare. However, a "buying climax" can be followed by a lengthy period of sideways price stabilization which later may turn out to be a distribution top. Common sense would tell you that selling into this kind of price advance is very hard for most investors. It certainly won't guarantee you the highest price; but, by the time the majority gets really enthusiastic about a stock, most of the good news may have discounted in the future.

Most investors will only watch their "cake" grow as prices move higher, but will never enjoy the "eating" of it. Why not? Because they will never sell and take their profits. The stock becomes an extension of their ego. As it moves higher and higher, they envision more and more riches. They become mesmerized by greed. They are congratulating themselves on their brilliant decision. Sell the stock? Ridiculous! They'd have to pay too much in taxes. Besides, since it's going up so rapidly, they are conditioned to believe that it will continue to do so at that rate in the future. Unfortunately, the PSYCLE usually takes care of their dilemma.

It must be understood that price movements reverse themselves from up to down only in light of the most favorable news and investor sentiment. It has to be that way in order for markets to function at all. In order for a few to be right, many must be wrong. If every shareholder of a company woke up one morning and decided to sell, the price would immediately collapse. So distribution must take place when the majority of owners are happy to hold and reluctant to sell.

As the price peak passes and movement begins downward, investor *complacency* with regard to the stock is predominant. The news for the company is still favorable and the outlook is positive. They don't understand why the stock is not at new highs, but they have been through reactions before and always the stock has recovered. They're satisfied that their investment is sound and will do well over the long term. Greed is still alive and well. Some investors even rationalize the setback as a "healthy reaction." As the price drops, some owners may add to their positions. The buyers who "missed the boat" the first time eagerly make new commitments. Everyone remembers higher prices and sees no reason why they can't be attained again. Under these circumstances, the rallies may be sharp, exciting experiences and the price erosion is slow. Everyone is still focusing on the long term.

As the stock continues to react, greed begins to melt

into fear. Investors now feel *concern* about losing more money. All the way down they have believed the stock looked cheap; they felt it had so much inherent value. It was beyond their comprehension that it could drop this low in price. Unfortunately, now the news on the company is beginning to deteriorate.

As we have observed, price movement is the major stimulus to investor sentiment. Downward prices now reinforce negative feelings and investors begin to give serious consideration to selling. Some are forced to liquidate because of margin calls. However, those who can hang on are not quite ready to "throw in the towel." This is the "ostrich," or stick-your-head-in-the-sand phase. That is, they stop checking the stock quotes because they can't face up to a potential disaster. Although investors are very concerned, they are still willing to ride it out. Selling would be an admission of a disastrous mistake. They tend to cling to a fanciful hope that the price will move back up. If it does, they then resolve to sell. Unfortunately, from this point in the PSYCLE, they are rarely accommodated. Prices are now moving steadily downward.

As the end approaches, greed completely vanishes and investors and speculators become sick with fear. All thoughts of profits disappear and they are now only worried about further losses. As the price continues to fall, panic forces some of the staunchest holdouts into *capitulation*. By now, the news is turning from bad to worse. A "selling panic" is just the reverse of a "buying climax."

As prices accelerate on the downside, potential buyers back away, and sellers become aggressive. Now they want out at any cost. "Never mind the cheese, just let me out of the trap," typifies their thinking. They end up taking a much greater loss than they would have if they'd sold when they originally began thinking about it. It doesn't seem to matter now because at least the mental anguish is over. However, the financial and emotional pain was necessary before they would liquidate their stock. This give-up stage is seen most visibly through a sharp price break toward the end of a down-trend. It could be precipitated by an unexpected large loss or dividend omission. By the time such news is available to the majority, the worst may already be reflected in the price of the stock.

At this point, the major buyers may be the specialists and floor traders who must trade against the crowd anyway. Since most of the urgent sellers have been satisfied, the stock can eventually produce a sharp rally on almost no volume. Under these circumstances, the professionals can unload their stock fairly easily. Then a new wave of selling may return the price to its former lows.

After the panic has passed, prices should begin to stabilize. Sometime during the contempt phase, prices may break marginally below the "benchmark low" set during the capitulation phase. This may be necessary in order to get some of the remaining holdouts to liquidate their stock positions. Instead of waiting for a rally, they are scared of another substantial price drop. Now, fear has raised the emotional and financial pain high enough so that they can justify (to themselves) selling at these low levels. The stock is now "moving from weak hands into strong hands."

This old Wall Street adage means that the majority of buyers at this point are investors in the truest sense of the word. They are bargain-hunters. They are buying value at distressed prices according to their own individual perceptions. They are buying for the long term and have adequate staying power. In most cases, their stock will only be pried away from them at much higher prices.

Conversely at the top of the PSYCLE, stock tends to move "from strong hands into weak hands." Investors are selling and speculators are buying. Margin tends to be used a lot more at this point so staying power is reduced. Also, buyers may focus more on price movement. Therefore, some buyers may be inclined to dump their stock quickly if it starts to drop. In general, the expectations at the top of the PSYCLE are much higher than at the bottom.

There is another very interesting phenomenon of the PSYCLE. That is, certain phases tend to be "mirror images" of each other. This means that the price movement would be exactly opposite. The capitulation and conviction phases are the most obvious. Respectively, the emotional extremes of fear and greed produce accelerating price movement to the downside and upside. The relationships of other phases are more subtle.

The caution and complacency phases tend to reflect each other. Why is that, you may wonder? Remember, at the top, the majority is committed to the long term. However, near the bottom they are nervous and tend to trade more. At the top, greed makes the buyers step in aggressively, but at the bottom, they tend to vanish quickly. In the caution phase, the stock moves up grudgingly and then reacts sharply. Just the opposite occurs in the complacency phase. The stock goes down slowly but then rallies up sharply. This tends to keep the majority worried at the bottom and contented at the top.

The confidence and concern phases also tend to reflect each other. However, now supply and demand tend to be more even but with a respective upward and downward bias. In the confidence phase, buyers become increasingly positive so they keep reactions shallow. This produces a steady uptrend in prices without much volatility to the downside. In the concern phase, sellers become increasingly negative, so they keep ralllies truncated. This produces a steady downtrend in prices without much volatility to the upside.

As prices move steadily upward, confidence increases to the point where it becomes conviction. Now price volatility will occur to the upside. As prices move steadily downward, concern increases to the point where it becomes capitulation. Now price volatility will occur to the downside. Each phase of the PSYCLE seems to set the stage for the following one.

The PSYCLE is a model. This means it is a structured arrangement of principles and terms that tries to represent the elusive shifts in crowd psychology. It attempts to define a process that otherwise would be undefinable. No model is absolutely perfect because each has some inconsistencies. Although few stocks may ever trace out an idealized PSYCLE, many will follow it closely. By accepting it as *your* reality of the marketplace, you'll be forced to buy low and sell high. If that's true, then you've found the "magic key" to stock market success.

7

Stock Market Success

DECISION STRATEGY

Now that we understand the PSYCLE, the three cornerstones of my investment approach should make more sense to you. Actually, if you believe point one, then two and three follow in a logical manner. (1) If the majority of investors will always be wrong at major turning points; (2) then it must be assumed that consistently predicting future stock price movements will be extremely difficult for most of the players; (3) therefore, long term profits in the stock market are best realized by attempting to minimize risk, not in trying to maximize gain. Now, let's examine a decision strategy that should enable us to make money within this frame of reference.

Consider buying a stock only when it is near its lows of the last ten or twenty years. The reason for this is pretty simple. We are trying to minimize price risk. That is, we are hoping that the stock will not go much lower than what we paid for it. Only when the stock is in what we feel is a "low-risk" buy zone, will we consider a purchase.

The low-risk buy zone has evidence of substantial long-term support. This means that in past years, at the chosen price level, there has been buying power in sufficient volume to stop the downtrend in prices. The reasons for this phenomenon may not be precisely explained. This is because the circumstances that produced the past price drops were obviously different each time. Thus we are talking only of observable data.

I am not saying the cycles are perfect; because they are not. If they were, many people would use the cyclical system and its usesfulness would therefore be destroyed. Long-term price charts are simply a way to *monitor* the PSYCLE. Price movement is the best frame of reference to use in trying to identify extremes in crowd psychology. Although the amplitude and the wave length of the price cycle can vary, it is our contention that human nature won't.

Trying to determine the buy zone is an art, not a science. Turn to Exhibit 7.1, "Price Leverage." The top part shows a chart of our old friend, Outboard Marine. We are using it again because you are familiar with the accumulation and distribution phases. Also, it is more or less a classic example and should be easier to understand. The best way to create a buy zone is to simply draw a straight line across the bottom of the chart. Try to include as many former lows as possible. Also, be sure to leave yourself some room on the bottom so you get to buy the stock.

Stock prices have a tendency to go to extremes, both on the upside and downside. They can go higher than anyone could ever believe possible, and they can go lower than anyone can imagine in his nightmares. By the time conviction has turned into contempt, most of the price damage has already been done. Now you must have the cash and guts to buy when the opportunity presents itself. This is easier said than done. Here's why.

You're going to be scared, too. Fear is the predominant emotion at the bottom and you should feel it to some degree, just like everyone else. That means you may have "butter-

Exhibit 7.1 ***Price Leverage***

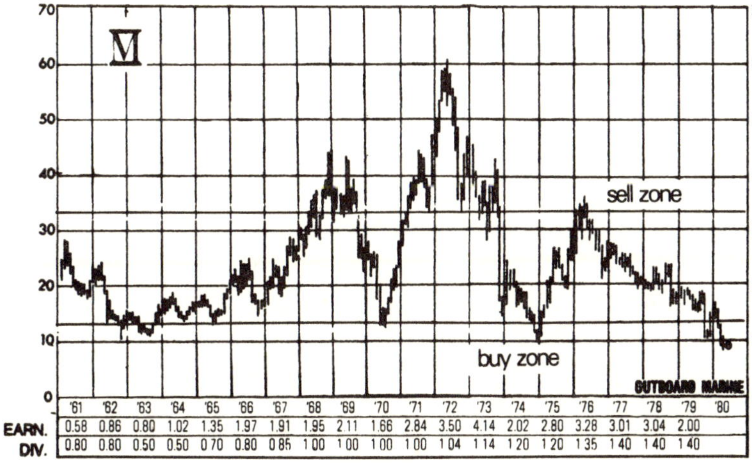

Buy	$ Price	Sell	$ Price	Years	% Profit
1980	10	1986	30	6	200
1981	15	1986	30	5	100

Courtesy of Moody's Handbook

flies" in your stomach when you place the order to buy. If you don't, there could be something wrong. It probably means that you're early and that the stock hasn't been "blown out" enough. Your best buy decisions will probably turn out to be the ones about which you are the most nervous.

If you are aggressively accumulating the stock based on a quick turnaround in price, it's likely you'll be disappointed. Obviously, you are buying motivated by greed. This is exactly what the crowd is doing. In today's sophisticated market environment, people know that they shouldn't be part of the "crowd," so, many investors may *think* that they act contrary to the other players. Yet this can't be true. There is only one way to tell if the price of a stock is close to its lows. You must be gripped with fear when you buy the stock.

Do you know the difference between courage and cowardice? In a stressful situation, both individuals may be equally afraid. The coward loses control and runs. The brave man stays and does what has to be done. At a good price trough, this is how you will feel. As you pick up the phone to call your broker, your hand may be shaking. As you tell him to execute the order, your voice may quiver from lack of conviction. After you have placed the phone on its hook, you may feel like throwing up your breakfast. That's fine. You'll get over it shortly. You probably have made one of the best buy decisions of your life. The bottom of the PSYCLE won't have arrived until fear is a real experience for you, too.

Buy only seasoned, viable companies. Since we will only consider the stock when it is distressed in price, this approach has one very positive advantage over most other ones. It severely restricts the number of potential investment candidates. This gives us a substantial edge over the rest of the players. The majority of people spend their time trying to find stocks that will achieve big gains. This means they must choose from a large number of opportunities; therefore, they have less time, energy or other resources to investigate an individual company. This can increase the likelihood of making a mistake.

Our strategy is based upon the conviction that most of our stocks will eventually recover in price if we don't buy any that get into severe financial difficulties. Since we are risk-adverse, our research efforts should be used to uncover negative information. Bunkruptcy comes when a corporation runs out of cash. So companies with a high percentage of debt on their balance sheets should be thoroughly investigated. Another advantage of this strategy is that by the time the stock has dropped into the buy zone, the news is already pretty bad. So, it is possible for a more realistic analysis of the situation.

This is where the fundamental security analyst can be of the most help to the individual investor. It is also one of the most important reasons to do business with a full-service brokerage firm (we'll discuss the relationship with your stockbroker in more detail in the last section of this chapter). Although the fundamental sescurity analyst is not always able to predict the price movement of the stock, he is very qualified to assess the viability of the corporation. If it is in serious trouble, the stock should be avoided until the difficulties are over. This policy will mean some missed opportunities, but remember our strategy is not to buy losers.

You must not expect the analyst to be too optimistic about your stock when it is in the buy zone. Of course, he *could* be positive, but this would be unusual since the near-term outlook will appear negative to the majority. This is a good reason why the stock is down in price. If the analyst is positive, so much the better. Yet he probably will be neutral or have a a faint buy opinion on the stock. He may feel (rightly or wrongly) that the stock won't be "doing anything" for a while. That's just fine because our investment time frame (up to 6 years) is much longer than the period covered by his opinion. Don't forget that analysts are judged on a performance record of one or two years.

Of course, you must expect to hear comments of gloom and doom about the company. This is natural at the bottom. Some people may feel that the company is a bankruptcy candidate. Certainly, there won't be any reason for the stock to go up in price any time soon. This is precisely where you must try to separate fact from fear. This won't be so easy. But, the higher the quality of the company, the less the risk of insolvency. This is one good reason why most of your selections should come from the New York Stock Exchange. Yet, no matter how rigorous your selection process, you'll probably buy a dud every once in a while. This risk is inherent in any equity investment.

So far, so good. But now you may be asking yourself, "What's going to make the stock go back up in price?" The answer is probably (1) a dramatic increase in earnings, (2) a perceived dramatic increase in earnings or (3) a takeover by another company. Large companies are very durable. In the majority of cases, a decline in earning power is not a permanent event. Management may be forced to make "painful" adjustments, but a strong asset base will enable the company to endure. Often, the company will emerge from a crisis a much stronger competitor. Occasionally, a larger company will come along and buy out the depressed company because it may be trading at a substantial discount of replacement value. Of course, you can't rely on this, but it'll happen more often than you might think.

Be prepared to hold your position for as long as six years. Hopefully, you'll be able to realize your profit objective much sooner. Certainly, that'll be true on many occasions. But, sometimes it is necessary to be very patient. Lack of patience is one of the major reasons most people don't do well in the stock market. Their Child Ego State requires instant gratification.

A year may often seem like an eternity when you think you're stuck in a dead stock. In most market environments, there will be at least a few "high flyers" that will be moving upward. Your Hungry Child may be tempted to buy them. Don't do it. Resist the temptation to join the "crowd." This is where investment maturity and discipline become extremely important. Remember that all substantial price moves usually begin from a period of low volatility or *contempt*. If you bought a seasoned, viable company at a distressed price, the chances are that the players will eventually bring it back into favor. Today's "dogs" can become tomorrow's "darlings." The reverse is also true.

Once a commitment is made, you shouldn't change it. Do you remember the amount of time that we spent discussing random price movements and the expectation of loss? Well, the more you trade, the more those forces work against you. Occasionally, there will be legitimate reasons to make an exchange. If the viability of the company becomes seriously questioned, then you should probably sell it.

One of the great virtues of this investment system is its lack of hassle. You'll have to put in some work, but it should be minimal. A vital reason to establish a six-year time frame is so that you won't be bothered by short-term random price fluctuations of the stock. All your worrying won't make the stock go up any sooner. Just relax and enjoy life. Let the PSYCLE work for you.

Each stock should have the potential to appreciate at least 100% in price. This figure may sound somewhat arbitrary, but there are some logical reasons for it. First of all, that means that the stock is down at least 50% from its highs. So the price is distressed. Second, our goal is to double our money every six years. Therefore, our objective is for the stock to go up at least 100% within that time.

Our approach is based on the theory that overall gains will be the greatest by optimizing price. You should try to buy the stock at the cheapest price possible. Although that may sound like common sense, it's not the way many players operate. The market technician tries to ride the price trends and the fundamentalist may rely on near-term earnings growth. Whatever the system, the player's techniques are designed to make money in the shortest possible time.

We believe that the price cycles will be forthcoming, but we just don't know when they will happen. The PSYCLE cannot help predict stock price movements in terms of amplitude or duration. However, it is an extremely valuable tool that can be used to identify extremes in investor sentiment. This can help us know when to buy and sell.

Turn back to Exhibit 7.1, "Price Leverage." Let's say

that you could have bought Outboard Marine at $10 a share in 1980. This is when people were sitting in line for two hours just to get gasoline for their cars. Now, let's assume that you have another alternative. You can buy the stock in 1981 when it reacts back to $15 after it has gone to $20. The outlook for the company is more positive. Assume, for argument's sake, the stock goes to $30 by 1986. Which trade would give you a better rate of return?

As we have noted, the rate of return is defined by dividing the profit by the original investment. If the stock goes from $10 to $30, you've made a 200% profit in six years. If it goes from $15 to $30, you have made only a 100% profit in five years. To get the simple annualized rate of return we must divide the 200% profit by six years and the 100% profit by five years. Respectively, we get 33% and 20%. Obviously, you are better off in the first case under the given assumptions. This is not the only reason to try and minimize price risk. It's possible that you may not have bought the stock on a pullback. Then you would have missed the profit opportunity altogether. Also, there were no assurances that the stock wouldn't have continued to react to $10 again. After much trial and error, it is this author's firm opinion that over the long term, the greatest profits will be made by buying at the cheapest price possible. To put it another way, price leverage is much more important than time leverage. Amen.

Diversify your portfolio in order to spread your risk. As we discussed earlier, this is an important aspect of any true investment program. You may find what you think to be the greatest value since gold sold for $32 per ounce. However, it would be imprudent to put most of your financial assets into one opportunity. And if you are that optimistic about the investment, your buying is motivated by greed. This means the PSYCLE has probably not run its course yet. There may be financial pain ahead.

The more stocks you own, the more relaxed you can be toward your investments. This is important not just for your peace of mind, but also for investment results. A nervous investor is prone to make irrational and emotional decisions. He may panic in a crisis, particularly if his assets are concentrated in a few stocks. His staying power is reduced. The diversified investor is far better able to "sweat out" a downswing in prices.

Since we can't predict stock price movements, we don't know what stocks the players are going to take up first. In the initial stages of starting this investment program, it will be easier for the investor to stay with it, if he has even one or two early successes. Hopefully, you would have at least a few stocks hit the sell zone within three years. This is why you start with at least six to eight positions with the same amount of capital in each one.

Avoid selling at a loss. This may seem like a simple-minded statement. Yet it is a vital rule of this investment strategy. The surest way not to ever have any losses, is just to refuse to take them. Stock losses once taken are real and must be offset by gains. However, a stock loss that is not taken will often disappear if you bought it according to this approach.

You must be prepared for price fluctuations in some of the stocks after purchase. Yet, if you bought stock in a viable company at near historic lows, it is much easier for you to remain committed to your position, knowing that patience is your only requirement for profits. There is an old market adage, "A stock well bought is half sold."

There is only one situation in which selling stock at a loss should be considered. This is if the financial health of the corporation is seriously threatened, and bankruptcy is a clear possibility. Unfortunately, by this time, the stock may have dropped substantially from where you bought it. A sale may thus be prudent even though the company eventually recovers.

Sell near levels of long-term resistance. When the stock reaches your price objective, you must close your eyes and "pull the trigger." This is going to be easier said than done if you haven't predetermined the sell zone. It can be done effortlessly when the stock is in the buy zone, because the sell price is a long way off. When you are buying the stock, it is natural to be a little afraid. Even though you are being objective, fear is still the predominant emotion at the bottom. So, you'll be happy to make at least 100% on your money.

When the stock approaches the sell target, greed will be your predominant emotion. You will enter a state of euphoria just like everyone else. You'll be thinking how brilliant you are, and how rich you're going to be. Your Child Ego State won't want you to sell because he is getting stroked. At this point, Mr. Macho won't help you because the rationale for staying in the stock will be overwhelming. You can't pay attention to your emotions or to conventional wisdom. You must execute your plan and sell. If you don't, then you'll be a face in a crowd, like everyone else.

Setting a price to sell your stock is an art, not a science. Reexamine the Outboard Marine chart in Exhibit 7.1 "Price Leverage." You want to sell your stock when it reaches long-term resistance. That means a price level where there has been a large enough volume of selling to keep the price from going higher. This will not be easy in many cases. However, you must draw a line across the top of the chart to indicate the sell zone. Be sure and leave some room on the upside so you can get out comfortably.

We still must use our knowledge of the PSYCLE. It is possible that the stock will get to the conviction phase before the sell zone is reached. This will be identified by an accelerating price movement to the upside. Under those circumstances, you should probably go ahead and sell. Remember that we are trying to minimize risk, not maximize gain. This means that we should move our capital from overvalued situations into undervalued situations. So leaving some "money on the table" is not as bad as riding the stock all the way down to the base again.

Assume that you'll almost always be wrong near-term. This sounds overly pessimistic, but it is better to be surprised at how good your decisions are than to be unhappy because the stock dropped three points right after you bought it. An important aspect of equity investing is achieving long-term capital gains. This means that you must hold the stock for at least one year. What difference does it make whether the stock goes up or down a few points in the meantime as long as the stock eventually goes up?

Common sense tells you that many stocks will go higher, at least short term, right after you sell them. Now is when your Child Ego State will want to second-guess your strategy. Don't pay any attention to him, he's just being greedy. Remember that you're not investing in the stock market to go on an ego trip. You're in it to make money. When you get a substantial gain, sell. What the stock does afterward is irrelevant. Hopefully, you've doubled your money after taxes. You've done what you intended to do. Just be thankful and look for another undervalued situation and do it again.

The principal reason most investors don't do well is because they don't have a consistent decision strategy of when to buy and when to sell. This is most apparent at major turning points. They want to be right near-term. After they buy, they don't want to see even one downtick. When they sell, they want the stock to stop going up at once. These are irrational emotions of their Hungry Child Ego State. You can profit handsomely from their confusion if you take a different approach. Simply acknowledge that you can't beat the near-term, random price movements. It will greatly increase your peace of mind and investment results.

PROFITS

Let's look at some specific examples. We will show the price movements of 14 different stocks. The profits are from actual trades that I made in my own account. In some cases, I didn't buy or sell all of my shares at the exact prices, but the transactions are representative of what happened.

I suggest that you get a Moody's Handbook or any other type of long-term chart and thoroughly examine the price action of each stock. The reason for examining these charts is so that you can have a more accurate understanding of what kinds of experiences you may have in both the buy zone and sell zones. Also, it will prepare you for some of the periods of frustration and inactivity that are inevitable with this approach. Altogether, I have owned more than 40 stocks that have appreciated over 100% after I bought them. There were a few instances in which I did not achieve the full 100% gain, but in most cases I did. Of course, there were many occasions where the appreciation was much greater than that. On the whole, the returns were entirely satisfactory.

Let's now review the overall stock market environment for the past 20 years. To do this, we will use the Dow Jones Industrial Average (DJIA). Although it only comprises the price action of 30 companies, it is the most popularly followed stock market indicator. As Exhibit 7.2 clearly shows, the DJIA has been locked in a trading range between 550 and 1050 for the past 20 years; but, as we shall see, there were many opportunities to profit from the PSYCLE.

The great bull that began in 1950 with the DJIA at 200 peaked between 1965 and 1968. With the DJIA around 1000, speculation was running wild and P/E ratios were very high. Just when everyone was anticipating that the DJIA would climb to 2000 during the 1970s, stocks prices collapsed.

By 1970, the DJIA had dropped to the mid-600s. Although the devastation in the market value of many stocks was nearly unbelievable, it turned out to be just the first half of the ball game. From 1970 to 1972, the DJIA rallied back to over 1000. Unfortunately, the price increases occurred mainly in the big capitalization, institutional stocks known as the

Exhibit 7.2 ***Dow-Jones Industrial Average (1962–1982)***

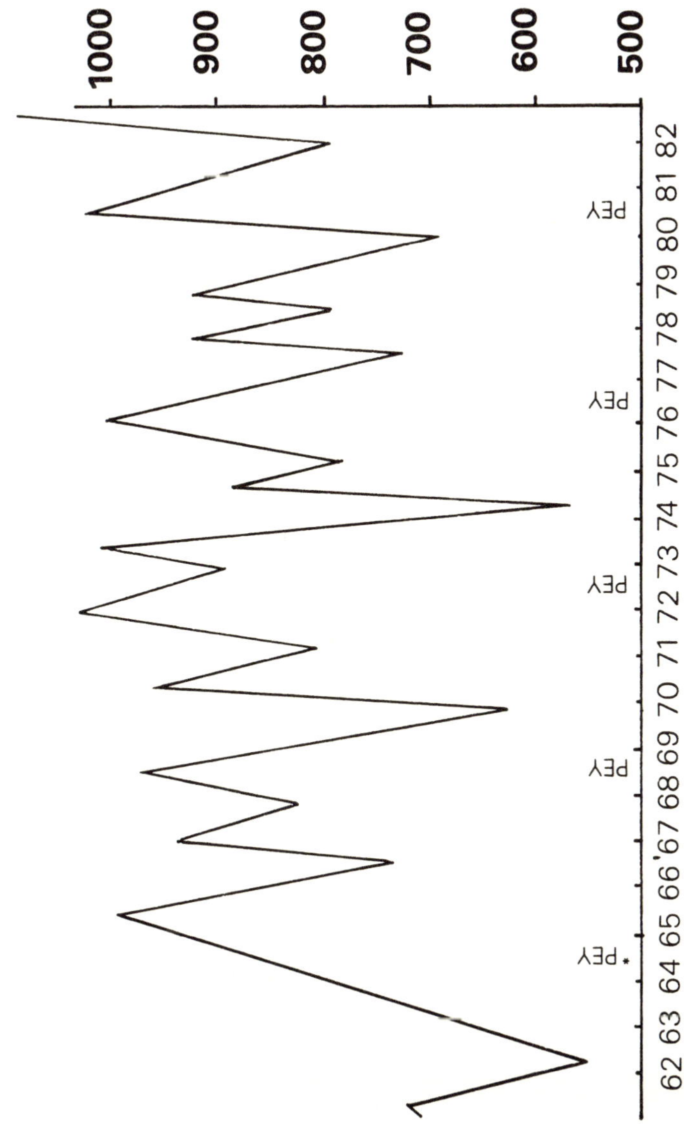

*Presidential Election Year.

Source: ***Wall Street Journal*** (Dow Jones & Co., Inc.)

"nifty fifty." Most secondary stocks moved up only modestly. Then the "killer wave" hit. In 1974, the DJIA dropped to about 550. However, within the carnage lay opportunity for substantial gains.

Many players would argue that the 1974 low of about 550 on the DJIA was the beginning of a bull market that has continued into the early 1980s. That may not seem apparent because it has been a truly sectionalized market environment. That is, there have been certain groups of stocks that have been going up, going down, or going sideways. Under these circumstances, it doesn't seem that much overall progress has been made. However, many stocks have had dramatic price swings over that period of time.

By 1976, the DJIA had returned to over 1000. Again, many investors were focusing on 2000. With everyone so bullish, the stock market had to prove the majority wrong, so it went down. In the first quarter of 1978, the DJIA made its low of about 750. At that time, many players were extremely negative. Many were looking for a recession that never came. Overall, investment advisers were very negative and institutions were loaded with cash. Many wondered if the DJIA would test its previous lows of around 550. The rest is history. In 1980, the DJIA was back at 1000.

Turn back to Bob Farrell's chart of the S&P 500 (Exhibit 6.6), you will see that the consensus was now fully invested and looking for the great bull market of the 1980s. Once again, the market obliged by dropping a few hundred points on the DJIA. Some of the precious metals, energy, and high technology favorites were massacred. Many dropped well over 60% from their price peaks. In the stock market, the "illusion of certainty often becomes the certainty of illusion."

Examine Exhibit 7.2 again and you will notice that a presidential election year (PEY) has pretty much marked the stock market peaks recently. Is the price movement a cycle or is it just random? Who knows for sure? We do know that predicting the future is extremely difficult for most of the players.

The one thing we do know about stocks is that they will fluctuate in price. If you buy *only* when they are down in price, you can sell when they go up. Exhibit 7.3 "Profits" illustrates seven years of price movement for six selected stocks. The year at the bottom indicates when the stock was sold.

Molycorp, Inc. primarily mines, processes, and markets molybdenum and rare earth metals. At the end of 1971, the stockholder's equity per share (SE/S) was about $23, but we felt the replacement value of their mines was worth much more than that figure. When we began buying the stock, the price had dropped into the low teens. In 1974 and 1975, Molycorp stayed in a trading range between the mid-twenties and mid-teens. In 1976, the company earned over $5 per share. Union Oil of California made a tender offer for the stock in 1977 and we sold when it moved into the fifties.

The Budd Company primarily supplies the automobile industry with a variety of bodies, chassis frames, wheels, and other parts. At the end of 1975, the SE/E was $31. When we began buying the stock, the price had dropped to under $10 and then recovered to the low teens. In 1978 the stock was bought out in the mid-thirties.

National Airlines was a major U.S. carrier. At the end of 1976, the SE/S was $22. However, some security analysts believed that the market value of their jet airplanes was almost twice that figure. The National Airlines debt load was only about 12% of its total capitalization, which was a fairly conservative figure for an airline. We bought the stock in the low teens after it had been in a trading range for several years. In 1978, Texas International Airlines began accumulating the stock. Then a takeover battle ensued as other airlines started buying stock. In a two-month period in 1978, the stock jumped from $20 to $40 and we sold. The company was eventually bought out by Pan Am at $50, but it dropped back to the low twenties first.

Milton Bradley is a large domestic maker of toys and

Exhibit 7.3 ***Profits (Yearly high-low)***

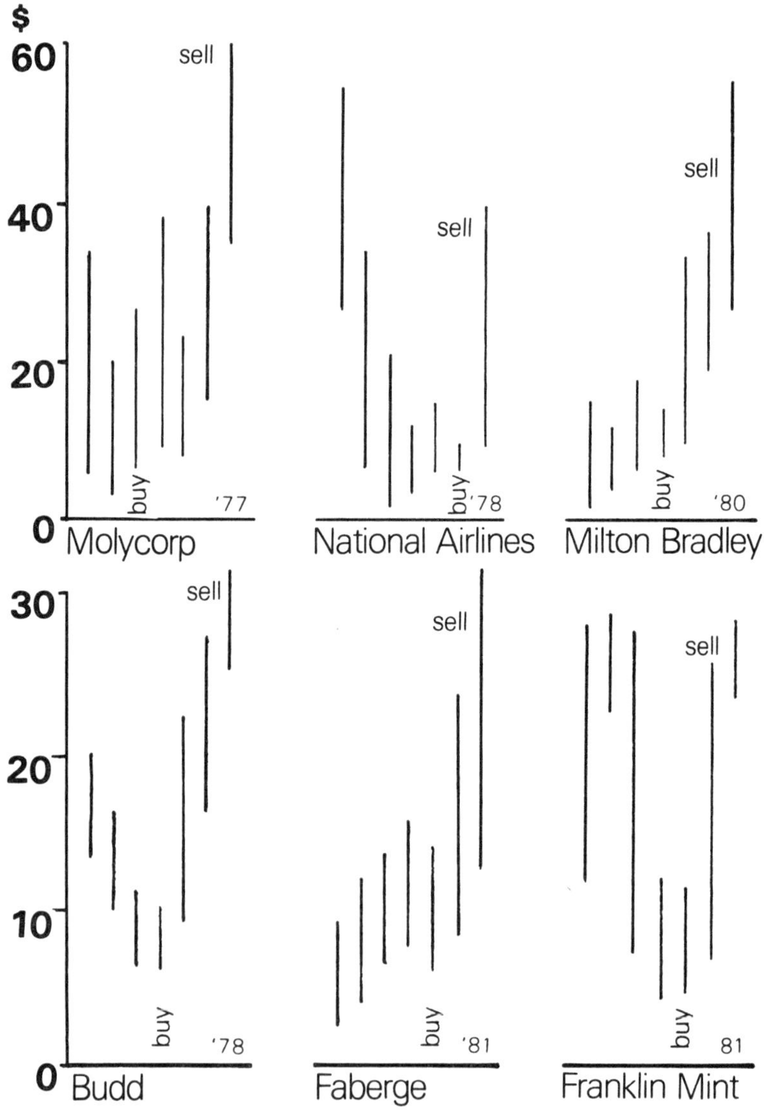

games. At the end of 1976, the SE/S was $13. When we began buying the stock, the price had dropped to the low teens. The company was making about $2 per share and paying a small dividend. The stock remained stagnant for about a year. Then along came the electronic game craze and the stock soared. Toward the end of 1979, the stock moved from the mid-twenties to the low forties and we sold it. By early 1982, the stock had returned to the mid-teens.

Faberge is a worldwide manufacturer and marketer of cosmetics and toiletries. At the end of 1978, the SE/S was $21. When we began buying the stock, the price had been mostly under $10 for a number of years. Then a subsidiary company developed a household device for the early detection of breast cancer. The stock jumped from the low teens to high twenties in a six-month period, so we sold it. By 1982, the stock had returned to the mid-teens.

Franklin Mint is the largest private mint in the world. It creates, produces, and markets limited edition collector's items. At the end of 1977, the SE/S was over $8. This company was a former institutional favorite that fell from grace when its earnings collapsed from $2.92 to $.85. We bought the stock when they "blew it out" in late 1978 and early 1979 to under $7. Warner Communications had bought some of the stock at much higher prices a few years earlier. As the earnings continued to improve, they bought more of the stock. They finally made a tender offer for the whole company at $27. We sold early at $25 and left a few points for the "arbitrage boys." You never can tell when a "deal" is going to fall through.

Exhibit 7.4 entitled "PSYCLE Profits" shows the price action of 14 stocks in which my clients and I have made substantial gains. Again, I would suggest that you get a long term chart book and examine each one carefully. They are representative of the type of experiences that you may have in the future. You're not going to be able to profitably utilize this approach until you understand it. So, do some homework. It'll be more fun than you might think.

Exhibit 7.4 ***PSYCLE Profits***

STOCK	BUY	PRICE	SELL	PRICE	YEARS	PROFIT
ALLIS CHALMERS	2/72	$14	8/78	$37	6.5	164%
REYNOLDS METALS	9/72	$17	3/76	$40	3.5	135%
MOLY CORP	10/73	$22	7/77	$59	3.8	168%
BUDD CORP	1/76	$13	1/78	$31	2.0	138%
NATIONAL AIRLINES	4/77	$10	9/78	$38	1.5	280%
MILTON BRADLEY	5/77	$13	2/80	$41	2.8	215%
READING & BATES	9/77	$13	11/79	$26	2.2	100%
FABERGE	7/79	$ 9	3/81	$27	1.8	200%
SEABOARD COASTLINE INDUSTRIES	3/79	$26	9/80	$54	1.6	107%
PULLMAN	4/80	$20	8/80	$40	.4	100%
FRANKLIN MINT	1/78	$ 6	1/81	$25	3.0	316%
ROHM & HAAS	10/77	$32	6/81	$70	3.8	119%
NEWMONT MINING	12/77	$17	1/80	$47	2.1	176%
PHELPS DODGE	5/78	$22	2/80	$48	1.8	118%

PATIENCE

When the stock market averages go down over an extended period of time, usually the best we can hope for is that our stocks hold their own. However, because it is a market of stocks, sometimes we will be more fortunate. My recommendations, when I was a guest on *Wall Street Week*, on August 15, 1980, are a case in point. I mentioned only three stocks, but they substantially outperformed the DJIA over a two-year period. The table below tells the story.

Table 7.1 ***Three Stocks***

	8/15/80	8/16/82	% Change
DJIA	966.72	792.42	−18%
Outboard Marine	13¾	21⅛	+54%
McLean Trucking	10¼	17½	+71%
Mohasco	8	10¼	+28%

The average gain of my *Wall Street Week* recommendations was a 51% increase versus an 18% decrease in the DJIA. At the end of 1982, the portfolio had appreciated about 95%. In that 2.4 year period, the DJIA had exceeded its August 1980 figure by less than 9%. The *Wall Street Week* selections did over *ten* times better than the DJIA. I would be willing to take that kind of relative performance anytime. Of course, it doesn't always happen that way but, by following this approach, we will have many more surprises on the upside than on the downside. Now, let's examine some positions that hadn't worked out by the summer of 1982. Remember that I own all these stocks in my own personal portfolio; so do many of my clients.

Bell & Howell makes and distributes a variety of products and services that facilitate communications and learning. At the end of 1973, the SE/S was $30. When we began buying the stock, the price had dropped to about $21 and continued to drop to about $10. Since we bought it, the stock has been trading from the mid-teens to the mid-twenties. In 1980, the stock traded in the mid-thirties for a short time. It has been one of the "slowest" moving stocks that we've had. The company originally was a manufacturer of high-quality cameras that ran into stiff overseas competition; it has been trying to diversify into other areas. In midsummer of 1982, the stock was trading around $20. Obviously, we haven't made any money in the stock over the past eight years.

Ford Motor Company is the second largest automobile manufacturer in the world. At the end of 1979, the SE/S was $86. When we began buying the stock, the price had dropped to the low twenties. In 1980 and 1981, Ford lost about $2 billion. Several times the stock dropped into the teens. Also, the company completely eliminated its dividend. However, in the summer of 1982, the stock was trading around $24, which is about the price that it was when we began to accumulate it.

Goodyear is the largest tire and rubber manufacturer in the world. At the end of 1979, the SE/S was $30. When we began buying the stock, the price had dropped to the low teens. The stock had come back down to test its lows made in 1974. The drop had occurred probably because investors felt that skyrocketing oil prices would dramatically impact on profits. This is because petroleum is used extensively in its products. Regardless of the rationale, it was possible to buy a leader in its industry at less than 50% of SE/S. The price was as cheap as it had been in 20 years. By midsummer of 1982, the stock was trading around $24. It was up over 80% from where we had bought it.

Outboard Marine is the world's largest maker of outboard engines. At the end of 1978, the SE/S was $32. Do you remember the gasoline shortage of the late 1970s? That's when you had to wait in line for an hour just to partially fill up your car. People were panic-stricken that there wouldn't be enough fuel even to get back and forth from work. Cruising around the lake in your boat seemed to be a "thing of the past." Nevertheless, that's when we were buying the stock. It had dropped into the low teens. The company had to cut the dividend in 1980, but they still made EPS of $.28. Unfortunately, they had to lay off about 25% of their work force to do it. In 1981, the company earned $2.70 per share and the stock had traded into the low twenties. In the summer of 1982, the stock was trading around $23.

Sears, Roebuck & Company is a leading merchandiser that has expanded into insurance and other financial services. It is another example of a fallen "glamour growth" stock of a past decade. When we bought it in the mid-teens, it had dropped about 75% from its 1972 highs. The SE/S was $23 in 1979. In the summer of 1982 the stock had moved back to about $20.

Skyline is the nation's largest builder of manufactured housing. At the end of 1978, the SE/S was $9. However, the company had no long-term debt and over $5 a share in cash and equivalents. In 1981, the stock traded to almost $20. Many of my clients sold at least part of their positions and some sold all of their stock. Unfortunately, there was no follow-through to higher prices and the stock slipped back into the low teens. So we did okay on this one. We just need to wait for the price to get back up again.

Exhibit 7.5 "Patience" summarizes 18 stock positions that haven't reached their price objectives. Again, I would strongly suggest that you individually examine each long-term price chart. Which ones have done well since the summer of 1982? It's been my experience that many stocks will make their move within 2 to 4 years. Why don't you check and see how well my "dogs" have performed?

An important ingredient of this approach is waiting. You have to wait for the stocks to get into the buy zone. After you've bought them, you have to wait for them to move out of the buy zone. Then you have to wait for them to get into the sell zone or exhibit accelerating price movement to the upside.

Exhibit 7.5 *Patience*

STOCK	BUY	PRICE	PRICE MID '82	YEARS
COLGATE PALMOLIVE	2/80	$13	$17	2.4
BELL HOWELL	5/74	$21	$20	8.1
EASTMAN KODAK	1/80	$47	$72	2.5
FEDERATED DEPARTMENT STORES	2/80	$23	$44	2.4
GILLETTE	2/80	$21	$35	2.4
HEUBLEIN	7/77	$23	$40	5.0
ARMSTRONG WORLD INDUSTRIES	3/79	$16	$16	3.3
FORD MOTOR CO.	4/80	$23	$24	2.2
GOODYEAR TIRE	2/80	$13	$24	2.4
OUTBOARD MARINE	10/79	$12	$23	3.7
MOHASCO	3/79	$11	$11	3.3
MCLEAN TRUCKING	3/80	$ 9	$17	2.3
K-MART	2/80	$19	$19	2.4
SEARS	10/80	$16	$20	1.7
U.S. STEEL	12/80	$22	$20	1.8
UAL, INC.	12/80	$16	$21	1.8
SKYLINE	3/79	$10	$14	3.3
XEROX	9/81	$42	$33	.7

However, there will be occasions when the patience of Job won't do you any good.

Yes, you're probably going to occasionally encounter a few disasters using this technique. This will happen when the financial situation of the company deteriorates so badly that it is forced into bankruptcy. By that time, the price will have dropped to less than 50% of what you paid. Even if the company recovers, it may take a very long time. By then, you probably will have already used it as a tax loss candidate. Business risk is the reason that you must diversify. It is a risk you have with any equity investment.

If you want to avoid business risk as much as possible, then stay with higher quality companies. These are seasoned companies with relatively low amounts of long-term and short-term debt. For instance, Eastman Kodak and Federated Department Stores are much higher quality companies than McLean Trucking or Mohasco. However, you will also forego a number of legitimate profit opportunities if you buy only "brand names." Now, we're going to try to show you how to balance risk and reward in the implementation of this approach.

A PORTFOLIO APPROACH

Do you remember my friend Bart? He's the guy that helped me shelter my income in the Magic Oil deal. In fact, it was so "sheltered" that I'll never see any of it again. He was a compulsive salesman. When he got excited about an investment, he could be very persuasive. Unfortunately, he was one-dimensional. That is, he could focus on only one idea at a time.

In the late 1970s he found a little Houston-based oil company that was destined to soar in price. Although the price action will be correct, we will mercifully change the name to Go-Go Oil Company. Let's say the ticker symbol is

GOL. Bart never tired of telling the story of GOL to anyone who would listen. This included his customers, other brokers, and even the clients of some of the brokers in the office. As the stock began to move upward, people began to pay more attention to Bart. He became the recognized authority on GOL.

There was a client of one of the other account executives who used to come into the office everyday at lunch to check the market. Let's call him Big George. He was a tall, nice-looking guy in his late forties. He was always smoking a $2 cigar. Big George really liked to play the stock market. He was a dream client of any stockbroker. He had a lot of money and could buy in size. That means thousands of shares at a time. He also had "nerves of steel." He would use margin and keep on increasing his position as the stock climbed in price. The stock market was a passion with him. He carefully studied any situation in which he invested. All things considered, he was a very competent speculator.

Guess what happened? You're right again! Bart got Big George interested in GOL and he began to buy the stock. In 1977, the stock traded from $3 to $7. In 1978, the stock traded as high as $9. For most of 1979, GOL traded between $10 and $12. However, in September it jumped to $20. By December, it had traded over $30. Big George was buying it all the way up and he was making a "killing."

In January 1980, I saw Big George at a prestigious luncheon club. He was beaming: "Yesterday was a big day," he said (GOL had jumped from $30 to $32.) When I guessed he must have made over $100,000 he just smiled. Then I asked him, "When are you going to sell?" His face produced a shocked expression as if I had just kicked him in the groin. He looked at me in disgust and said, "The stock will be over $60 by the summer. Besides that, there were several major oil companies that want to buy out Go-Go Oil," he told me. "But George," I said, "the stock has gone up over 1000% in two years." "Just the beginning," he said as he rushed off. That was the last time I ever saw Big George smile.

It later turned out that most oil stocks had made their highs at about that time. Then prices collapsed. By March, GOL was back to the teens. Big George had run out of money and had to liquidate 40,000 shares to meet his margin calls. Unfortunately, he had the same disease as many other speculators. He loved to buy all the way up, but no amount of profits was ever enough. He sold only when he was forced out.

By 1982, "oil fever" had wiped out many of the clients of my friends in the brokerage business. Some of the brokers had also seen their own personal fortunes evaporate. Although GOL recoiled upward to the low forties at the end of 1980, few investors sold their stock. All the way up, Bart was optimistic. He "fanned the fires" of the takeover rumors. He must have spent at least two hours a day talking to stockbrokers all over Houston urging them to buy the stock. By the summer of 1982, GOL was trading at $5. Bart had wiped out his clients and himself. He had watched his own personal equity in Go-Go Oil Company start at nothing, rise to over $1 million, and then return to nothing. Maybe we can learn a few lessons form the experiences of Bart and Big George with GOL.

One of the problems with a company like Go-Go Oil Company is that it invariably attracts a lot of "hot money." What's that? Well, it's speculative money that is further leveraged by the use of margin. Also, in many cases, there is a very heavy concentration of the stock in the client's account. The rationale is that since the selected stock is doing so well and has such great prospects for the future, why own anything else. Remember that it is much casicr to scll a clicnt a rising stock with a good story.

The faster a stock rises, the more "hot money" is attracted to it just as flies to honey. Leverage works great when the stock is rising. It is a tool to dramatically build the speculator's equity. As the price invariably starts down, it quickly turns into a sword that hacks their capital into oblivion. Just ask Bart or Big George, if you don't believe it.

We don't want to be too hard on the speculators because we need them. They'll be there eagerly bidding for our stock when it's soaring into the sell zone. Also, we'll be taking their stock off their hands when it's in the buy zone. They'll be "puking" it up because they can't stand any more loses or because they are being forced out through margin calls. We certainly don't want to change their behavior.

Now, there is nothing wrong with using financial leverage, but it must be used properly and with moderation. That means at least six to eight positions in your portfolio. Never concentrate in one or two stocks with high leverage. You're just asking for financial pain. In general, you should not use leverage until you become a very seasoned investor. The best time to use margin is when it's the hardest. That is, when stocks in general have taken an extended drop. Always leave yourself leeway so that you'll have plenty of staying power.

I am fortunate to know a number of highly professional account executives in my business. I also know some that have absolutely no idea what they're talking about. Regardless, I have never met one who has convinced me that he, or she, could consistently predict stock price movements. Even if there were some that could, the emotions of fear and greed produced by the PSYCLE would get in their way. Most of the ones who do a good job for their clients are conservative. However, a good AE will be an important ingredient in your stock market success.

I would suggest that you choose your AE with a great deal of care. No matter how determined you may be to follow through with this program, he will have more effect on your decisions than you may realilze. Most individuals date several people before they select their spouse, so, you may want to talk to a number of AEs before your make a selection. Although changing brokers is much easier than getting a divorce, making the wrong choice can be as expensive.

First of all, you should narrow your selection to a full-service firm with a good research department. You want to feel confident that you have a viable company when it's time to buy your stock. A good place to start is to call the branch office manager of several firms. Tell him that you are a conservative investor who likes to buy quality companies at distressed prices. Ask him to recommend an AE to you who has the same philosophy. He will be more than happy to try and accommodate you. If you are starting with a small amount of money, you may get one of the newer brokers in the business. That's just fine. There are many sincere and dedicated individuals that enter this profession every year.

One of the most important ingredients in this relationship is for your AE to be compatible with your investment philosophy. The best way to find that out is to ask him, or her, about their approach. Once he knows what you're looking for, a good AE can show you stocks that you may want to consider. Of course, you must decide if it fits our investment strategy. After he observes a few of your successes, he may become more interested in our approach. Anyway, just having someone with whom you can share your victories makes the winning more fun.

In reality, you're going to have to do some work to make this approach viable. You're going to have to develop a system to select and follow your stocks. Many private, part-time investors simply do not have the time to follow their investments. They are too busy making a living. The paradox is that many work hard for their money only to squander it on emotional investment decisions. This approach should help you avoid that trap. It should also leave you plenty of time for pursuing your profession and having fun (we'll discuss that in more detail in the next chapter).

The most necessary tool of this approach is the long-term price chart. In my opinion, the best place to find the chart of the stock you want is *Moody's Handbook of Common Stocks*. It provides easy access to the financial information on over 900 stocks. The charts cover price data of about 20 years and are adjusted for splits and dividends. You can get one new book every quarter for a subscription price of about $140 per year. That's very little compared to most other investor publications.

Next, we need a systematic way to follow our stocks. I would suggest that you use a weekly data form as shown in Exhibit 7.6 (the left side is shown). You can design your own or copy this one. It doesn't have to be fancy. As you begin to follow a stock, simply place a sheet in a three-ring notebook. Across the top you can record the current year, number of shares outstanding, the name of the company, and the ticker symbol. There are 52 weeks in a year. That means that there are 26 weeks from January through June and 26 weeks from July through December. Wherever you are within the year, you simply start on that Friday's close.

The next thing to do is to cut the chart out of your Moody's book and place it on your weekly data sheet (you may find tape that sticks on both sides helpful). The form is designed to be able to alternate your charts on either side. This makes your pages lie flatter. I would also draw lines at the top and the bottom of your price chart to indicate the buy zone and sell zone. There is a place to record other pertinent information if you want to use it, however, it's not necessary.

It is also helpful to have a file for each of your stocks. In it you can keep annual reports, quarterly reports, research comments, and news articles. Do not keep anything in your notebook but your weekly data sheets. Everything else related to your chosen company goes into your file. If you don't follow this suggestion, your notebook will soon become messy and cumbersome.

Exhibit 7.6 *Weekly Data Form*

CURRENT YEAR **NAME**

JAN–JUN DATE	CLOSE	1 WK CHG/%	4 WK CHG/%	13 WK CHG/%	26 WK CHG/%	52 WK CHG/%
1						
2						
3						
4						
5						
6						
7						
8						
9						
10						
11						
12						
13						
14						
15						
16						
17						
18						
19						
20						
21						
22						
23						
24						
25						
26						

If you don't do anything else, go through the weekend edition of your local paper and record Friday's close, one week change, and the date. You should be able to do at least two per minute. After you've recorded all the data, then you may go back and spend more time with an individual stock if you desire. You should make a sincere effort to record the data every week. The best way to do this is to set aside 20 or 30 minutes at the same time on the weekend or on Monday. However, if you do miss a week, don't worry about it. Just skip that slot and do next weekend's data. Otherwise, the task may seem too burdensome.

The rest of the columns across the page are used only when you feel that they are necessary. They are used to get sudden price moves into perspective. It is a technique to measure the magnitude of crowd psychology and is most helpful when you have a stock approaching a price where you have predetermined that you want to take action.

The Annualized Percentage Change (APC) is pretty much my own theory. I've never seen anyone use an approach that resembles this one; certainly not in the way that I use it. Remember that the faster that prices go up, the more most of the players think they will continue to go up. In my opinion, the evidence points to just the opposite.

If you go back and examine the actual uptrend and downtrend phases of the charts, you will see that the stocks usually reach their bottoms or tops in less than two years, once they start to move. Remember, we expect the most volatile price movement to the upside (conviction) at the end of an uptrend phase. This is when the majority is the most optimistic. The buyers are aggressive and the sellers are reluctant. Also, we expect the most volatile price movement on the downside (capitulation) at the end of a downtrend phase. This is when the majority is the most pessimistic. The buyers are reluctant and the sellers are aggressive. The use of APC will help us keep in focus that we're supposed to buy low and sell high.

To use Annualized Percentage Change, you must convert the time period you are using into an annual rate. This assumes that the rate of change would continue for the whole year. To do this, simply multilply the one-week percentage change by 52, the four-week percentage change by 13, the thirteen-week percentage change by 4, and the twenty-six-week percentage change by 2. Of course, the 52-week percentage change is the number that we want. APC is based on the conclusion that the steeper the price movement, the less likely it is able to sustain itself. For example, it is rare to see a stock go up more than 100% in a year or drop more than 50% in a year. There are no hard and fast rules for APC. It is simply an intuitive tool. You will gain skill and perception as you use it.

Let's look at Rohm & Haas as an example of how we may have used APC in order to buy and sell a stock. In 1976, the stock dropped form $76 to $44. That was an APC of 42%. Toward the end of 1977, the stock dropped from $51 to $30 in a twenty-six-week period. That's 41%. Multiplying by 2, we get an APC of 82%. That's a pretty steep drop. Also, the stock is in what we consider the buy zone because it is testing the 1970 lows. Sure enough, the stock stopped going down and began to go sideways for a couple of years. In other words, an APC of 82% would mean that the stock would drop to zero in approximately one year and three months. That doesn't make good sense.

In a twelve-month period from early 1980 to early 1981, Rohm & Haas went from $33 to $55. The APC was 66%. In the first six months of 1981, the stock went from a low of around $47 to $71. The APC was 102%. That's a pretty good move, especially since the stock was getting into long-term resistance. In a four-week period that ended in late June, the stock moved up from about $62 to $70. The APC was 154%.

The stock also gapped up $2 in price during one week; in other words, it closed at $68 one day and opened at $70 the next. The buyers were acting very aggressive. It was time to sell.

Getting started with this approach may produce some mental anguish. This will be expecially true of investors who already have a portfolio of stocks. You will have emotional attachments to some of your stocks. You willl probably have some losses. However, all of them will have to be considered a source of funds for PSYCLE stocks. The first step is to examine the price charts on all your companies. Then try to determine where they fit on the PSYCLE.

Stocks that may be deemed to be somewhere in the confidence, conviction, or complacency phase should be watched very carefully or sold immediately. Other stocks should be sold as new buying opportunities present themselves. This is going to require some judgment calls. They won't be perfect even after you've been doing it for years. But, you have to start somewhere. The only way that you gain any skill is through practice. Don't get discouraged. It's going to take a while for you to internalize this approach and execute it in a confident and seasoned manner.

Now, add up the value of the cash and securities that you're going to commit to this approach. Of course, you may be starting with only money. That's fine. Just take the number and divide by 8 to determine your position size. For instance, if you had $50,000, you would divide by 8 and get $6250. To give yourself a little margin for error, assume that you'll put about $6000 into each position. So, you would buy $6000 worth of a stock even if you had to buy an odd lot amount (an odd lot is less than 100 shares). What if you only have $500 to get started? Then, you put about $60 in each position. Of courses, if you have $500,000 to invest, you may want to consider 20 positions. In general, the more money you have to invest, the more stocks you should own.

Some investors may prefer to operate entirely by themselves. That is, they don't want anyone else's opinion. They want to make their own decisions. One helpful independent source is *The Value Line Investment Survey*. It has a lot of basic factual data. It can be found in the business section of most libraries. Also, Standard & Poor's Corporation has individual information stock sheets on most NYSE, ASE, and OTC stocks. The price charts are for only 7 years, but they're better than nothing. You should be able to get them from your stockbroker or local library.

If you examine the monthly bar charts of the companies in the last two sections, you may be hard-pressed to find a relationship between earnings and stock price movements. We bought stocks with good earnings and stocks with no earnings. We sold stocks with low P/E ratios and stocks with high P/E ratios. The only consistency was that all the stocks had fluctuated fairly dramatically over time. Rationalizations in retrospect are always available for those who believe that they can predict stock price movements. The one conclusion that you can get for sure from the price charts is that there must be many, many players who can't do it.

There is one final note. There will be those players who criticize this approach. They may argue convincingly that this strategy will only work in the topsy-turvy market environment of the past 15 years. In a long-term bull market, they will say that the investor will miss many profit opportunities by selling too soon. My advice would be not to pay too much attention to these players. They're the same ones that only get interested in buying stocks when they get to their highs. Just nod and smile as if in agreement with them. Let them continue with their Child ego fantasies. We'll need them when it's time to unload our stocks as they accelerate into the *conviction* phase.

One of my longtime clients recently remarked to me that he thought that we had been a little "lucky" (preparation meeting opportunity) over the years with the stocks that we had owned. He told me that it seemed that his friends and co-workers took massive losses with some regularity. He further observed that although we've had setbacks, the value of his account continues to increase over the years. He felt that we had, indeed, been fortunate.

After dutifully listening to his remarks, I had to remind him of several of our past conversations. Although he rarely questions my advice now, that was not always the case. I pointed out to him that I had had to twist his arm on a few occasions to get him to buy such stocks as National Airlines and Franklin Mint. Later, I had to plead with him to keep him from selling for a five or six point profit. Finally, when it came time to get out, he was reluctant because he felt they were going higher. I told him the only luck involved with his stock portfolio was that he had me for a stockbroker. That sounds pretty egotistical, doesn't it? I thought I had *earned* the right to say that to him.

How had I done that? Because I had to suffer many failures, much frustration, emotional and financial pain before I became successful in the stock market. I had to examine and reject many preconceived notions commonly held about making money in stocks. Unfortunately, this was only internalized by trial and error. Before you break into tears, I might tell you that these mistakes were all necessary ingredients in my learning experience. Although my dues seemed unfairly high, I wouldn't change even one trade. I'll own up to every one of them. I embrace every one of my disasters as a learning experience. You see, I had a particularly fanciful Child Ego State. It just took an undue amount of pain before I could freely admit that I couldn't predict stock price movements. This investment approach is my reality of the stock market. It is simply the only way that works for me. It will also work for *you*, if you let it.

8

A Balanced Lifestyle

INVESTMENT GOALS

Definite goals are necessary for achievement. Success can only be measured against a predetermined frame of reference. It is important that any financial goals be realistic and attainable. We all want to accumulate wealth, but how fast can we expect to do it? Remember that one of the biggest problems for most investors is that they have an unrealistic expectation about the return that they should receive on their capital.

John Templeton was ranked the number one mutual fund manager from 1955 to 1980. Over the 25-year period, a $10,000 investment in his Templeton Growth Fund would have increased to $243,881. The original investment was multiplied 24.3881 times. How did he attain that enviable performance record? All he did was increase his investment base by about 14% every year on average. In other words, he achieved a compound growth of 14% on the $10,000. This is a before tax rate of return.

The miracle of compound growth is the only way people will accumulate wealth over a long period of time. It is the rate at which you should expect your capital to grow when you average your good investments with your bad ones.

There may be years that you actually lose money. That's okay, because there should be years when you will do very well. The question is to be answered is simply this: What is the continuous rate of return that you should expect on your capital?

Lets examine some historic data. A good benchmark would be the performance of the pension fund managers. These are the professionals who are paid to manage retirement funds. On Tuesday, April 15, 1980, the results of a study done by A. G. Becker's Fund Evaluation Service was published in the *Wall Street Journal*. Becker tracks the quarterly performance of about 3,500 tax-exempt pension and profit sharing funds with more than $90 billion of assets. According to Becker, the annualized return for the median equity portfolio was 4.3% per year for the 15-year period from 1965 to 1979. This 4.3% rate of return only represents the mid-point of investment results. By definition, half of the funds did better than the median and half of the funds did worse.

That kind of performance is not exactly "shooting out the lights." Over half the funds would have been better off if their money had been in a passbook savings account at 5%. Also, they probably would have saved a lot of management fees. John Templeton's track record of 14% return looks pretty remarkable against the median fund performance of 4.3%.

To come up with some idea of the returns that we can try to achieve, let's go back and examine the recommendations that I made on *Wall Street Week*. The price increases are easily documented. The portfolio is not a totally fair comparison because there were only three recommendations over a 2.4-year period ending December, 1982. Nevertheless, the stocks also did well in a down market which should give the approach some credibility. The DJIA increased less than 9%. However, the average gain of the *Wall Street Week* picks was 95%. If it were possible to continuously get that compound rate of return, you would double your money, after taxes, about every 3.25 years; but that's not a realistic expectation.

Before we try to come to a final conclusion, let's go back and reflect on the nature of financial markets. It is important to understand that the vast majority of money that flows into stock and bond investments was made *someplace else*. That's correct. Financial markets were never designed to make people rich overnight. Very few investors have ever made and kept a lot of money by "playing the stock market." Financial markets are best utilized for the preservation and slow accumulation of wealth. It is unrealistic to expect much more than a 10% to 15% pretax compound rate of return on your capital over a long period of time.

Within the framework of our discussion, it is my personal belief that an investor should be able to double his money, after taxes, every six years. That means you would compound your money at 12.25%, after taxes, every year. Believe it or not, that is a very high rate by historic standards. Even if you did only half as well as the 12.25%, you would have done much better than the median retirement fund in Becker's survey. Also, don't forget that the problem for many investors is losing money, not relative performance. It's possible that you may do better than 12.25% using this approach. However, when setting investment goals, it is better to get ones that you feel are attainable. Then you can be surprised on the upside.

What will it take to double your money after taxes every six years? It's not as hard as you may think, using this approach. Here's an example that doesn't include commissions. Let's assume that you buy 100 shares of a stock at $20 a share and then you sell it six years later at $40 per share. You now have a long-term capital gain of $2000. Further, let's assume that the stock paid $100 per year in dividends. That's a 5% yield on your cost basis. Now, how much money would you have after taxes?

Let's assume a marginal tax rate of 40%. That means you keep only $60 out of your $100 in dividends. So, over six years you would receive $360 after taxes. When you sell your stock, 60% of the $2000 is excluded from taxes. So, 40% of $800 is $320 and that's what you owe Uncle Sam. You are left with $3,680. However, you have the $360 that you received in aftertax dividends. So, your total amount of tax free cash is $2,040. If you compounded the dividends at 12.25%, you would have at least another $100 that would cover the commissions. The point is that you can get an approximate 12.25% aftertax compound on your money if your stock doubles in six years. This estimate assumes payment of a moderate dividend.

If you go back and examine Exhibit 7.4, PSYCLE Profits, you'll see that a six-year time period from bottom to top is not unreasonable. Of course, some will go up much faster and there will be a few that won't make it all. However, it has been my experience that if you put all the trades together, you will have a realistic shot of at least doubling your money every six years. Past performance can be no guarantee of future success, but this approach is still a conservative and consistent way to invest your money.

There are two ingredients necessary for the accumulation of wealth. The first one is that you must have a reasonable way to make your money grow. We've certainly discussed that subject. The second one is that you must have a systematic plan to add new money every year. If you can project how much money you can invest every year, you can come up with the final figure. It is very important that you go through this exercise in projecting your wealth. Having written, defined long-term goals is the most important ingredient of success. To make this task easier, we need to understand compound growth tables.

Let's assume that you have just turned 29 years of age. You have $1000 to invest now. Your objective is to accumulate $1,000,000 and then retire. Further, you project that you will be able to add $1000 each year for the next six years, $2000 per year for the following six years, $3000 per year for the six years after, $4000 per year for the next six years, and $5000 per year for the final six years. Also, once your capital is greater than $500,000, no more new money will be added after you complete that six-year increment. The question is, How old will you be when you retire?

There are two problems to solve in order to get the correct solution. The first one is a lump sum compounded at 12.25%. The second one is an annuity (annual payment) compounded at 12.25%. Turn to Exhibit 8.1 "Aftertax Compound Growth."

Let's examine the first six years in both cases (the cents have been dropped to simplify the example). In the case of the lump sum, simply multiply $1000 by 1.1225 to get $1122. In other words, by the end of the year, $1000 has increased by 12.25% to $1122. In the second year, the $1122 increases by 12.25% to $1260. This goes on for six years until the $1000 has grown to $2000. In other words, it has doubled. The annuity table is the same except that you must add $1000 at the beginning of the year. Over a six-year period, you added $6000. At the end of that period, it has grown to $9166. By adding $2000 and $9166 you have accumulated $11,166. You started with an initial investment of $1000 and added $1000 each year for six years. You put in a total of $7000 aftertax dollars and it is worth $11,166 after six years. That's not too bad.

Now you have a lump sum of $11,166 which you know will double in six years to $22,332. You also have an annual contribution of $2000. To see how much money you would have, simply multiply the $9166 figure by 2 to get $18,332. The annuity table is based on a $1000 annual contribution. So just multiply the six-year figure of $9166 by the number of $1000 contributions. In this case it would be 2. By adding the

Exhibit 8.1 *Aftertax Compound Growth*

YEAR	LUMP SUM OF $1000 @ 12.25%			ANNUITY OF $1000 @ 12.25%		
	Begin Year	***End Year***		***Begin Year***	***End Year***	
1	$1000	$1122		$1000	$1122	
2	$1122	$1260		$2122	$2382	
3	$1260	$1414		$3382	$3796	
4	$1414	$1587		$4796	$5384	
5	$1587	$1782		$6384	$7166	
6	$1782	$2000		$8166	$9166	
		$2000	plus		$9166	equals
	a lump sum of *$11,166* @ 12.25%			Annuity of $2000 @ 12.25%		
12		$22,332	plus		$18,332	equals
	a lump sum of *$40,664* @ 12.25%			Annuity of $3000 @ 12.25%		
18		$81,328	plus		$27,498	equals
	a lump sum of *$108,826* @ 12.25%			Annuity of $4000 @ 12.25%		
24		$217,652	plus		$36,664	equals
	a lump sum of *$254,316* @ 12.25%			Annuity of $5000 @ 12.25%		
30		$508,632	plus		$45,830	equals
	a lump sum of *$554,462* @ 12.25%					
36		$1,108,924				

two figures together, you would have accumulated $40,664 aftertax dollars in 12 years. So far, your cash contributions would be $19,000.

For each six-year period thereafter, we repeat the process. In the next six years, your $40,665 would have increased to $81,328. When you include the value of your $3000 annuity, your capital increases to $108,826 on a $37,000 contribution. In 36 years, or by the time you are 65 years old, you've accumulated $1,108,924. The total amount of your aftertax contributions over your lifetime was $91,000. Most of that came in your latter years when you should have been able to afford it. Exhibit 8.1A shows graphically how your equity would grow in value.

There is another way to accumulate $1 million by the time you retire: It's called an Individual Retirement Account (IRA). Anyone can contribute as much as $2000 a year and you can write it off your income taxes. That's right! It's tax deductible. A $2000 annuity compounded at 12% would grow to $1,049,087 in 37 years. So, all you have to do is start when you're 28 years old. However, there is one difference in the IRA: you must pay taxes when you begin to withdraw the money. Regardless, it is a very good way to accumulate wealth.

If you're 41 years old, you have 4 six-year periods until you are 65. If you have $67,500, you can accumulate $1,000,000 without adding any more money. All you have to do is be able to compound your capital at 12.25% after taxes.

Table 8.1

Age	Portfolio Value
41	$ 67,500
47	125,000
53	250,000
59	500,000
65	1,000,000

Exhibit 8.1A ***Accumulating $1,000,000***

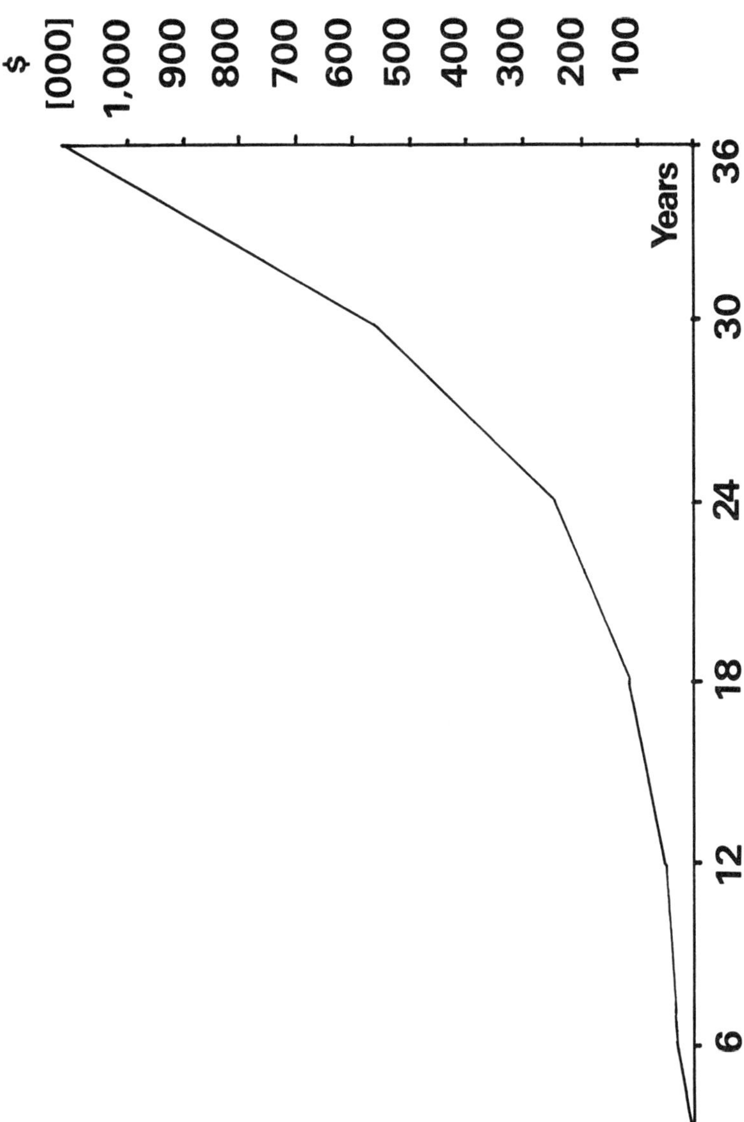

Table 8.2

Age	Portfolio Value
47	+ $91,660
53	$ 183,320 + 91,660 = $ 274,980
59	$ 549,960 + 91,660 = $ 641,620
65	$1,283,204 + 91,660 = $1,374,900

Let's assume that you are 41 years old but you don't have any money to invest. However, your children are now able to pay their own way and you just got a big raise. You decide that you can save and invest $10.000 aftertax dollars every year. Let's go back to our compound growth tables to get the answer. By the time you're 65 years old, you will have $1,374,900.

What we have shown you is the slow way to become a millionaire. Admittedly, we have assumed that this investment approach will double your money after taxes every six years. That may seem optimistic, but it is well within my experience level of the past 10 years.

YOUR PSYCHOLOGY OF MONEY

Do you sincerely want more money? Yes, of course, you do. Doesn't everybody? But, how much *more* is enough? Why do you want it? What will you do with it? How will it make you feel? Do you think having more money will make you happier than you are now? What personal sacrifices will you be willing to make in order to accumulate more money? These are complex questions that each of us should examine and answer truthfully to ourselves. There is an important reason for this. The more realistic and healthy your attitude toward money, the easier it will be for you to control your fear and greed emotions when dealing in the stock market.

Our value system is a product of the conditioning that we received in the socioeconomic environment in which we were raised. Every adult has developed a certain psychology of money. We all have an ingrained belief system about money operating at an unconscious level. Many of our feelings are a result of the illusions and fantasies of our Child Ego State. In order for money to meaningfully contribute to our overall happiness, we should challenge these irrational beliefs.

Here are a few of the thoughts that we all have flashing through our minds in one form or another: "When I can afford a Cadillac, I'll be happy." "When I get a lot of money, I can associate with the 'beautiful people' in high society. That will make me feel important." "I've got to save for a rainy day." "People will like and respect me when I get rich." "My family will love and appreciate me because of the money that I make and the lifestyle that I provide for them." "I need to leave my kids a lot of money so they won't have to go through the tough times that I had to do. They will really love and appreciate me for that." Of course, some of our thoughts and feelings about money have certain amount of validity to them. However, some of them make us feel guilty and some of them are misconceptions.

The Hungry Child, in many of us, thinks of money as a "cure-all" for most of his inadequacies. He knows that money can buy a certain amount of personal prosperity. It can acquire a spacious and comfortable house. It gives one the opportunity to travel on exciting vacations. It also gives one the ability to buy fine clothes, jewelry, furs, and other luxury items. Money can be used as a tool to try to "buy" the love and admiration of family members by giving them maximum advantages in life. Of course, money is also seen as the ultimate symbol of success. Your Hungry Child may think that the more money you have, the more admiration you will have from friends and people in your business life. The power of money to provide financial independence, freedom from worry, and personal self-esteem often is misunderstood.

If you doubt the validity of the last statement, then why did the premature deaths of Elvis Presley and John Belushi occur? Despite fame and fortune, both men poisoned themselves with drugs. It seems evident that money, power, prestige, and professional success didn't do much to solve their feelings of inadequacy. Otherwise, why did they need to stay "high" most of the time in order to avoid reality. There must be a better explanation.

Let's examine how your psychology of money might fit into your hierarchy of needs. Abraham Maslow uses this model (Exhibit 8.2) to explain man's behavior. His theory postulates that man will work to satisfy his lowest level of needs. Once that has been accomplished, a higher level of needs or desires will emerge. He will then focus on satisfying that set of needs. For example, you can't think about your safety needs if you're starving to death. You might be driven to steal food, even knowing the consequences might be severe. In *Motivation and Personality* he cautions against applying this hierarchy of needs in a rigid manner. The boundaries are often vague and people feel the desire to satisfy these needs with varying degrees of motivation. For instance, an individual may satisfy only 50% of his safety needs before attending to his love and belonging needs.

In today's cosmopolitan society, high achievers basically can satisfy most of their psysiological, physical and acquisitive needs. As soon as these needs are taken care of adequately, they cease to motivate behavior. It is rather the desire to satisfy lofty goals and fulfill an unexpressed need for self-actualization that propel these people into the world they love.

By examining Maslow's hierarchy of needs, one must come to the conclusion that, at some point, money will provide only *marginal utility* in satisfying one's needs. What does that mean? Well, it's a term used in economics to define a small increment of benefit. Let's discuss an example in order to explain it better.

Do you know what one of the proudest days in a man's life is? It's the day he gets his own automobile. It gives him instant independence and mobility. It is a symbol of his ascendancy into adulthood. It doesn't matter whether the car

Exhibit 8.2 *Maslow's Hierarchy of Needs*

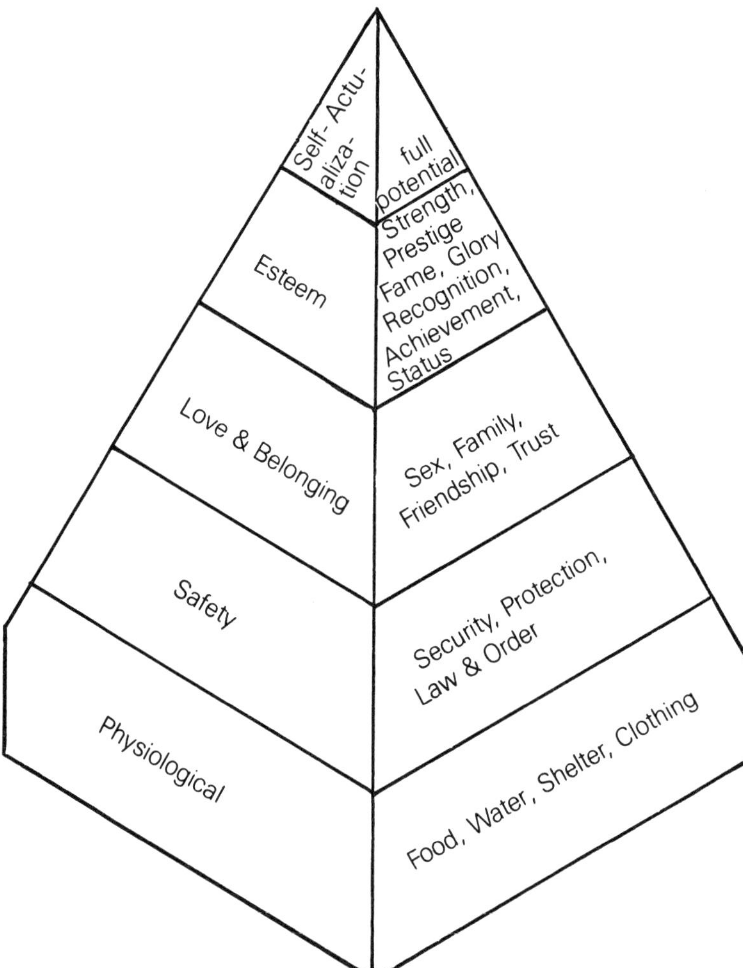

Data for diagram based on Heirarchy of Need in "A Theory of Motivation" in MOTIVATION AND PERSONALITY by Abraham H. Maslow. Copyright 1970 by Abraham H. Maslow, reprinted by permission of Harper & Row Publishers, Inc.

is an "old clunker" or a new one. Few moments in his life will have as much significance or pleasure. From then on, each new car that he acquires can only have marginal utility. If he buys an expensive Cadillac 20 years later, it could certainly help satisfy is esteem needs. However, the transportation and independence aspects of the automobile haven't changed. Certainly, buying two Cadillacs won't provide twice as much joy. Therefore, more money could only provide marginal utility under these circumstances.

Once you have enough money so that spending it, in a reasonable manner, is not an issue, then it can only provide marginal utility to many aspects of your life. This means that if you are married and can provide adequate food, shelter, and clothing for your family in a safe, secure environment, having more money will not add dramatically to your enjoyment of life. Some psychologists believe that incomes over $35,000 produce only very marginal improvements in the quality of one's life.

Of course, money can be an important ingredient in satisfying your esteem needs. If you acquire enough money to move from a $50,000 house into a $250,000 one, it will change your socioeconomic status. It means you might develop a new set of friends that are more affluent. Our Hungry Child wants to be part of the "beautiful people" in high society. When you proudly drive your new Cadillac, you feel important. Your Hungry Child views all of these prestige symbols as a source of strokes that can bolster his inadequate self-esteem. He is saying "Look at me. I'm important. I am succesful. I am worth something." But, we have to be careful because this false bravado may not be lasting.

Everyone desperately wants to have a positive self-esteem. This can be defined as a deep down feeling of one's own self-worth. However, the feelings of inferiority of our Hungry Child can frustrate us from attaining a healthy self-esteem. In today's buy-it-now and pay-for-it-later world, acquiring material prestige symbols may actually lead to neuroticism, not happiness. If you have a tendency to "flash" the trappings of material success, it may tell people that you're trying to compensate for a low self-esteem.

There is an incredible paradox that comes with professional success and the accumulation of monetary wealth. Often, the achievements are motivated by the desire of our Hungry Child for strokes, admiration, and respect. After the hard work, personal sacrifices, and pain, a cold reality may become apparent at the moment of triumph. Instead of accolades, our successes may generate envy, resentment, and jealousy from those we thought would have wished us well.

If you doubt the validity of that statement, then examine your feelings about someone whom you know is "doing better" than you are. If you are truthful, it's more likely that you'll feel at least slight resentment, envy, and jealousy rather than respect and admiration. It's a natural reaction of your Hungry Child to feel inadequate when comparing yourself against someone else who is "doing better."

There is not much that can be done about this phenomenon except to be as humble as possible about any successes that we may have. Also, our Adult must be aware that there will be few sincere well-wishers to applaud our victories. The people in our lives who really care about us will be the ones whom we have stroked and nurtured. In other words, the belief that monetary wealth can "buy" the admiration, respect, and love of other people is just a fantasy of our Hungry Child. Once we understand this sad reality, we can develop a healthier psychology of money.

There is another paradox when it comes to having money or the things that you can acquire with it. Once you possess something, it ceases to motivate your behavior. Your socioeconomic situation and the "toys" you can acquire only become a frame of reference. Eventually, they stop being as meaningful as they once were to you. This is a natural phenomenon that keeps us asking, "Is that all there is?"

It seems to me that the high achiever has a natural drive to increase his *personal power*. This could be defined simply as his inner forces and knowledge that help him to control his destiny. Maslow would define this as the highest need, which is his need for self-actualization. This means that Man has a natural drive to seek his full potential, whatever that may be. This is why no amount of money or material possessions will produce contentment. Unless a man or woman is continuously trying to raise themselves to a higher level of consciousness, they will be unfulfilled.

Henry Clay Lindgren wrote a book *Great Expectations: The Psychology of Money*. In it, he explored many misconceptions and myths people have regarding money. One of his most important findings was that the people who acquired wealth did not have it as a priority. Their money came to them because they focused their main attention on excelling in their chosen field of endeavor. Another way of saying this might be that money can be a by-product of self-actualization; but self-actualization rarely, if ever, comes from acquiring wealth.

It appears that the continuous pursuit of self-actualization is a way for men and women to transcend the feelings of inferiority of their Hungry Child. Self-actualization can be achieved only after one has satisfied his lower-level needs. We all want to experience the expansive emotions of happiness, success, self-confidence and peace of mind. How can we attain this? The answer is simple: We must continuously strive for personal growth. When we stop growing we naturally become frustrated. We allow ourselves to feel guilty, suffer anxiety and self-condemnation. When we cease growing, we start dying. William Butler Yeats said it best: "Happiness is neither virtue nor pleasure nor this thing nor that, but simply growth. We are happy when we arc growing."

It is natural for every high achiever to strive to accumulate wealth. However, money should be seen as a means to an end, not as an end in itself. For some, it is only a way to keep score. If we believe that material possessions will make us happy, we may be doomed to frustration, anxiety, or neurosis. At some point, more money is not necessarily better. Money can free us from many of the trivial details and drudgeries of life. In the sense that money gives us financial independence, it can satisfy our physiological and safety needs. After we've accumulated a certain amount of wealth, some of our esteem needs will be met. This can free us somewhat from certain fears, anxieties, frustrations, and failures. This should give us the time, opportunity, and energy for creative growth. That, of course, is the main ingredient in self-actualization.

In order to achieve our full potential, we must be able to simultaneously focus on the three important dimensions of our lives. We must be capable of setting and attaining professional goals, investment goals, and personal goals. This is the only way that we can become a self-actualized, balanced high achiever.

SUCCESS IS A PROCESS

When will you become a success? If you asked that question of a number of high achievers, you may get an answer like this: "I'll be a success when I become rich and happy." For many people, both the question and the answer contain complex misconceptions. It's probable that the terms success, rich, and happy are only vague fantasies of our Child Ego State.

To most people, success is a mystic goal line somewhere in the future. When they cross it, everything is going to be all right. Unfortunately, no matter how far they may climb up Maslow's Hierarchy of Needs, they never seem to get to the top. There is a reason for this. Success is not a static point in time and space for everyone. It is a process. That is, it's a step-by-step series of achievements (small successes) whose ultimate result is continuous self-actualization.

Now, let's define the term success as *the attainment of a predetermined goal*. Therefore, by definition, you must have a clear-cut objective or goal in mind before you can have a successful experience. When you attain a predetermined goal you will get a "winning feeling." This can be defined as a very positive sensation of self-worth. Depending on the importance of the goal, it can be almost euphoric. All high achievers want to feel like winners. This is because for an instant in time and space, they can feel self-worth, self-confidence, and self-esteem. The attainment of predetermined goals is one of the ultimate experiences of self-realization. There is nothing to match it.

Incidentally, the vast majority of people do not understand this relationship between success and predetermined goals. It is for this reason that some corporation presidents occasionally jump out the window of their 50th-floor offices. As long as they were striving to get to the top, they were vitalized. Once they reached their objective, the letdown was tremendous. They were incapable of setting other goals. Also, it is for this reason that many corporate executives go downhill rapidly after retirement. The average life expectancy is only about seven years. In actuality, there is no reason to ever stop feeling like a winner. As long as we can set and achieve even the smallest goal, we can continue to have successful experiences.

Our culture has scripted many of us to believe that the words rich and success mean the same thing. That is, your worth as a human being is the same as your "net worth" on your personal balance sheet. Yes, it sounds ridiculous when you say it, but subconsciously many indviduals believe it. People can engage in fraud, cheat, steal, or kill for money and still get a certain amount of respect because they are protected, in a sense, by their affluence.

Unfortunately, no matter how much wealth we accumulate, few of us will ever feel rich. It's a relative term. There will always be somebody with more material possessions and money than we have. It seems to me that the most important thing is to try and appreciate the value of money we have now. The man, or woman, who can give worth to all they possess is, indeed, rich.

Happiness is another relative term. It is not determined so much by outside circumstances, but rather by how we feel about our existing conditions. This means that happiness is purely a state of mind. You will be happy or unhappy depending on what's going on between your ears. So, we could define happiness as a state of mind in which we feel pleased about our current situation and positive about our future. Happiness is not something we can earn. It is not something we will deserve when we accomplish some future event. Happiness comes from within. More often than not, it is a by-product of the feelings we get when we are striving toward a goal that is important to us.

Some individuals believe that the "American dream" is to make a million dollars and then retire to a life of luxury and inactivity. Of course, this is another illusion of our Child Ego State. The joys of doing nothing are vastly overrated. When you work hard all week, your leisure time is enjoyable and relaxing. It is needed to "recharge your batteries." However, extended periods of living without trying to accomplish something would become incredibly boring. This would be especially true for the motivated high achiever who could make a million dollars in the first place.

There appears to be a lot of empirical evidence that creative people live longer than others. It seems that goals may increase the vitality of such groups as painters, writers, and inventors. For instance, Michelangelo did some of his most famous paintings after he was 80 years old. At 90, Edison was still actively inventing. In his 90s, Shaw was still writing plays. The creative accomplishment of goals increases our personal power and "turns us on" to life.

If the above discussion is valid, then we must view life as a long-distance journey. It is not a race where the prize is a million dollars and retirement. We are like the marathon runner without a final goal line. Each milestone is considered a successful accomplishment. The more we strive, the farther we can run. The more we work and learn, the more pathways are open to us. Our objective is to develop the endurance to go as far as possible. Life can be considered a game whose winners are the ones who enjoy the action day-by-day and keep on playing the longest.

Everyone who reads this book is a potential high achiever. What will enable him to become a high achiever? He must be willing to develop his skills of concentration, creativity, persuasion, intuition, and self-discipline. He must be able to use his imagination to visualize his intended results long before they are realized. He must use written goals to keep a definition of purpose and maintain a positive mental attitude. He must have enough insight to welcome his failures as necessary learning experiences. Under these circumstances, he can remain challenged and motivated throughout his life. This will contribute to his enjoyment and peace of mind.

What does all this have to do with making money in the stock market? Well, in my opinion, living a balanced life style is much more important than being consumed with the obsession of wealth. Money is transitory. It can be lost just as fast as it is made. There are many people who work hard and make a lot of money professionally. Unfortunately, they lose it through irrational "investments." Also, it is hard to accumulate wealth if you have a disastrous family life. You can be assured that you'll have to give over half of it to your former wife when you are divorced. Finally, millions of dollars won't be any good to you if you drop dead from a heart attack at 50 because you lead a stress-filled life. The balanced high achiever has a much better chance to increase his wealth if he's comfortable with the other aspects of his life.

The balanced high achiever should partition his life into three separate and distinct success areas or arenas. He will have to divide his time and efforts accordingly. This is necessary so that he may focus his psychic energy to achieve maximum results according to his own predetermined goals. An imbalance in one area can dampen his overall performance. The balanced high achiever should strive to be a professional success, an investment success, and a personal success. Let's briefly discuss some considerations in each area.

The creation of most wealth originates with one's chosen profession. That is, unless you inherit it, marry it, or steal it. Realistically, these are not options for the vast majority of people. As you save money apart from your living expenses, you create an investment capital. This will be the source of your future wealth. The more aftertax money that you can generate, the faster you can increase the amount of your wealth. Therefore, it is vital that you have a profession that you like and one that motivates you to excel.

This may be hard to belive, but many people give more thought to planning their summer vacation than to planning their career. A lot of individuals just stumbled into their job by blind chance. They don't like it, but are afraid to change. Writer Henry Thoreau said that these are the people who "lead lives of quiet desperation." Sadly, some are in professions because they are trying to satisfy family members. If you're just showing up every day for a 9-to-5 job, it's unlikely that you'll ever generate much excess investment capital.

Earlier, we said that people who acquired wealth did so because they excelled in their chosen field of endeavor. Therefore, if you have a profession in which you are intensely interested, feel creative, and are excited about going to work almost every day, then the chances are that you will be a high performer and the monetary rewards will be forthcoming.

It doesn't seem reasonable to expect a 22-year-old to make an accurate long-term decision about his life's work. Yet, somehow many think they should. In actuality, it may take several years, more formal education and a few bad decisions before one finds one's niche. The important thing is to keep on trying until one finds his chosen field. Most high achievers are happiest when they're working and being productive. So, the professional self-actualization will satisfy many needs besides producing monetary rewards.

This is not to say that you should turn into a workaholic, far from it. This is why the emphasis is on a balanced lifestyle. For the high achiever, work is a vital outlet for his aggressive juices. However, if it drains all his energies so that there is nothing left for the other areas of life, it can be self-destructive. The balanced high achiever must learn to know when to stop working, how to manage stress, when to take a vacation, how to delegate the work load, and how to say no to overcommitment. It's not easy, but it can be done.

Now that you are generating investment capital, how will you make decisions on where to employ it? That's a big problem for high achievers. Not that there is a lack of "investment opportunities." There are plenty of ways to squander one's hard-earned money. There are two reasons why the high achiever may not be an investment success. The first is his time and the second is his ego. We have talked about both before, but now let's focus on them individually for emphasis.

Even if they aren't workaholics, high achievers spend a considerable amount of their time and energy professionally. Fifty-to-sixty-hour work weeks are not uncommon. If they are making decisions on an "investment" by "investment" basis, they just don't have the time, energy, expertise, or inclination to make objective decisions. They may put some money into a situation just to "save taxes." Often, the "investments" are highly speculative and sold on "hype." Rarely are the risks involved totally understood. Each new investment requires a certain amount of "start up" time to get it into focus. Sadly for the high achiever, it is simply not available. Therefore, he may make an emotional decision instead of an objective one. It is little wonder that he may end up in bogus tax shelters or owning stocks that drop 50% in value.

Because he is good in his professional arena, he somehow believes that that expertise applies to his investment decisions. Also, he may feel that he must be a winner in the investment arena in order to be a "real man." Somehow, he is supposed to be "whiz" at making a lot of money in a very short period of time. When the inevitable disasters come, they are particularly painful. They tear away at the very foundations of his self-esteem and self-confidence. In my opinion, this is one of the main reasons why the high achiever should be very conservative with his money.

When you lose money on an "investment," you are a loser. Of course, everyone should expect a few bad decisions. The danger comes when an individual has a string of losses in a row. In this case, he may start to *feel* like a loser. This negative reinforcement can spread to his professional and personal life with unfavorable consequences. I've had investors tell me that they didn't mind losing the money nearly as much as they hated feeling like a loser. Who needs it?

This investment strategy is perfect for the balanced high achiever. It's conservative, consistent, and should produce a reasonable return on investment capital. It doesn't require a lot of time and effort to implement it. Also, the investor will save a substantial amount of time, energy, and future aggravation by simply refusing to consider other "investment deals." It very much lends itself to long-range financial planning. A man, or woman, with investment goals and a plan of action, as we discussed earlier, stands a very good chance of being an investment success.

The human biological clock can run as long as 110 to 120 years. That is, there's documented evidence of people living that long. Yet, many high achievers die in their 60s and only a small percentage reach their mid-70s and beyond. Do we have to "burn out" so early? Perhaps not, if we can become a personal success.

This is a broad area. It encompasses everything not directly related to earning money. Let's further subdivide this area to include the following: family success, health success, leisure success, educational success, social success, religious success, and retirment success. Obviously, these cannot be rigid divisions. Some areas will complement each other and some will be interrelated with each other. However, let's examine some of the things that a balanced high achiever might want to consider.

The one-dimensional high achiever who is driven to acquire wealth, power, and status often pays a high personal price for his accomplishments. Unfortunately, he may only be able to relate to the world when he is striving, struggling, or building. When it comes to interpersonal relationships, he may be unable to be sensitive or tender, and therefore, his family life may suffer.

The high achiever often comes home drained both physically and emotionally. He selfishly may think of his work world like that of a boxer in a ring. Every day the bell sounds and he has to go out and do battle. He thinks of his home life as a haven or corner from the pounding struggle for survival. He may expect all family members to be sensitive to the beating he takes every day. He expects them to administer to his needs so he'll be able to go out for the next round. Such an attitude can produce a great deal of conflict, tension, and strife.

Instinctually, we all want to provide a good standard of living for our families. However, we shouldn't use this as a "cop-out" for our own feelings of inadequacy. Our family members also need our time and psychic energy. They desperately need our love and strokes. Don't forget that each one of them has a Hungry Child Ego State just as we do.

Many performance-oriented high achievers spend some of their family time criticizing their children's mistakes and failures. Successes are rarely praised because they are expected. Some psychiatrists believe this kind of system only encourages the child to avoid risk because the pain of failure is too great. Current thinking now believes that a parent should praise the *assumption of risk* and help the child view failure as an inevitable part of the learning process. Professional success or investment success will be hollow if our children run away and join a religious cult or overdose on drugs. Plenty of strokes and love are the best things that we can give to our children to help build their self-esteem and prepare them to face the realities of adulthood.

The biggest challenge for many balanced high achievers, besides professional success and investment success, may be staying married to the same spouse for more than 10 years. The statistics show that well over 50% of all marriages now end in divorce. At some point in all marriages, a power struggle will ensue. This usually occurs after romantic love has waned. However, this time of crisis can be the foundation for increased intimacy.

Every successful marriage has to eventually solve the conflict between love and power. For love to grow and mature, the Balanced High Achiever must be willing to relax his control over the relationship. This certainly won't be very easy for him. Because one of the driving forces in his life is the need to control his destiny. When we are in control of a situation, our Hungry Child does not feel inadequate. But when we give up power, our feelings of inferiority can return and we may feel very uncomfortable.

If two people are to build an open, intimate, and honest relationship, they must develop trust. Remember that each of us has a Hungry Child that *desperately* wants to be loved, appreciated, and accepted by other people. Positive strokes build trust whereas critical comments reinforce the old feelings of inadequacy. Positive strokes build intimacy, but negative strokes destroy it. Any form of criticism will make our Hungry Child feel inadequate, at least temporarily. Our Child Ego State may react with "defense mechanisms." Almost every argument betwen a man and a women starts with a perceived critical transaction from one to the other. Every emotional conflict in a marriage is between two angry, Hungry Child Ego States "fighting it out."

Many conflicts also arise because the Hungry Child of each partner has different expectations of what a "good wife" or "good husband" should be doing. One mature way to avoid conflicts is to have a predetermined monthly session. At this special time each partner should be able to discuss their feelings and expectations without reprisals. Perhaps the use of written contracts can be used to avoid tense situations. Also, each partner can feel that they will have a monthly forum to bring up anything that's bothering them. This should avoid venting hostilities at inopportune moments.

Most psychiatrists would agree that it is impossible to change anyone else's behavior through *criticism*. In fact, the only behavior that we have control over is our own. If we are not getting the kind of response we want from our spouse, then we must try to change *our* behavior to get it. In other words, it is our actions and reactions that create the actions and reactions from our spouse. If we want them to be more open, loving, and affectionate, then we need to be more open, loving, and affectionate.

There is little question that a good marriage and family life can make an important contribution to the performance of the Balanced High Achiever; whereas a poor one can be disastrous. It is a success area that requires goals, time, effort, and personal growth just like any other success area. In general, we should avoid all criticism of other family members as much as possible. We must also try to understand that our Hungry Child will never get all the positive strokes that he wants or feels he deserves. However, we can consciously give out sincere, positive strokes whenever possible. Intimacy is increased and conflict reduced when people feel good about themselves.

The high achiever also pays a high personal price in terms of the toll his professional success takes on his body. It probably won't show on the outside, for he will be well-groomed and crisply dressed. He may project the picture of success. Inside, it may be an entirely different story. His blood vessels may be clogged with cholesterol, which makes his blood pressure dangerously high. His liver may be crystallizing from alcohol while his lungs are choked with the tar from cigarette smoke. Also, his stomach could be burning from an ulcer. These physical problems, along with many others, are usually a result of stress and anxiety. It's pretty obvious that we can only play in the game of life as long as *all* of our vital organs continue to function normally. If even one stops working, we're out.

If you had to use one word to separate the winners in life from the also-rans, it might be the word *pain*. The winners know that they must challenge and conquer the many inevitable pains of life. The losers seek to avoid them. In today's world, we don't "fight it out" physically so those kinds of pain are rare. However, we do "fight it out" mentally, emotionally, and financially. Those kinds of pain are real and may be reflected internally in the form of anxiety and stress.

There is also a certain amount of pain that comes with personal growth. You've heard of "growing pains"? Well, they're real. Anytime we go from the familiar to the unfamiliar, there is pain in the form of stress, anxiety, or fear. Do you remember going to the circus and seeing the trapeze artist flying through the air? Well, the only way he can get to the other bar is to let go of the one that he is hanging onto. That's scary! Yet, we must do something very analogous to that throughout our life.

Psychiatrists know that all human personality development goes through a series of growth stages. There are predictable crises (a time of heightened potential and vulnerability) in adult life. Gail Sheehy labeled them "passages" in her book of the same name. They're real and we're called upon to try and work our way through them. Part of this process is challenging and disregarding archaic value systems and accepting new ones. Just like the trapeze artist, there will be points where there'll be nothing to hang onto, momentarily. We have to let go of the old values before we can grasp the new ones.

Besides having to "fight it out" in the jungle for professional and investment survival, the Balanced High Achiever is faced with the growth and development of his own personality. There is going to be a certain amount of pain and discomfort in the form of stress, anxiety, and fear. It can't be avoided entirely, but it can be reduced. Unfortunately, many people seek to escape from this pain through the use of tobacco, alcohol, or drugs. These solutions are only temporary, at best. Besides being unhealthy, they tend to reduce performance. No, there is a much better way.

It has now been proven beyond a reasonable doubt that a continuous aerobic exercise program will promote long life and reduce stress. Aerobic exercises are vigorous and repetitive activities like walking, jogging, or swimming. They should be done five or six days a week. You don't need to belong to a fancy athletic club to have a good exercise program. You can do it in your house or your neighborhood.

The two biggest killers of high achievers are heart attacks and cancer. A strong and healthy cardivascular system substantially reduces the probabilities of a heart attack. It also has been shown that cancer is six times more prevalent in inactive individuals than in physically active ones. Aerobic exercise improves the body's oxygen transport system. It keeps cells cancer resistant by keeping them well supplied with oxygen. Perhaps now the phrase "run for your life" will have a special meaning.

The right exercise program could add dramatically to your life expectancy. Now I know what you're going to say. You don't have time. Right? Well, besides feeling a lot better and being more productive when you're working, you'll spend a lot less time in bars. Also, your sleeping requirements should be less. The Balanced High Achiever should consider exercise as a serious part of his daily routine.

Besides relieving stress, exercise also builds endurance. There is no question that exercise will produce a certain amount of pain and discomfort. Endurance is the ability to withstand pain. It means to perservere even though it hurts. It means that you hold out even though you want to quit. It means that you continue to press on, because you know that nothing is more important than persistence. When we build our endurance to physical pain, we also build our endurance to emotional pain (anxiety). To parphrase Coach Vince Lombardi, "Fatigue makes cowards of us all." When we feel good about ourselves physiologically, it bolsters our self-esteem. Endurance gives us the abilitiy to work our way through the pain to obtain the rewards that we desire. Few experiences are more exhilarating to the balanced high achiever.

One way to look at life is in terms of a pain–pleasure relationship. This means that your concept of pleasure will be related to your experience of pain. It will be strictly relative. In other words, it's hard for most people to really appreciate or enjoy something unless they've been denied it. Unfortunately, we tend to take a lot of life's precious gifts for granted. Let's look at an extreme example to understand this point.

Dr. Viktor E. Frankl, one of Europe's leading psychiatrists, wrote a moving book *Man's Search for Meaning*, based on his experience as a longtime prisoner of the Nazi deathcamps. He found himself stripped to a naked existence. He lost every material possession. Daily, he suffered from hunger, cold, and brutality. Death could be expected at any hour. After the war, he discovered that his father, mother, brother, and wife died either in the camps or the gas ovens. It is not possible for most of us to even vaguely comprehend the pain he, and millions of others, must have suffered.

It is probable that Dr. Frankl has a much higher appreciation of the "little things" in life than many of us. For instance, he probably really enjoys just being able to eat when he is hungry or being able to put on a coat when he is cold. I'm sure that he doesn't let too many of life's trivialities get him down. He probably finds a lot of pleasure in just being alive.

This is not to suggest that we need to vacation for a month in a concentration camp to appreciate life. Although there is no question that a catastrophic experience does change our frame of reference, the point is that we cannot avoid pain; but we can challenge and control it. In the final analysis, there may be no way to experience pleasure unless it follows pain.

Finding pleasure in leisure is another challenge of the high achiever. Of course, he gets a certain amount of pleasure from his accomplishments. However, just "having fun" can be elusive for him. He is goal-directed in most aspects of his life. However, when it comes to leisure, he is strictly activity oriented. Otherwise, it is not leisure, it is work. The purpose of leisure is to relax the mind and reduce stress.

The high achiever must be careful not to get caught in the squirrel cage of always trying to win, win, win. It's not easy because he has been conditioned to always try to be a winner. He feels that he must always compete. He's got to have the "best" stamp collection, be the "best" tennis player at the club, or be the "best" singer in the choir. This kind of conditioning constantly keeps the individual under pressure to perform. It keeps him anxious and frustrated. To promote mental health, leisure is an activity that should be pursued as an entity unto itself. That is, the pleasure will come from the action without much thought of winning or losing. The goal is to try and have fun just playing, like an uninhibited child.

The other subdivisions of personal success will have varying degrees of importance to the high achiever. It will depend on his personal wants and needs. However, educational success, social success, religious success, and retirement success can be approached as a goal-directed activity, just like everything else.

One final thought in the process of success. It is easy to identify the tangible or material aspects of success that we want. It is fairly definite to want to be vice-president of marketing for your firm or to want to have a net worth of $500,000 by the time you're 50 years old. It is much harder—but just as necessary—to identify the internal changes you must make to achieve your tangible goals. The intangible goals of personality growth are an important part of the success process.

OPTIMAL SELF-REALIZATION

Do you know what separates the species Man from all other living creatures on Earth? Well, in the evolutionary process, we have lost something and gained something. In order to achieve unlimited potential, we've had to give up certain securities that shackled our ancestors.

Every living creature is born with instincts. That is, it has a built-in blueprint for survival. In other organisms, it is an extremely rigid frame of reference for life. A squirrel, born in the spring, gathers and stores nuts in the fall of the year. He does this even though he has never experienced winter. At the proper time, he will leave his parents and build a nest. He will seek a mate and procreate. Thus, the species survives. Obviously, he didn't attend a "squirrel school" to learn how to accomplish these tasks. He had inherited this knowledge for living through his instincts. Although this provides for a secure existence, he cannot expand his life beyond its confines.

As Man has accelerated into higher levels of consciousness, many of our instincts have faded into oblivion. In their place, we have acquired imagination. We have the ability to picture in our mind circumstances, objects, and realities different from what they may be at one point in time and space. In doing so, we have the power to create our own destinies. No other living creature has the power of creative imagination except Man.

As Man lost the security of his instincts, he sought to replace them with traditions. This would include doctrines, practices, and customs handed down from generation to generation. In order to feel secure, Man has sought to institutionalize the value systems of the past. That is, to hold up traditions as "the" right way to live. However, as technology and education have expanded conciousness, many traditions have been questioned and discarded. This has left Man with nothing with which to buttress his existence. There are few instincts to tell him what he has to do. There are few traditions to tell home what he ought to do. Under these circumstances, he is often confused about what he wants to do. Is there any wonder that there is so much anxiety and neurosis in today's modern society?

Creative imagination has given man perfect freedom, but its price has been the lack of structure. This can produce the feelings of inferiority that we all experience. This happens because we tend to judge ourselves and rate ourselves against unrealistic norms. This would be a "model of perfection" that we perceive is part of our society or peer group. In this situation, it is not possible to ever win because we're always trying to "measure up" to something that is always better than we are. It's hard to be happy when you feel second-rate.

Perhaps now, it is even more clear why a goal-directed life is necessary. Each of us is a unique individual. We have never been created before nor will we ever be again. We must establish our own frame of reference and norms. We must measure ourselves against our own potential to get what we want out of life. No one else's norms can matter, since no one can live our life for us. With the gift of perfect freedom comes the obligation to create our own destiny.

What we have been talking about is both the desire and the necessity of seeking optimal self-realization. It is a process of continuously becoming whoever we will be. It won't be easy. It will require a lot of hard work. However, the payoffs are incredible. But, how shall we go about it? What are the needed ingredients? What is the most effective approach? Well, without being presumptuous, I'm going to share with you the system that has helped me. Perhaps it will also help you.

In my opinion, there are three separate elements needed to attain optimal self-realization. (1) Clearly defined goals with a step-by-step plan for their achievement. (2) A weekly time budget appropriately to focus your energies. (3) A diary that will provide a feedback mechanism to monitor performance. Let's examine each item separately.

Do you know the difference between a daydream and a goal? A daydream is just a fanciful illusion of our Child Ego State. A goal is an internalized objective of our Adult Ego State. The paradox is that all goals begin as daydreams. The challenge is to make one into the other. Before we discuss that process, let's talk about our creative imagination and how it helps us to achieve our goals.

All goals are born as fantasies of our Child Ego State. These may be a tangible want, such as a new Cadillac. Or a desire to marry the beautiful blond that you have been dating. Or a need for status, power, and money, such as being president of your firm. This is a very necessary part of the process. That means that every goal that you achieve in life must first be pictured in your mind. *It also means that you must clearly visualize your success internally before you can attain it externally in the world of reality.*

Most of us have heard that everyone has both a conscious and subconscious mind. However, few people really understand how their subconscious mind affects their lives. Most of our creative thinking goes on at the unconscious level. Let's illustrate this point. All of us have had problems that we've worked on and worried about without finding a solution. Maybe we've even given up. Then one morning, perhaps while we're in the shower, the answer hits us like a "bolt out of the blue." That's our subconscious obediently solving our problem.

The subconscious mind is like having our own Creative Servant (CS). It automatically obeys our every wish and tries to get for us whatever we want. However, the only way that we can communicate with our Creative Servant is through conscious thought. If we think negative thoughts, our CS will help us to become a failure. If we think positive thoughts, our CS will help us to become a success. In other words, we create our own reality and we are the only person responsible for it.

The power of the subconscious mind to help us get anything we want in life is just beginning to be understood. It appears that once we focus on a goal or target, the subconscious mind will propel us forward like a guided missile. It will be self-correcting. This means that our inevitable failures or setbacks won't keep us off course for very long. As long as we keep visualizing the intended end result, our Creative Servant will keep working day and night to help us get there.

There are some mechanical ways that we can help our Creative Servant. By far, the most important one is through writing. Yes, I said writing, because writing crystallizes thought in a way that nothing else can do. It provides a record for our brilliant ideas. It is the best feedback mechanism to monitor our performance. Also, it seems to be the easiest way to communicate with our Creative Servant.

When you begin a goals program, you're going to need some materials from your local office supply store. Buy a medium-size three-hole notebook, dividers, and plenty of paper. Divide your notebook into six sections in the following order: Dream, Professional, Investment, Personal, Time, and Diary. Be sure to put some blank paper behind each divider for easy access. Affix your name, address, and phone number on the inside cover, in case you lose it. Now, you're all set to go. Actualizing your creative imagination will be one of the most exciting things that you'll ever do.

One word of caution: Don't ever, under any circumstances, show anyone your goals diary. Your thoughts that are transmitted into words are intended for your eyes only. This is important so that you can reveal your innermost feelings. It's like having a best friend whom you know won't tell anyone else what you've said. Also, writing out your thoughts and feelings is probably one of the best forms of psychotherapy that there is available.

Now, turn to the first section entitled Dream and let your imagination run completely wild. Write down everything you've ever wanted, needed, or desired. It doesn't matter how ridiculous it may sound to someone else. Remember, no one else will ever see what you've written down. If you want to be president of your company, write it down. If you want to have a million dollars, write it down. If you want to get married, write it down. If you want to go to the moon, write it down. Whatever spills forth from your fanciful Child Ego State, write it down. Obviously, you won't be able to think of everything at one time. Also, your desires will change as you become more and more successful. You can come back again and again for your own personal dream session. It goes on for a lifetime. Have fun.

The important thing here is to not let your critical Parent Ego State block your imagination. You'll hear voices in your head saying, "That's ridiculous!" "You'll never get to be president." "You're not smart enough to make a million dollars." "You're too ugly to get married." "You'll never get accepted in the astronaut program." Just ignore them. Don't judge your goals by whether you have the capability to achieve then now. Your're just trying to find out what you really want out of life.

Now, we must transform daydreams into goals. As you examine each want, need, and desire, decide into which success area it belongs. Then transform it into a specific written goal with a deadline for its achievement. Some will be easily transmitted and others will require a lot of thinking and planning. In order for goals to be effective, they must be written and specific. They must be your own personal goals and compatible with your value system. In order for them to motivate you, they must also be realistic.

Let's suppose that you were a weight lifter and you wanted to be able to lift 250 pounds. What would you do? Well, you'd probably start with what you could lift now, as a realistic frame of reference. Let's assume that it's 100 pounds. Let's also assume that you decided that you could add an additional 10 pounds each month. So, in 15 months, you'd reach your objective. This is analogous to what the goal-setter must strive for.

It is very important to have long-term goals in your life. They can help you to transcend the daily routine necessary for achievement. But it is also necessary to break those larger goals into much smaller goals. This is important so that you may experience progressive step-by-step successes. Each step of a long-term goal may turn into an intermediate term goal. Each step of an intermediate-term goal may become a short-term goal. The ultimate short-term goals will appear on your "to do" list every day. In this way, your large accomplishments are broken into much smaller day-to-day success experiences.

Each goal must be stated positively and specifically. You can't say, "I want to stop eating so much." You must say, "I want to weigh 165 pounds by September 30, 1982" (this assumes you might weigh 185 pounds). You can't say, "I want to be rich." You must say, "I will accumulate a net worth of $1,000,000 by January 1, 1989." This is necessary so that your imagination can clearly picture what you want.

Once you have a goal clearly in mind, you must decide if you're willing to pay the price to achieve it. How do you determine that? Well as we've said, the only reasons anybody does anything is to *gain something* or to *avoid losing something*. Psychiatrists can find no other reasons. So, now you must list the rewards that you will receive when the goal is attained. Also, you must list the costs in terms of personal sacrifices that must be made in order to achieve this goal. See Exhibit 8.3 "Will I Pay the Price?" Write the goal at the top of the page and answer the questions. After you've gone through this process, it will be pretty clear whether you really want to pursue this goal. You may decide that the costs are greater than the rewards. That's fine! At least you've cleared up the issue in your mind and you don't have to feel guilty about it. Just go on to the next goal. Believe me, you won't run out of them.

If you have a long-term goal, try to break it into as many steps or smaller goals as possible. Each step may have certain obstacles. List as many of them as you can think of. This gives your Creative Servant a more tangible problem to focus on. Often, if we can clearly define the problem, we are halfway to the solution.

Exhibit 8.3 *Will I Pay the Price?*

____

____

____

Sacrifices (costs)	Benefits (rewards)
1. ________________	1. ________________
________________	________________
2. ________________	2. ________________
________________	________________
3. ________________	3. ________________
________________	________________

Will the benefits to be gained outweigh the losses that will be incurred?

________ Yes   ________ No

Do I have a sincere desire to accomplish this goal regardless of the sacrifice?

________ Yes   ________ No

When will I start? ________________________

When will the goal be accomplished? ________________

Visualizations (mental pictures of the rewards)

1. __________________________________
2. __________________________________
3. __________________________________

Now, you've really prepared the way for your Creative Servant to go to work for you. Use your imagination to transmit the message to him as often as possible. Think about the rewards you will receive when the goal is achieved. Think about how you will feel and act. Absorb throughout your body the power of the accomplishment. Visualize your goals every day and they will soon become part of your life. Now nothing can stand in your way!

As you progress toward your goals, you will experience setbacks, failures, and pain. This is a completely natural part of the process because it builds your character and enables you to be worthy of the goal when you attain it. You can't get something for nothing and, even if you could, it wouldn't mean anything to you. The greater the struggle, the sweeter the victory will be when it comes. Also, it may come in a magnitude much greater than you could have believed possible.

Ambition could be defined as the fuel of achievement. It is the driving force that helps us attain the goals and rewards that we desire. That's why it is so important to be able to clearly visualize exactly what you want. Properly harnessed ambition can enrich our lives. This can only occur if we have thoroughly examined and internalized our own value system. Unbridled ambition can be self-destructive. Dr. Herbert J. Freudenberger described this phenomenon in his excellent book *Burn-Out*. He also examines the case histories of many individuals who have lost their zest for life. This condition is most likely to occur in high achievers who have intense, full schedules, but who are unable to deal with their limitations. Also, they tend to focus their energies into a narrow frame of reference, such as their profession. In the process of trying to achieve their goals, they exhaust their inner resources.

Human beings have a unique capability not given to any other animal. They have the capacity to perform past the limits of endurance. They can continue to push themselves beyond pain and get a "second wind." The high achiever has a tendency to drive himself to the point of mental and physical exhaustion. When this happens, the flame of ambition seems to burn out. This leaves him in a lethargic and frustrated state of mind. Living a balanced lifestyle can help to avoid this destructive condition.

In order to attain our goals, we must systematically focus our energies on the activities that will produce the end results. There may be several goals in different areas of our lives that we are working on simultaneously. We need a frame of reference in which to operate so we can effectively control our time. In other words, we want to work when it's time to work and play when it's time to play.

The best solution to this problem that I've found is the Weekly Time Module. A week is a time unit in which we should be able to "touch all the bases." It is continuously repetitive. If you're 40 years old and you're going to live until you're 72 years old, you have only 1664 weeks to go. That's it! That's all the time you've got, so you'd better get at least a little of everything that you want out of life every week.

When we set goals, we focus on end results. However, when we structure our time, we must concentrate on those activities that will produce the desired end results. This means we must identify those tasks that will make the most important contribution to the many successes that we desire. This is not easy and will involve a continuous effort. However, the increase in effectiveness and peace of mind will be dramatic.

Creating a weekly time module has many advantages. First of all, it forces you to set specific time priorities regarding all aspects of your life. Second, it helps you reduce stress by forming good work habits. Third, it makes you much more aware of the smaller time segments of your day. Therefore, it creates an urgency to get the needed tasks done in the allotted time.

In order to make your Weekly Time Module work effectively, you must divide your 24 hour day into small "airtight" compartments. They should be generalized periods of time in which you will focus effort on a specific group of activities. You must treat them like a football game. That is, when the allotted time runs out, the game is over. There never has been a touchdown counted 30 seconds after the final gun. Once your time unit has been consumed, you must move on to the next group of activities. After you begin to experience this sense of loss, your effectiveness will improve dramatically.

The Weekly Time Module is a necessary tool for the balanced high achiever. He must set aside specific time units for his investment goals and personal goals. Otherwise, his professional goals may tend to "crowd out" the rest of his life. Even if the one-dimensional high achiever attains "success" in terms of society's norms, he may find himself unfulfilled, if the other aspects of his life don't bring him any joy.

The Weekly Time Module should be seen as a flexible frame of reference, not as a rigid structure. It should be built around *your* existing lifestyle. Start with very large time units and then gradually get more specific as you become more skilled at utilizing your time. You may never have a "perfect week," but you will continue to become more and more efficient. Your WTM needs to be fluid because it will change as your priorities change. Just keep analyzing it a little bit every week and you'll have a lot more control over your life.

Your work day should be divided roughly into five separate segments: (1) planning, (2) activity, (3) wind-down, (4) personal, and (5) sleep. Planning is the most important and what most people fail to do. It forces you to set your priorities within your given time units. One hour a day of uninterrupted planning dramatically improves effectiveness. During the activity phase, you should concentrate upon achieving your daily goals. During the wind-down, you may want to read, or attend to administrative details. Personal time is your time. Forget about work and enjoy yourself. Tomorrow is another day. Finally, an adequate amount of sleep gives the mind and body the needed rest that it deserves.

Examine Exhibit 8.4 "Weekly Time Module," and you'll see the WTM that I'm using right now. Travel time is structured to avoid peak traffic hours. Planning is done early when the subconscious is the most creative. Exercise is scheduled in the afternoon to relieve the stress that has built up during the day. Finally, I try to take care of my work week from Monday through Thursday. Friday is left open for emergencies. That way, I have some flexibility. Usually, I try to focus on my educational and creative needs that day. Creative learning is vital for optimal self-realization. My reward for achieving my goals during the first four days of the week is to take all, or part, of Friday off from the daily grind at the office. That motivation makes for an exciting and effective work week.

The time that you spend in creative learning will become the fuel that will increase your personal power. This is how you will expand your consciousness about the world around you. This is when your Creative Servant will help you to decide what your life's goals should be and how you should focus your energies to attain them. During this period of time you will read, write, think, plan, visualize your goals and find the special meaning for your life. Systematically tapping your creative energies will make you a "winner" in life's journey.

When you first think about the WTM, it may appear ridiculously rigid. However, many people feel that the disciplined man is a truly happy man. This is because he utilizes his time most effectively and concentrates on the task at hand. Unfortunately, many low achievers do just the opposite. They daydream about playing when they should be working. Then they feel guilty when they should be relaxing and enjoying themselves. The WTM will minimize this type of stress. At every point during the week, you'll know what activity you should be focusing your efforts upon. Once you get accustomed to it, you'll wonder how you ever did without your Weekly Time Module.

Exhibit 8.4 ***Weekly Time Module***

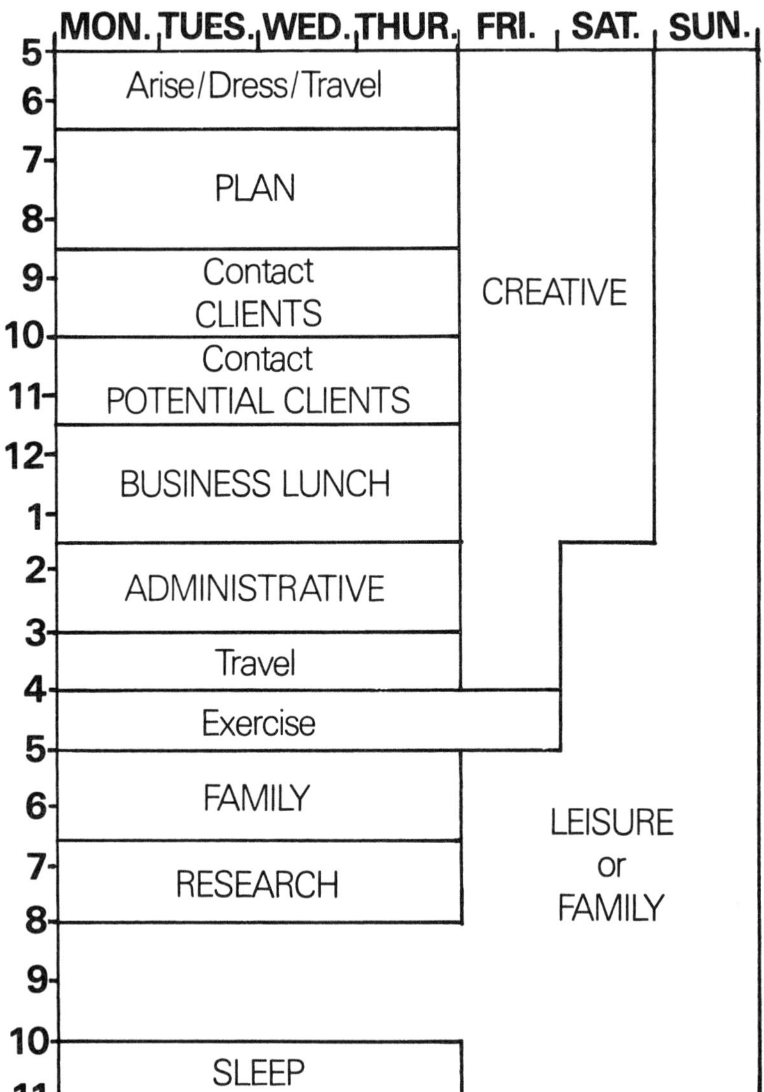

Source: Paul J. Myer, *The Dynamics of Personal Leadership* (Success Motivation Institute, 1970)

Now, let's examine the last tool for optimal self-actualization, your very personal feedback diary. Properly utilized, it will dramatically increase your levels of consciousness and personal growth.

Have you ever been to a psychiatrist? If you haven't, here's approximately what would happen. Each time you talked about something, the doctor would ask you, "How do you feel about that?" That question would be asked a number of times during your session. The object would be for you to get "in touch" with your feelings. That's something we all need to do. Your feedback diary can help monitor your performance and feelings about all aspects of your life. It can help you reinforce positive and eliminate negative behavior.

Behavioral psychologists believe that all of our thoughts, feelings, and actions have been learned. They are based on our past living environment and cumulative experiences. They believe that if we change our behavior, our thoughts and feelings will also change. In other words, you just have to "fake it until you make it."

They estimate that it takes about three months to change old habits into new ones. This has some startling implications. For instance, you may think writing in your diary is a waste of time. However, if you just force yourself to do it for three months, it will become part of your life. Also, you may feel that you hate to exercise but, if you just do it every day for three months, you'll probably discover that the benefits far outweigh the effort. At the end of three months, it will be easier to keep doing it than to stop. That is, it will be a habit.

It just takes about 20 or 30 minutes to go over what you've done for the day. Think back on your activities and accomplishments. Then, you should express your feelings about what you've done in writing. You must be as honest as possible. Write them down even if you tear the page up immediately. Remember, no one else will see it.

Try to articulate exactly how you feel. You can be euphoric or hostile. Use tender words or vulgar ones. On paper, try to critically examine your feelings. Perhaps they're not totally rational. Write about the problems you are having in your profession or with your spouse. Now, write down the proposed solutions. You'll be amazed at how your Creative Servant will come up with the answers.

You may have many success areas that you want to improve. The key is to focus on only one or two at a time. You can't change everything at once. Remember that we want to be long-distance runners. You've got the rest of your life ahead of you to grow and be self-actualized.

The vast majority of people are caught up in the "web" of life's trivialities. They don't have long-term goals, an overall game plan or a real commitment to getting the "goodies" that they want from life. Yet, everyone is a master of their own destiny. All they have to do is pay the price for success. If you didn't before, you certainly now have a mechanism for optimal self-actualization.

Today *is* the first day of the rest of your life. Whatever your past failures, they should be viewed as learning experiences. Whatever personal inadequacies that you may have now, they can be improved. However bad your present circumstances, they can be changed. Within you lies the *personal power* to attain every professional goal, investment goal, and personal goal that you can conceive and in which you can truly believe. Go for it!

It may seem that we've discussed many things that aren't applicable to making money in the stock market. However, it's my own personal opinion that you can't separate your investment goals. They are part of the total life process for the high achiever. The thrust of our message is simply *awareness of reality*. To make money in the stock market you must be aware of the psychological forces that produce price movements. In order to profit from the PSYCLE, you must be aware of your own thoughts, feelings, and behavior. It's the only way that you can take advantage of reality.

As a high achiever, you are probably driven first to pursue your professional goals, and second, your investment goals. Only when you are reasonably satisfied in those two areas will you turn your attention to your personal goals. This is unfortunate, but it's true in many cases. For the vast majority of private, part-time investors, this approach will produce much better results than anything else. With that kind of comfort, you can properly focus your energies on both your professional goals and your personal goals.

You can profit from the PSYCLE in many ways. Of course, the monetary rewards will be important. However, your peace of mind and internal awareness will also make positive contributions to your journey toward optimal self-realization. Good luck! You've got an exciting trip ahead. Just take it slow and easy and set your goals progressively higher in a reasonable step-by-step manner.

If you set aside time every week for your own education and creative growth, you will experience a dramatic increase in your personal power. This expanded knowledge that will come from your higher level of consciousness will provide you with access to the tools that you need to get whatever you want from life. It will require hard work, dedication, persistence, and patience; but the rewards will be incredible. Just be aware that increased monetary wealth will only be meaningful if it is accompanied by personality growth.

One last word of advice. Many wonderful things in life are possible if you just remember to *buy low and sell high*!

Publishers Weekly

THE MYSTERY OF BANKING

Murray Rothbard. Richardson & Synder (Dutton, dist.), $19.95 ISBN 0-943940-04-4

When economist Rothbard (*The American Depression*) is finished, there isn't much mystery left. He sets out the basics of economics, banking, money and credit, then traces modern-day inflation back to an 18th century inheritance case in which a British court ruled that bank deposits were bank "debts" and not property held in trust. Thus, more than one promissory bank note could be issued against the same pound of gold; bank failures were merely insolvency, not theft. From then on, as Rothbard tells it without shrinking from such words as "fraudulent," banks and governments printed money "out of thin air" to finance wars and economic expansion. It is a story of manipulation, politics, boom and bust, eventually somewhat stabilized by the Federal Reserve system of the last 70 years. Rothbard, however, urges the "Fed" be abolished and gold returned to a true current-market value, with a 100% par value bank note money system free of government's inflationary dominance.

[*September 30]*

Contact: Dianitia Hutcheson, Director of Publicity, Richardson & Snyder, 25 Broad Street, New York 10004

THE MYSTERY OF BANKING

Murray Rothbard. Richardson & Synder (Dutton, dist.), $19.95 ISBN 0-943940-04-4

When economist Rothbard (*The American Depression*) is finished, there isn't much mystery left. He sets out the basics of economics, banking, money and credit, then traces modern-day inflation back to an 18th century inheritance case in which a British court ruled that bank deposits were bank "debts" and not property held in trust. Thus, more than one promissory bank note could be issued against the same pound of gold; bank failures were merely insolvency, not theft. From then on, as Rothbard tells it without shrinking from such words as "fraudulent," banks and governments printed money "out of thin air" to finance wars and economic expansion. It is a story of manipulation, politics, boom and bust, eventually somewhat stabilized by the Federal Reserve system of the last 70 years. Rothbard, however, urges the "Fed" be abolished and gold returned to a true current-market value, with a 100% par value bank note money system free of government's inflationary dominance.

[*September 30]*

Contact: Dianitia Hutcheson, Director of Publicity, Richardson & Snyder, 25 Broad Street, New York 10004

Notes

1. Accumulating Wealth

1. H.G. Wells, *The Outline of History: The Whole Story of Man* (Garden City, N.Y.: Doubleday, 1971), pp. 1–133. [Ref. pp. 6–7]
2. Horace C. Levinson, *Chance, Luck and Statistics* (New York: Dover, 1963), pp. 1–110. [Ref. pp. 10–14]
3. John Scarne, *Scarne's Complete Guide to Gambling* (New York: Simon and Schuster, 1961), pp. 1–29 [Ref. pp. 14–15]
4. Warren Weaver, *Lady Luck: The Theory of Probability* (Garden City, N.Y.: Anchor Books, 1963), pp. 324–348. [Ref. p. 16]
5. Benjamin Graham and David L. Dodd, et al., *Security Analysis* (New York: McGraw-Hill, 1962), pp. 47–58. [Ref. pp. 20–22]

2. Investment Techniques

1. Benjamin Graham and David L. Dodd, et al., *Security Analysis* (New York: McGraw-Hill, 1962), pp. 24–35. [Ref. pp. 38–44]

2. Jerome B. Cohen and Edward D. Zinbarg, *Investment Analysis and Portfolio Management* (Homewood, Ill.: Dow Jones-Irwin, 1967), pp. 87–188. [Ref. pp. 38–44]
3. Robert D. Edwards and J. Magee, *Technical Analysis of Stock Trends*, 5th ed. (Springfield, Mass.: John McGee, 1966), p. 5. [Ref. p. 53]
4. Martin J. Pring, *Technical Analysis Explained: An Illustrated Guide for the Investor* (New York: McGraw-Hill, 1980), pp. 1–10. [Ref. pp. 53–56]
5. Garfield A. Drew, *New Methods for Profits in the Stock Market* (Wells, Vt.: Fraser Publishing, 1966), [Ref. p. 61]

3. Predictability

1. Burton G. Malkiel, *A Random Walk Down Wall Street* (New York: Norton, 1975), pp. 15–203. [Ref. pp. 85–91: Random Walk Section]
2. Clive W. J. Granger and Oskar Morgenstern, *Predictability of Stock Market Prices* (Lexington, Mass.: Heath/Lexington, 1970), p. 3, pp. 41–42. [Ref. p. 88: Exhibit 3.1 Random Walk Theory]
3. John Templeton, interview in *Forbes*, November 27, 1978 [Ref. p. 92: quotes]

4. The Player's Problems

1. Barbara Wheeler, ed., *The New York Stock Exchange Fact Book 1982* (New York: New York Stock Exchange, 1982), pp. 1–33. [Ref. p. 106]
2. Burton G. Malkiel, *A Random Walk Down Wall Street* (New York: Norton, 1975), pp. 73–175. [Ref. pp. 119–121]
3. David N. Dreman, *Psychology and the Stock Market* (New York: Warner Books, 1979), pp. 99–213. [Ref. pp. 133–138]

4. Robert J. Farrell, "Weep Not for the Individual Investor," *Forbes*, January 1977. [Ref. pp. 135–138]
5. George W. Bishop, Jr., *Charles H. Dow: Economist* (Princeton, N.J.: Dow Jones Books, 1967). [Ref. p. 139]
6. John Kenneth Galbraith, *The Great Crash, 1929* (Boston: Houghton Mifflin, 1961), p. 75. [Ref. p. 139: Fisher quote]

5. All Markets Are the Same

1. Eric Berne, *Games People Play* (New York: Ballantine, 1964), p. 23 [Ref. pp. 147–148], 27 [Ref. p. 151], 29 [Ref. p. 152]
2. ______, *Transactional Analysis in Psychotherapy* (New York: Ballantine, 1961), pp. 1–292. [General Ref. pp. 145–161]
3. ______, *What Do You Say After You Say Hello?* (New York: Bantam, 1980), pp. 1–439. [General Ref. pp. 145–161]
4. Muriel James and Dorothy Jongeward, *Born to Win: Transactional Analysis with Gestalt Experiments* (Reading, Mass.: Addison-Wesley, 1971), pp. 1–274. [General Ref. pp. 145–161]
5. Thomas A. Harris, *I'm OK—You're OK* (New York: Harper & Row, 1969), p. 44. [Ref. p. 158]
6. Gustave LeBon, *The Crowd* (New York: Viking, 1960), pp. 41–66. [Ref. pp. 161–162: quotes]
7. Charles Mackay, *Extraordinary Popular Delusions and the Madness of Crowds* (New York: Farrar, Straus & Giroux, 1932), pp. 89–97. [Ref. p. 163]
8. John Kenneth Galbraith, *The Great Crash, 1929* (Boston: Houghton Mifflin, 1961), pp. 1–199. [General Ref. pp. 164–165]

9. Frederick Lewis Allen, *Only Yesterday* (New York: Harper & Row, 1931), p. 315. [Ref. p. 164]

10. John W. English and Gray E. Cardiff, *The Coming Real Estate Crash* (New Rochelle, N.Y.: Arlington House, 1979), pp. 1–182. [General Ref. pp. 165–167]

11. Robert J. Farrell, interview in *Barron's* April 20, 1981, pp. 1–5. [Ref. p. 177: Quote/Ref. Chart: *Bonds vs Gold]*

6. Cycles

1. Carl Sagan, *Cosmos* (New York: Random House, 1980), pp. 233–235. [Ref. pp. 183–184: Three quotes]

2. Edward R. Dewey, *Cycles: The Mysterious Forces That Trigger Events* (New York: Hawthorne Books, 1971), p. 200. [Ref. p. 186: quotes]

3. N.D. Kondratieff, "The Long Wave in Economic Life," *Review of Economic Statistics* (November 1935). [Ref. pp. 189–192]

4. Dick A. Stoken, *Cycles: What They Are, What They Mean, How to Profit From Them* (New York: McGraw-Hill, 1978), pp. 1–54. [Ref. pp. 192–195]

5. Robert J. Farrell, interview in *Barron's*, March 1, 1982, pp. 1–5. [Ref. pp. 196–198: quote]

6. Don Guyon, *One-Way Pockets: The Book of Books on Wall Street Speculation* (New York, Capstone Publishing, 1917; Burlington, Vt.: Fraser Publishing, 1979), pp. 5–64. [General Ref. pp. 208–213]

8. A Balanced Lifestyle

1. Abraham H. Maslow, *Motivation and Personality* (New York: Harper & Row, 1970), pp. 1–369. [Ref. pp. 265–266, Exhibit 8.2]

2. Vance Packard, *The Status Seekers* (New York: Pocket Books, 1965), pp. 1–317. [Ref. pp. 263–268]

3. Henry C. Lindgren, *Great Expectations: The Psychology of Money* (Los Altos, Calif.: William Kaufman, 1980), p. 76. [Ref. p. 269]

4. Maxwell Maltz, *Psycho-Cybernetics* (Hollywood, Calif.: Wilshire Books, 1965), pp. 1–245. [Ref. pp. 270–273]

5. John Bradshaw, "The Palmer Lecture Series 1981–82" Houston: John Bradshaw, 1982), sound cassette. [General Ref. pp. 275–280]

6. Herb Goldberg, *The Hazards of Being Male: Surviving the Myth of Masculine Privilege* (New York: New American Library, 1976), pp. 1–184. [General Ref. pp. 273–282]

7. M. Zussman, "Hope for Workaholics," *Success Unlimited*, May 1981, pp. 37, 40, 41, 58. [General Ref. pp. 275–276]

8. Gail Sheehy, *Passages: Predictable Crises of Adult Life* (New York: Bantam, 1977), pp. 1–514. [Ref. p. 281]

9. Jackie Schwartz, *Letting Go of Stress* (New York: Pinnacle, 1982), pp. 1–105. [Ref. pp. 280–281]

10. Viktor E. Frankl, *Man's Search for Meaning* (New York: Pocket Books, 1963), pp. 1–211. [Ref. pp. 283–284]

11. Joyce Brothers, *How to Get Whatever You Want Out of Life* (New York: Ballantine, 1980), pp. 1–243. [General Ref. pp. 270–299]

12. Joseph Murphy, *The Power of Your Subconscious Mind* (Englewood, N.J.: Prentice-Hall, 1963), pp. 1–224. [Ref. p. 287]

13. Denis E. Waitley, *The Psychology of Winning* (Chicago: Nightengale-Conant, 1978), sound cassette. [General Ref. pp. 270–299]

14. Ernest Dimnet, *The Art of Thinking* (Greenwich, Conn.: Fawcett, 1923), pp. 1–202. [General Ref. pp. 285–299]

15. Jospeh Epstein, "Ambition," *Success Unlimited*, March 1981, pp. 55–59. [Ref. pp. 292–293]

16. Herbert J. Freudenberger, *Burn-Out: The High Cost of High Achievement* (Garden City, N.Y.: Anchor Books, 1980), pp. 1–211. [Ref. p. 292]

17. Paul J. Meyer, *The Dynamics of Personal Leadership* (Waco, Tex.: Success Motivation Institute, 1970), pp. 85–131. [Ref. pp. 287–292]

18. Frank E. Sullivan, *The Critical Path to Sales Success* (Indianapolis: Research and Review Service of America, 1970), pp. 23–39. [Ref. pp. 293–296]

19. Aaron Hemsley, *There's More to Success Than "Pop" Psychology* (Santa Ana, Calif.: Aaron Hemsley, 1981), pp. 1–4. [Ref. pp. 297–298]

Bibliography

Anonymous Investor. *Wiped Out: How I Lost a Fortune in the Stock Market While the Averages Were Making New Highs*. New York: Simon and Schuster, 1966.

Bean, Louis H. *The Art of Forecasting*. New York: Random House, 1969.

Brutus. *Confessions of a Stockbroker.* New York: Bantam, 1973.

Crane, Burton. *The Sophisticated Investor.* New York: Simon and Schuster, 1963.

Durant, Will and Ariel. *The Lessons of History.* New York: Simon and Schuster, 1968.

Ellis, Charles D. *The Second Crash: How the Stock Market Went the 1929 Route in 1970*. New York: Simon and Schuster, 1973.

Goleman, Daniel, and Speeth, Kathleen R. *The Essential Psychotherapies: Theory and Practice by the Masters*. New York: New American Library, 1982.

Hall, Calvin S. *A Primer of Freudian Psychology.* New York: New American Library, 1979.

Hill, Napoleon. *Think and Grow Rich*. New York: Fawcett, 1963.

Jaynes, Julian. *The Origin of Consciousness in the Breakdown of the Bicameral Mind*. Boston: Houghton Mifflin, 1976.

Lechner, Alan. *Street Games: Inside Stories of the Wall Street Hustle*. New York: Harper & Row, 1980.

Leuthold, Steven C. *The Myths of Inflation and Investing*. Chicago: Crane Books, 1980.

Neill, Humphrey B. *Tape Reading and Market Tactics*. New York, B.C. Forbes, 1931; Wells, Vt.: Fraser Publishing, 1960.

Ney, Richard, *The Wall Street Jungle*. New York: Grove Press, 1970.

Peale, Norman Vincent. *The Power of Positive Thinking*. Greenwich, Conn.: Fawcett, 1963.

Schultz, Harry D. *Panics and Crashes and How You Can Make Money Out of Them*. New Rochelle, N.Y.: Arlington House, 1974.

Selden, G.C. *Psychology of the Stock Market: Human Impulses Lead to Speculative Disasters*. New York, Ticker Publishing, 1912; Burlington, Vt.: Fraser Publishing, 1965.

Stobel, Robert. *Panic on Wall Street: A History of America's Financial Disasters*. New York: Macmillan, 1970.

Wilson, Sloan J. *The Speculator and the Stock Market*. New York: Investor's Library, 1963.